International Trade Centre

Business and the multilateral trading system

Business Guide to Trade Remedies in Canada

Anti-dumping, countervailing and safeguards legislation, practices and procedures

Revised edition

Geneva 2006

ABSTRACT FOR TRADE INFORMATION SERVICES

2006   C-20 124
                                            BUS

INTERNATIONAL TRADE CENTRE UNCTAD/WTO
Business Guide to Trade Remedies in Canada: Anti-dumping, countervailing and safeguards
legislation, practices and procedures. – Revised ed.
Geneva: ITC, 2006. xvi, 181 p. (Business and the Multilateral Trading System)

Guide focusing on the Canadian trade remedy system – provides an overview of the world trading
environment and the WTO trade remedy system; highlights Canada's anti-dumping and
countervailing measures systems; provides details concerning the information that must be supplied
by exporters to the Canadian authorities, and the factors taken into account in making dumping and
subsidy calculations; deals with the Canadian International Trade Tribunal (CITT) injury
decision-making process; examines temporary emergency measures available to Canadian producers
faced with a surge in low-priced imports; provides information on Canadian law, procedures and the
role of the CITT in considering safeguard measures; includes bibliographical references (p. 183).

Descriptors: **Canada, Safeguards, Anti-Dumping, Countervailing Measures, Agreement on
Safeguards, Agreement on Subsidies and Countervailing Measures.**

English, French, Spanish (separate editions)

Palais des Nations, 1211 Geneva 10, Switzerland

ITC/P207.E/TSS/BAS/06-IX

ISBN 92-9137-334-6
United Nations Sales No. E.06.III.T.2

Foreword

Under the WTO Agreements, Members have the right to apply trade remedies in the form of anti-dumping, countervailing or safeguard measures subject to specific rules. The importance of these rules was highlighted at the WTO Ministerial Conference in Doha, where Members agreed to 'negotiations aimed at clarifying and improving disciplines under the Agreements on Implementation of Article VI of GATT 1994 and on Subsidies and Countervailing Measures...' (paragraph 28 of the Ministerial Declaration).

From 1995 to 2005, records maintained by the WTO Secretariat indicate that approximately 2,840 anti-dumping investigations were initiated worldwide. Over two-thirds of these cases, exporters in developing and transition countries were the main targets. According to experience gathered under ITC's World Tr@de Net programme, businesses in developing countries and transition economies engaged in producing and exporting 'sensitive' products consider anti-dumping investigations, or the threat thereof, as a significant market access barrier to a number of major markets.

Parties involved in anti-dumping and other trade remedy proceedings, namely exporters, importers and domestic producers of the product in question, often know very little about the procedures themselves and what they entail. They are unaware of the basic substantive rules of the relevant WTO Agreements and/or implementing national legislation, and hence have very limited knowledge of their rights and are thus ill-equipped to defend their business interests. There has been a steady demand for a publication explaining to business people the essential laws applicable and practices followed in such proceedings.

It is in response to this demand that ITC has published this series of Business Guides to Trade Remedies. The three publications of this series concern the relevant trade remedy rules and practices of the European Community, the United States of America and Canada, which are among the biggest traditional users of trade remedy measures. However, over the last few years, an increasing number of developing countries and transition economies have begun to implement trade remedy actions at an accelerated pace. In order to reflect this trend, ITC has also published two additional technical papers which present along the same format the trade remedy rules and practices of Brazil and South Africa.

This guide focuses on Canada, which is an important market for many developing countries and transition economies and a frequent user of trade remedy measures. The main objective of this guide is to highlight those aspects of the law and practice of Canada and the appropriate provisions of the relevant WTO Agreements, which may be of practical interest to business managers, exporters and importers in developing countries and transition economies. This guide is not for specialists; special emphasis is therefore given to practical definitions, problems and recommendations.

Patricia Francis
Executive Director
International Trade Centre

Acknowledgements

W. Roy Hines (W.R. Hines & Associates Inc., Ottawa, Canada) wrote and updated this publication. He is entirely responsible for the views expressed herein.

The first edition of this publication was supervised by **Peter Naray**, former Senior Adviser on the Multilateral Trading System. This edition was coordinated by **Jean-Sébastien Roure**, Adviser on the Multilateral Trading System.

R. Badrinath, Director, Division of Trade Support Services, provided strategic guidance in the planning and preparation of this publication.

Alison Southby edited the guide. Isabel Droste prepared the copy for printing.

Contents

CHAPTER 2

The Canadian trade remedy system

CHAPTER 5
The Canadian safeguards process   97

Appendices

References

Note

Unless otherwise specified, all references to dollars ($) are to Canadian dollars, and all references to tons are to metric tons. The term 'billion' denotes 1 thousand million.

The following abbreviations are used:

CBSA	Canada Border Services Agency
CITT	Canadian International Trade Tribunal
CUSFTA	Canada-United States Free Trade Agreement
DSU	Dispute settlement understanding
EP	Export price
EU	European Union
FD	Final determination of dumping or subsidization
FOB	Free on board
GATT	General Agreement on Tariffs and Trade
GATS	General Agreement on Trade in Services
GSA	General selling and administrative expenses
ITO	International Trade Organization
MFN	Most favoured nation
MTN	Multilateral trade negotiations
NAFTA	North American Free Trade Agreement
NGO	Non-governmental organization
NTB	Non-tariff barriers
NV	Normal value
PAP	Profitability analysis period
PD	Preliminary determination of dumping or subsidization
POI	Period of investigation
SCM	Subsidies and Countervailing Measures
SIMA	Special Import Measures Act
SOR	Statement of reasons
The Code	The Anti-Dumping Code
WTO	World Trade Organization

Executive summary

This guide was written for exporters to Canada. It provides a comprehensive guide to what is important in order to do business and successfully navigate Canadian trade policy and law. For exporters identified in a Canadian dumping, subsidy or safeguard investigation, this guide provides the essential information needed to understand and optimally participate in these processes. Specifically, it sets out the who, what, where, when and why that exporters need to know to make their case, to be heard and to effectively position themselves to manage the trade dispute process in Canada.

Beyond the law and the administrative processes, the sectors particularly sensitive to Canadian business that represent the bulk of the trade actions are examined. The principal sector where exporters have encountered challenge is steel. However, actions have also been taken against a variety of other industrial and agricultural goods including footwear, laminate flooring, fasteners, potatoes and refined sugar. To be clear, there are major opportunities in the Canadian market for imports, but there are also some obstacles.

Canada is a major trading country with 37.8% of gross domestic product and one in every five jobs accounted for by international trade in 2005. The Canadian economy has experienced significant growth in the past decade and international trade has played a major role in that expansion. On average, Canada does $2.5 billion worth of trade daily. In 2005 exports of goods and services increased by 5.2% to reach $516 billion and imports to Canada increased by 7.4% to reach $463 billion. The United States is by far Canada's dominant trading partner, representing 81% of Canada's merchandise exports and providing more than half of its imports in 2005. The Canadian market is expected to continue to grow and provide exporters with new opportunities to participate in the economy.

At the end of 1995 there were 41 injury findings in place in Canada, covering a total of 97 actions and affecting imports from 33 countries. At that time, the value of imports affected by anti-dumping and countervailing measures was estimated to be $1 billion, two-and-a-half times as much as in 1990. Nevertheless, they accounted for only 0.51% of total Canadian imports, which was down from 0.54% in 1994. The value of Canadian domestic shipments affected by trade remedy actions was estimated at $4.3 billion in 1995 and accounted for 2.1% of total domestic shipments.

These numbers highlight the fact that anti-dumping and countervailing measures have actually adversely affected only a very small percentage of Canadian imports and domestic shipments. Indeed, these values have not changed significantly in recent years. In 2004, the value of imports affected by anti-dumping and countervailing measures was $1.047 billion or 0.32% of total imports. Moreover, the number of investigations launched in recent years has declined and it seems reasonable to conclude that this trend will continue at least while the economy continues to grow. Nonetheless, the mere threat of trade remedy actions can have a more profound negative impact on trade than the number of actual investigations indicates.

Of the 24 CITT findings in place at the end of March 2005, 10 cases were related to steel products imported from many countries mainly in Eastern Europe, South Africa, South America and the Pacific Rim. These cases affected imports from 22 different countries, many of which were either transition or developing country economies. Only one case, stainless steel wire, involved imports from the United States. Four other cases were against American goods, and included iodinated contrast media, dishwashers, whole potatoes, and refined sugar. Other products subject to these actions included women's boots, waterproof footwear, garlic, bicycles and frames, and wood Venetian blinds.

Until the last few years, steel and steel products were the areas of high sensitivity in the Canadian market. This no longer appears to be the case and, as far as remaining products are concerned, it is not possible to isolate product areas that are especially sensitive to imports. Investigations have covered a wide spectrum of goods. The most that can be said is that exporters should examine the market carefully before attempting to sell dumped or subsidized goods to Canada.

Canadian industry, even those in relatively small sectors, is familiar with Canada's trade remedy laws and does not hesitate to use them. Exporters shipping product into Canada that is dumped or subsidized run a risk of being caught up in these investigations especially because, in a relatively small economy, only a limited number of firms compete in any given sector and imports take on a high profile.

Import sensitivity in the Canadian market in areas such as textiles, steel and footwear has been high for a number of years and these continue to be areas of concern. Agricultural products, especially dairy and poultry, are another sector where the normal trade rules do not apply and exporters should be aware of marketing constraints before shipping these products to Canada. In this connection, it is worth noting that Canada has not taken any safeguard actions since WTO was created in 1995.

This guide is focused on the Canadian trade remedy system. It examines what exporters might expect when identified in a Canadian trade dispute and the factors to consider when entering the market for the first time. The guide is in five chapters: (1) The world trading environment and the WTO trade remedy system, (2) The Canadian trade remedy system, (3) The Canadian Border Services Agency (CBSA) questionnaires and the calculation of margins of dumping and subsidies, (4) The Canadian International Trade Tribunal (CITT): the injury decision-making process, and (5) The Canadian safeguards process. In each section there is information about specific Canadian trade actions, detailed process information, key points for exporters to consider and a focus on maximizing opportunities for exporters identified in Canadian trade investigations.

Chapter 1, The world trading environment and the WTO trade remedy system, examines globalization and economic integration, and provides a historical perspective on the evolution from GATT to WTO. This section considers the WTO trade remedy agreements on safeguards, dumping, subsidies and countervailing measures. It also provides an overview of the anti-dumping and countervailing agreements investigation processes.

Chapter 2, The Canadian trade remedy system, is focused on Canada's anti-dumping and countervailing measures systems. The entire process is documented, from the proper filing of a complaint by a domestic producer through to the issuance of a final determination by CBSA. This section differentiates the dumping and subsidy investigations, outlines the decision-making framework and the time frames associated with this framework, and examines possible solutions such as undertakings.

Chapter 3, CBSA questionnaires and the calculation of margins of dumping and subsidies, provides details concerning the information that must be supplied by exporters to the Canadian authorities and the factors taken into account in making dumping and subsidy calculations, and provides specific illustrations of valuation methodology followed by Canadian officials. The focus is on Canadian government research processes as well as on exporter information and verification requirements. It provides an understanding of how dumping, subsidy and normal value figures, among others, are calculated, and gives exporters specific guidelines on how to handle requests for information.

Chapter 4, CITT: the injury decision-making process outlines the second half of Canada's bifurcated trade remedy protection system. Anti-dumping and/or countervailing duty measures may be imposed on imports only when two conditions are met: (1) a positive determination of dumping or subsidization; and (2) demonstrable proof that the dumping or subsidization is injuring the domestic industry. CITT is responsible for the ruling on injury and the causal link to unfair imports. The paper describes the process, the injury criteria considered and the manner in which CITT members make decisions on injury.

Chapter 5, The Canadian safeguards process, examines temporary emergency measures available to Canadian producers faced with a surge in low-priced imports. Information is provided on Canadian law, procedures and the role of CITT in considering safeguard measures.

CHAPTER 1

The world trading environment and the WTO trade remedy system

Overview

Globalization, trade and economic integration

International trade, services and investment are linked

Globalization of trade in goods and services, finance, production and investment is continuing to occur at a rapid pace. Success in the international trade arena in today's world involves much more than the traditional import and export of goods. It encompasses direct linkages between trade, services investment, technology partnerships and commercial collaborations dealing with all aspects of finance, production and distribution. World trade expanded in 2005 with the value of merchandise exports increasing by 13% to exceed the $10 trillion mark and commercial services exports rising by 11% to $2.4 trillion. Trade and investment liberalization efforts are integral components of this process that affect developed countries as well as economies in transition (former State-trading countries) and developing economies. The WTO and its agreements were essential to these developments. Exporters, especially those in developing countries, need to be aware of changes taking place in world markets and be aware of their rights under the WTO rules-based trading system.

Economic interdependence will continue with globalization

All forecasts suggest that the trend towards greater economic interdependence will continue. Increasing globalization of business operations is anticipated as corporate interrelationships expand, industries continue to develop new international alliances, and intra-industry trade in goods and services, production, technology and marketing along value-added lines is promoted.

With enhanced globalization, technology and capital are becoming more diffused; service industry and personnel activities are less constrained by national boundaries; and information/communication and computer advances are rapidly disseminated worldwide. Improved modes of transportation continue to reduce distances and border obstacles to the movement of goods and services. Most economic activities now carried out in any one country can be organized and directed from anywhere in the world.

Dynamic economic change may lead to new risks for continued trade liberalization

Dramatic change is also taking place in individual countries. New technologies and new approaches in manufacturing and production mean the decline of some industries and the rise of new ones, changes in employment patterns and skills requirements, and extensive industrial restructuring. Policy initiatives, including new bilateral free trade agreements, are promoting market forces and efficiency as the way to achieve sustained economic growth. However, pressures have been mounting in recent years to constrain this process as some small and developing countries debate the likely economic benefits of continued trade liberalization for their countries. These concerns, together with the lack of new substantive progress in multilateral initiatives toward further trade liberalization, pose dangers for exporters and for growth in world trade.

Current developments have created a situation in which market access to foreign markets is now viewed by governments and the private sector as covering all the laws, rules and regulations affecting the terms of entry for foreign goods, services, investments, ideas and business people. The WTO rules-based system go some distance towards meeting the new challenges; however, much more needs to be done to promote the continued liberalization of world trade.

GATT/WTO – a historical perspective

Following the worldwide depression of the 1930s, characterized by extreme trade protectionism and the upheavals of the Second World War, the 1947 United Nations Havana Conference considered a proposal to create an International Trade Organization (ITO). The aim was to establish a functioning multilateral trading system that would promote trade expansion and an institution with strong decision-making and dispute settlement powers on trade matters. No major trading country ratified the ITO charter and it never came into existence.

Establishment of GATT

Fortunately however, the process of lowering trade barriers among countries was started. At that time, 23 countries adopted a provisional arrangement, the General Agreement on Tariffs and Trade (GATT). GATT was a modest beginning but included (1) an international agreement that sets out the rules for conducting international trade, and (2) an informal structure to administer the agreement. The term GATT was applied to both the agreement and the structure. A version of GATT exists today as part of WTO.

Basic GATT principles

GATT laid down the very important general principles of non-discrimination, 'national treatment', and progressive trade liberalization. These principles, with certain exceptions, ensured that GATT parties enjoyed equal treatment under 'most-favoured nation' (MFN) terms; that imported products, after payment of any applicable duty, enjoyed equal treatment with domestically produced goods; and that border measures were transparent, price-based (tariffs not quotas), bound against increases and reduced or eliminated over time.

Throughout the post-war period, Canada was a major supporter of the GATT system because it served the objectives of providing a relatively predictable set of international trade rules and procedures that facilitated participation in a global trading system. GATT was particularly helpful in advancing the interests of small and medium-sized countries such as Canada, and continues to benefit smaller exporting countries.

Initial GATT trade negotiations

The most visible role of GATT during its first decades was as a forum for periodic 'rounds' of negotiations to lower and remove tariffs and other customs impediments to trade. The first five rounds of negotiations were of relatively short duration and focused on tariff reductions. The sixth, the Kennedy Round (1963–1967), accomplished deeper and wider cuts in industrial tariffs and brought developing-country demands to the fore. It was also noteworthy for shifting the focus away from tariffs to non-tariff barriers (NTBs) when agreement was reached by a limited number of countries on the Anti-Dumping Code.

Non-tariff measures agreements

The Tokyo Round (1973–1979) also cut tariffs substantially and introduced a series of 'codes' or agreements on non-tariff barriers. These were negotiated mainly among industrialized countries and were binding only on those who signed them. They covered subsidies and countervailing duties, customs valuation, government procurement, import licensing procedures and technical barriers to trade.

Launching the Uruguay Round of trade negotiations

The Uruguay Round (1986–1994) was by far the most comprehensive and difficult negotiation ever undertaken in GATT. It addressed inadequacies in the GATT organization and the difficult issues of agriculture, services and other trade-related issues such as investment and intellectual property. It was a complex agenda that at the time was regarded by many as bold, daring, cutting-edge and stretching the limits of GATT. Indeed, only after a breakthrough on certain agricultural issues did a final agreement become possible in December 1993, over seven years after negotiations had been launched in Uruguay.

The Uruguay Round results

In April 1994, the Final Act – incorporating some 40 Uruguay Round agreements and 26,000 pages of individual country schedules of commitments – was signed by representatives of 111 GATT countries. With a few exceptions, it was binding on all parties. Four of the agreements, covering bovine meat, civil aircraft, dairy and government procurement, had no membership obligations.

The Uruguay Round also led to the establishment on 1 January 1995 of the World Trade Organization (WTO) to succeed GATT. As at 1 January 2006, WTO membership stood at 149 countries, three-quarters of which are developing countries. About 30 applicant countries are at various stages of the WTO accession process. The establishment of the WTO as part of the round was an important step forward since it was the first new international institution created in the post-war years designed to deal with global trade issues.

WTO gives order to international trade and provides a forum to discuss trade problems

WTO continued and expanded the original GATT. It provides two main functions as an institution. First, it contributes to order and predictability by overseeing and managing the application of internationally agreed trading rules and provides various mechanisms for resolving disputes. Second, in keeping with its primary aim of liberalizing world trade, it provides a forum in which countries can discuss trade problems and negotiate the removal of impediments to freer trading arrangements.

Some trade policy experts argue that the organization's highly complex structures of councils which include all members and numerous subsidiary bodies are cumbersome, inefficient and require further renovation. The problem could grow worse as WTO expands unless arrangements are negotiated to correct the current problems. At the same time, NGOs and some smaller countries continue to be concerned that WTO represents a closed culture dominated by the commercial interests of the largest and most powerful industrial countries.

The evolution of the WTO trade remedy system

Building on the GATT provisions

Trade remedy provisions part of original GATT

Trade remedy provisions have been an integral part of GATT since 1947. As noted above, the early GATT was mainly concerned with reducing and removing tariffs and dealing with customs border issues. Very little attention was given to the trade remedy provisions that are found in GATT Article VI covering anti-dumping and countervailing duties, Article XVI on subsidy practices and Article XIX dealing with emergency safeguard measures.

When GATT was first negotiated, the trade remedy provisions were regarded as essential to the trade liberalization effort. Some countries needed to satisfy their domestic industries that governments would be able to protect them if imports caused injury. Little has changed in this regard in the past 60 years. Firms still seek this kind of assurance against injurious imports caused by foreign government subsidies, dumping or rapid unanticipated changes in market conditions. In particular, trade remedy actions by developing countries have increased dramatically in recent years reflecting the concerns of their local industries about competition from foreign produced goods.

Complainants often comment that individual firms cannot and should not be expected to compete with the financial resources of governments. Nor should they have to compete against private sector firms determined to eliminate competition or who sell products in foreign markets for prices below that which they sell for at home. In the same vein, it is argued that where market conditions change quickly, firms should be afforded some breathing space to adjust to these new circumstances. The validity of these claims is recognized by WTO through the provisions of the Anti-Dumping Agreement (ADA), the Subsidies and Countervailing Measures Agreement (SCMA) and the Safeguards Agreement (SA).

Anti-Dumping Code was first GATT Non-tariff Agreement

In the latter part of the 1960s dumping became a real concern for the international community. As a result, certain GATT members decided to initiate discussions during the Kennedy Round to establish rules governing the application of anti-dumping duties.

These negotiations resulted in the Anti-Dumping Code (the Code), which was agreed to by a limited number of countries, and provided common rules and procedures to be followed by them in anti-dumping cases. In many respects, the Code, which was itself renegotiated in the Tokyo Round, became a model for subsequent negotiation of other non-tariff agreements in the Tokyo Round.

First Countervailing Agreement negotiated in Tokyo Round

The Code, however, dealt only with one part of Article VI. The countervailing duties portion of the Article and subsidy practices under Article XVI did not become a focus of attention until the Tokyo Round negotiations. Bringing greater discipline to the use of countervailing measures and subsidy practices became a central objective for these trade remedy negotiations, which were very difficult because of the interface involved between government practices and programmes, eventually led to the SCMA.

The Agreement was relatively comprehensive in spelling out the rules and procedures to be followed in countervailing duties investigations and generally followed the procedures set out in the Anti-Dumping Code. However, it fell considerably short and did not come to grips with issues relating to subsidy practices particularly their definitions and what subsidy practices should or should not be permissible in international trade. This Agreement was also limited in membership.

ADA and SCMA renegotiated and SA negotiated in Uruguay Round

In the Uruguay Round, the ADA and SCMA were renegotiated and a new agreement on Article XIX safeguard measures was adopted. These agreements are now commonly known as the three pillars of the World Trade Organization's trade remedy system. The three agreements are now the subject of further renegotiation in the Doha Round. If agreement can be achieved on the full package of measures being negotiated, some adjustments may be required in the trade remedies area.

What are trade remedies?

Trade remedies are duties or other measures imposed to counteract injury from imports

Trade remedies are the rules, other than tariffs, under which countries can apply measures or duties that affect the price or volume of goods they import. Trade remedy actions by governments are important because they are basically inconsistent with the primary trade liberalization objective of WTO, can directly influence business decisions affecting goods in international trade and can have an immediate and commanding impact on business and government decisions relating to the sale of goods in the marketplace.

Anti-dumping, countervailing and safeguard measures are approved trade remedies

Dumping is the export sale of a product by a private party at a price lower than the price at which the same good is sold at a profit in the exporter's domestic market. Subsidizing usually means that government funding (e.g. loans at preferential rates, grants or tax incentives) has contributed, in one way or another, to lowering the price of a product whether it is sold in domestic or in foreign markets. In both instances, the impact is to make selling prices lower than they would be under normal market conditions.

Trade remedies may be imposed only to offset injury

If dumped or subsidized imports cause or threaten material injury to a domestic industry in an importing country, the government of that country is permitted by the WTO Agreements, under relatively strict conditions, to offset the impact of the dumping or subsidy through an import duty or other measures, i.e. restore 'fair' trading conditions. The third support mechanism covers emergency safeguard actions that offset 'serious injury' caused by unexpected high volumes of 'fairly' traded imports.

Although by no means perfect, the ADA, SCMA and SA now represent a comprehensive framework of rules that enable governments to respond to injurious import problems. It is important to note that, for the most part, the WTO Agreements are concerned with controlling the use by governments of anti-dumping, countervailing and safeguard mechanisms rather than limiting the acts of dumping or subsidizing. At the same time, under the rules all WTO Member governments can be reasonably confident that their exports to other countries will be treated fairly. All WTO members are now automatically members of the three trade remedy agreements.

How are trade remedy agreements implemented?

Governments establish laws and procedures to implement rules

The ADA, SCMA and SA effectively require national governments to establish specific administrative processes and procedures in their trade remedy laws in order to carry out their commitments. Since the Uruguay Round, many countries are now signatories to these agreements for the first time and all new countries that join WTO must become signatories. Because the agreements do not require a country to have trade remedy laws, governments signing on to these agreements for the first time individually face the decision of what to do with them. They have two basic choices: (a) decide not to implement them as a matter of trade/import policy; or (b) take measures to put in place domestic laws, regulations and administrations consistent with WTO to impose trade remedies when imports are injuring their domestic industries.

Governments have discretion as to how they implement the WTO rules

Some countries have incorporated the WTO Agreements as an integral part of their domestic legislation. These laws are sometimes supported by regulations that provide a greater amount of specificity than is found in the Agreements. Most new WTO member countries are opting for this approach. Others, including Canada, have written and adopted specific laws, rules and regulations to give effect to the Agreements. These take into account the unique domestic judicial requirements and other national concerns of these countries such as time limits for investigations, retroactivity and assistance to domestic producers.

The World Trade Organization trade remedy system

Distinctions between the Agreements

The ADA, SCMA and SA set the general shape and parameters of the process that must be followed by all WTO countries in applying trade remedies. Dumping and subsidizing investigations are significantly different from safeguard inquiries. This difference is directly related to the nature of the activity under review. Dumping and subsidy investigations concern 'unfair' activities involving exporters either selling their products abroad at prices below the prices at which they are sold in their domestic market or selling them at subsidized prices. In safeguard cases, dumping or subsidizing does not enter the picture as the imported goods involved are sold at their normal 'fair' prices.

Three major differences between safeguard and anti-dumping or countervailing cases

Three major differences should be noted between safeguard cases and dumping or subsidy cases. First, safeguard inquiries are usually carried out entirely within the domestic market of the importing country. It is not necessary to examine price levels or other data in the country of export. Second, because the application of a safeguard measure alters the balance of rights and obligations between the importing country and the exporting country(s), the importing country must consult with its trading partners and, if the measure exceeds three years, they must enter into discussions regarding compensation with exporting countries to offset the adverse impact on their exports. In this process, the government(s) of the exporting country(s) should consult their individual exporters in making their assessment of the trade damage involved. Third, because progressive liberalization of a safeguard measure is required under the SCMA, domestic producers must put in place measures that will enable them to adjust to the import competition within a reasonable period of time.

General observations about the WTO Agreements

Before focusing on the substantive elements of the Agreements, the following general points should be kept in mind:

First. Both economically and within the WTO/GATT framework, dumping and subsidizing are generally acceptable activities in international trade.

Second. Anti-dumping and countervailing measures may only be applied to counteract imports that are causing or are threatening to cause material injury or material retardation to a domestic industry. Safeguard measures can only be implemented to deal with fairly traded imports that are causing or threatening serious injury to a domestic industry.

Third. Dumping relates to business activity between two private sector companies. It has nothing to do with government. Government becomes involved only when a decision is taken to adopt anti-dumping actions. Countervail, on the other hand, concerns an action by one government to offset a subsidy policy or practice of another government. Thus, the nature of the two is significantly different. Countervail is particularly sensitive and usually requires extensive government-to-government consultations. Safeguard actions also involve discussions and consultations with foreign governments.

Fourth. Even though anti-dumping, countervailing and safeguard measures are intended to offset different international trade practices, their *price and/or volume effects* are generally the same in the marketplace.

Fifth. Since trade remedy actions are generally characterized as being inconsistent with the primary trade liberalization objectives of WTO, one of the main preoccupations of the WTO trade remedy negotiations was to place constraints on the ability of governments to use these measures.

Sixth. The Agreements provide a set of rules to be followed by all WTO Members. As such, they involve both rights and obligations so that all member countries can expect fair treatment from their trading partners. That is, a country's exports should be treated the same in foreign markets as that country treats imports from other countries.

Seventh. While these Agreements are quite specific in certain respects, considerable scope is left for member governments to take decisions on how they implement them in their domestic laws.

Eighth. The ADA and SCMA generally follow the same processes in terms of investigation procedures and decision-making. As a result, most countries have established parallel administrations for carrying out these investigations.

The Agreements in brief

The Subsidies and Countervailing Measures Agreement

Countervailing measures

The countervailing duties provisions of the SCMA are intended to protect producers in an importing country from unfair competition due to subsidized imports that are causing or threatening injury.

It permits the imposition of countervailing measures, i.e. duties, limits on exports or undertakings, to counteract the effects of a subsidy given by a foreign government on an exported product.

Subsidy defined

The terms of the Agreement in respect of subsidy practices were extensively revised and made more precise in the Uruguay Round. The Agreement contained for the first time an internationally agreed definition of subsidy. It established three categories of subsidy practices – prohibited, actionable and non-actionable. The prohibited category includes subsidies contingent on export performance or those requiring the use of domestic over imported goods. The actionable category encompasses subsidy practices that cause 'serious prejudice' or 'injury' to the interests of other WTO members and these can be subject to countervailing measures. The non-actionable category was established for a five-year period, subject to review, and included subsidies for regional development, environment and research. These would not attract countervailing duties provided they were administered in a way that was consistent with the prescribed criteria set out in the Agreement. Since the review did not take place in 2000, this category is no longer valid. The Agreement includes detailed rules and procedures relating to the investigation of subsidies and their amounts.

The Anti-Dumping Agreement

Essence of Anti-Dumping Agreement

One of the basic objectives of the WTO, is to create conditions for fair competition among firms between different countries. The Agreement provides that 'dumped' goods that cause or threaten injury to an industry in an importing country may be subjected to the imposition of anti-dumping duties. The Agreement sets out in considerable detail the rules and procedures that are to be followed by governments in (a) investigating complaints received from domestic producers and deciding what constitutes the domestic industry, (b) assessing and measuring the degree of dumping, if any, that may be involved, (c) examining the factors that must be taken into account in deciding the question of injury, (d) establishing transparency provisions covering investigations and decision-making, and (e) providing interested parties with opportunities to defend themselves.

The Safeguards Agreement

Background to the Safeguards Agreement

The WTO Safeguards Agreement was one of the major accomplishments of the Uruguay Round (1986–1994). A major issue for negotiation in the Uruguay Round was concern over the proliferation of so-called 'grey area' measures, (voluntary export restraints, orderly marketing arrangements, etc.), which had no legal basis under GATT. The Safeguards Agreement clarified the rules governing grey area measures and provided for them to be phased out by the end of 1998.

Conditions governing the use and duration of safeguards

The SA allows governments to apply import safeguard measures on an MFN basis to a product for temporary periods, after an investigation, if it is determined that the product is being imported in 'such increased quantities, absolute and relative to domestic production, and under such conditions as to cause or threaten to cause serious injury to the domestic industry that produces like or directly competitive products'. These measures, which may be either tariffs or quotas, are permitted in order to give protection to the domestic industry while it adjusts to the increased competitive situation. The Agreement sets a maximum period of 8 years for the application of a safeguard measure by developed countries, and 10 years for developing countries.

What does 'serious injury' mean?

Serious injury means a significant overall impairment in the position of domestic producers. In considering this issue, the authorities examine whether there has been a significant increase in imports or significant price undercutting, depression or suppression. Other important factors examined include the impact of the imported goods on domestic producers with respect to their output, sales, market share, profits, capacity utilization, inventories and employment. The Agreement also provides that the increased imports should be in such quantities as to be a principal cause of serious injury (that is, there must be a causal link between the increased imports and the serious injury or threat thereof). A principal cause is an important cause that is no less important than any other cause of injury.

Provisional safeguard measures

Provisional safeguard measures may be applied for a maximum of 200 days if a preliminary determination is made that critical circumstances exist in which delay would result in damage that would be difficult to repair and that there is clear evidence that the increased imports have caused or threatened to cause serious injury to domestic producers.

The Safeguards Agreement and developing countries

Safeguard measures cannot be applied to products originating in a developing country as long as that country's share of imports of the product in the market of the importing country does not exceed 3%. However, if individual developing countries with less than 3% import share each collectively account for more than 9% of total imports of the product then safeguard action may be taken against them.

Article XVIII of GATT 1994 recognizes that developing countries may find it necessary to provide assistance to new or infant industries or for further development of existing industries through temporary safeguard actions. Stringent conditions govern the use of such measures. This provision was rarely used in the past and, following the Uruguay Round, developing countries wishing to invoke these provisions must obtain the prior approval of WTO.

The WTO anti-dumping and countervailing investigation procedures

Phases of investigations

Investigation procedures under the ADA and SCM A generally involve four separate phases:

Phases in typical anti-dumping or countervailing investigations

Phase I. This is the period, prior to the initiation of an investigation, when the domestic industry complainant alleges that dumping or subsidizing is taking place and that it is causing injury. During this phase the domestic complainants provide evidence of dumping or subsidizing and injury in support of their request for the initiation of an investigation. They also submit whatever data may be requested by the authorities to determine whether there is sufficient evidence to launch an investigation. This phase concludes when the authorities decide on the adequacy of the information and either initiate an investigation or deny the request.

Phase II. This is the period between the initiation of the investigation and the preliminary determination. During this phase, the authorities gather evidence and examine the dumping or subsidizing and injury issues to establish the facts of the case. This usually involves direct contact by the authorities with exporters and importers and may require visits to the exporter's place of business. Throughout the investigation, the authorities must ensure that there is evidence of a causal link between dumping or subsidizing and injury or threat of injury or retardation. This process is completed when either the investigation is terminated or a preliminary determination is made and a decision is taken on whether or not to impose provisional measures.

Phase III. This is the period between the preliminary determination and the final determination. During this period the authorities continue to assemble whatever information is required to finalize decisions on the dumping margins or the amount of the subsidy and on the injurious impact of the dumping or subsidizing. Depending on the complexity of the case, this may involve face-to-face meetings between officials and the interested parties, including exporters, to discuss the details of the findings. These are referred to as disclosure meetings. If public hearings are provided for, they usually occur during this phase of the investigation. The publication of the final determination and the detailed statement of reasons explaining the decisions taken mark the conclusion of the investigation process.

Phase IV. This is the period following a positive final determination when measures are applied and procedures are put in place to enforce and monitor the decision. It is during this period that appeal processes are activated if these are provided for in domestic law.

The detailed procedures envisaged in the WTO Agreements are set out in flowchart I at the end of this chapter.

Elements of procedures

Complaints

Dumping and subsidy cases almost always begin with a complaint received from domestic producers of goods that compete with the imported goods. The reasons for complaints may vary, and result from:

❑ Dramatic import volume increases;

❑ Downward price pressure;

❑ Lost sales and markets;

❑ Negative impact on employment, production and inventories or other factors.

Properly documented
complaint

The Agreements require that the complaints be properly documented. That is, the allegations made by the domestic industry must stand up to analysis and verification. The onus is on the domestic industry to 'make its case'. Complaints must be made by or on behalf of the domestic industry and must be supported by (1) producers whose collective output of the goods represents 25% or more of total domestic production and (2) more than 50% of the producers who voice an opinion. The agreements require that the complaints be supported by evidence of dumping or subsidizing. The complainant(s) must also provide reasonable evidence that the imports are causing injury to the domestic industry.

The complaint phase is most critical in the investigation process

This is the most important and critical stage of the process for all elements of the business community involved. The domestic industry must put forward a case on both injury and dumping or subsidizing. Particular care is required in properly defining the products concerned since this definition establishes the scope of the investigation in terms of product coverage. It also has a direct impact on the time periods during which values will be established. Normally, if a complainant is unsophisticated and unfamiliar with the legal requirements, the time needed to complete the complaint phase of the process can be quite long. Much depends on the experience, size and resources of complainants. It is important to remember that there are no time limits on this phase of the investigation. Indeed, no formal investigation has yet begun and the public, exporters, importers and foreign governments are usually not aware that a complaint is being considered unless the complaining industry makes the matter public or the commercial intelligence networks within the industry detect possible actions against imports.

In general the Agreements provide that a request for a dumping or countervailing investigation must normally include:

Issues that must be covered in an investigation request

❑ A description of the imported goods, including the name of the country of export of the goods, names and addresses of known foreign producers, exporters and domestic importers;

❑ Names and addresses of domestic producers of the goods, total estimated domestic production and estimated total domestic market (including imports);

❑ Evidence of dumping, including the estimated price at which goods are being sold to importers in the importing country, the estimated price at which the goods are being sold in the domestic market of the exporter or the estimated cost of production of the imported goods; or evidence of subsidizing, including a description of the subsidy programme and supporting details of the subsidy and the estimated amount of subsidy;

❑ Evidence of injury such as increased market penetration achieved by the imports allegedly dumped or subsidized, sales lost to dumped or subsidized imports, depressed market prices, declines in profitability, loss of market share and other such evidence. Persons submitting a complaint must also submit a non-confidential version that will be provided to concerned foreign governments, exporters and importers.

Length of time for investigations

Time limits provided for in WTO Agreements

The WTO Agreements establish three main timelines or limits for investigations.

❑ Provisional measures cannot be taken until 60 days after the initiation of an investigation.

❑ Provisional measures cannot be applied until a preliminary determination has been made and they can remain in effect only for a maximum period of four months or, if requested by exporters representing a significant percentage of the trade involved, a period not exceeding six months.

❑ The overall time frame for conducting an investigation is limited to one year unless there are exceptional circumstances, in which case it may be extended to 18 months. These time frames are shown in flowchart II at the end of this chapter.

A complete investigation normally takes between seven and twelve months from the date of initiation of the investigation. It is important to note that the period prior to the initiation of the investigation is not reflected in this time frame. Thus, the clock is not ticking throughout the period when the complaint is being examined and the authorities are deciding whether or not to launch an investigation.

Clock does not begin until investigation formally launched

Major decisions in the process must be announced and interested parties must be notified. Once the actual investigation is begun, the matter is in the public domain and public pressure can be brought to bear to ensure that time limits are met. This is important since there is no limit on how long the authorities might take between the date of initiation and the preliminary determination even though the investigation may be having an adverse effect on trade. By the time the investigation reaches the preliminary determination point, the authorities are in a position to either make a preliminary determination or terminate the investigation. Following a preliminary determination, price or volume undertakings may be accepted.

Exporters should be ready to act when investigation announced

Determination and calculation of the margin of dumping

A decision of dumping requires the establishment of two separate figures: **normal value** and **export price**. The difference between these is the **margin of dumping**.

Normal value defined

The normal value is generally defined as the price at which the imported product is sold for consumption in the country of export under conditions similar to those that apply to the importer. The Anti-Dumping Agreement prescribes various methodologies to be used in determining normal values. These include the selling price in the country of export, selling prices to third countries, or costs of production, plus a mark-up for selling, administrative and all other costs, plus an amount for profit.

Export price defined

The export price is usually based on the price at which the goods are sold to the importer less all charges and expenses incurred after the sale of the goods. Export prices are determined by making various adjustments to the exporter's sales price and importer's purchase price or by using an adjusted resale price for the imported goods in the country of import.

The ADA sets out precise rules for the authorities to follow in making calculations to ensure that prices are comparable in terms of trade levels, quantities, style, product design, materials, warranty and performance guarantees, etc. and to ensure that the transactions reflect prices between unrelated firms, determined under competitive market conditions.

Determination of the existence of a subsidy

Existence and amount of subsidy

The process of substantiating the existence and amount of subsidies involves consultations with government officials of the country of export, examination of records of the exporting firms and the completion of extensive questionnaires seeking detailed information on all aspects of the subsidy programme. The analysis of these data leads to a calculation of the amount of subsidy on a per unit basis with respect to the imported goods.

It is crucial that exporters fully cooperate with the authorities to ensure that calculations in both dumping and subsidy cases accurately reflect the true values and costs relating to the subject goods. A lack of attention to detail at this stage in the process could prove particularly harmful to the interests of exporting firms.

Determination of injury

The ADA and SCMA incorporate a number of indices and criteria that must be examined by the authorities in arriving at a judgement as to whether injury or retardation exists or is threatened. They include:

Factors affecting injury decision

❑ The effects of the dumping or subsidizing on prices, production, sales, market shares, profits, employment and capacity utilization;

❑ The magnitude of the margin of dumping or the amount of the subsidy; and

❑ The actual or potential negative effects on cash flow, inventories, employment, wages, growth and the ability to raise capital or investments.

The Agreements require that a decision be based on positive evidence and involve an examination of the impact of the volume of the dumped or subsidized imports on the domestic producers of like goods. A determination of material injury or threat of material injury must be based on facts and not mere allegation, conjecture or remote possibility. A causal relationship must also be established between the imports and the injury. The authorities also examine any factors other than dumping or subsidizing that may be having an adverse effect on the domestic industry. Here again, it is very important that exporters, importers and foreign governments ensure that all of the facts relating to the economic situation facing the domestic industry are accurate and substantiated by evidence and analysis.

The injury decision process must be transparent and allow parties to defend their interests

Governments are free to choose the kinds of procedures they wish to follow in making injury decisions. The main criteria, however, are that the process be transparent and that the involved parties have a full opportunity to defend their interests. Some countries, such as Canada and the United States of America, use a bifurcated approach in which the injury assessment is carried out by a body that is independent and separate from the authorities investigating dumping or subsidizing. The majority of countries however rely on a single administrative body to make decisions on both dumping or subsidizing and injury.

Definition of domestic industry

Definition of domestic industry

In injury determinations, the impact of the dumped or subsidized imports must be assessed in relation to their effects on the 'domestic producers as a whole of the like products or to those of them whose collective output of the like products constitutes a major proportion of the total domestic production of those products'.

Effectively, this means that dumping or countervailing duties cannot be imposed when only one or a few producers in the industry are injured. A 'major proportion' of the industry usually means more than 50% must be injured. The Agreements contain special rules for dealing with related producers and regional markets.

The investigation process

Requests for information or questionnaires

Once a complaint has been accepted the request for information is sent to all known exporters and importers as soon as possible following the initiation of the investigation. The request or questionnaire for exporters describes in detail the necessary information that must be prepared and it provides an opportunity for exporters to fully explain and document their pricing practices on sales to the country of import. The information requested from importers may vary depending on whether the importer is related to the exporter. If they are not related, the request is focused on the importer's purchase price for the goods under investigation. If related, the request is focused on the resale of the goods in the importing country, including information describing the general selling and administrative expenses associated with these sales. In subsidy cases, a request for information is forwarded to the foreign government at the time the investigation is initiated.

Time permitted to respond to questionnaires

Exporters, importers and foreign governments are usually given a specified number of days to respond to requests for information. This time limit is essential given the relatively short period available to assemble and analyse all the information associated with these cases. The Agreements provide that the authorities must allow at least 30 days for exporters to respond to questionnaires. These days are counted from the date the party receives the request for information, which is deemed to occur one week after it is sent. Extensions of time limits are permissible under the Agreements.

Authorities provide reasons for decisions

De minimis values or negligible volumes

When a preliminary determination is made, a *statement of reasons* is usually issued explaining in detail how normal values and export prices were determined and the authorities' assessment of the evidence of injury to the domestic industry. The evidence of dumping or subsidizing and injury must be considered simultaneously in the decision whether or not to initiate an investigation and, thereafter, during the course of the investigation. Cases must be terminated as soon as it is discovered that there is not sufficient evidence of dumping or subsidizing or injury, or if the margin of dumping or the amount of the subsidy is found to be *de minimis* or the volume of dumped imports is negligible.[1]

Provisional measures

The Agreements allow for the imposition of a provisional duty or the posting of a security or bond in the amount of the provisionally estimated duty if these measures are necessary to prevent injury during the investigation. Such action cannot be taken for at least 60 days following the initiation of an investigation and cannot normally be in place for a period exceeding four months.

Undertakings

Types of undertakings and applicable conditions

The ADA and SCMA provide for two possible types of undertakings in dumping cases and several types in subsidy cases. In dumping cases, the undertaking may involve the exporter increasing the selling price of the goods to eliminate the dumping or increasing it sufficiently to offset the injury. In subsidy cases, the consent of the foreign government must be obtained but can include undertakings to eliminate the subsidy on future shipments of the goods, limit the amount of the subsidy or quantity of the goods shipped in future, or to otherwise agree to eliminate the injurious effects of the subsidizing on production in the country of import.

Undertakings are usually accepted only if given by exporters or governments representing all or substantially all of the trade of the product under investigation. In some countries, the undertaking must cover at least 85% of the volume of the dumped or subsidized imports. The terms of undertakings must be sufficiently precise to allow them to be effectively monitored.

Final determination

In most investigations, the time between the preliminary determination and the final determination is taken up in verifying the informational base, visiting exporting firms not previously investigated, seeking clarification of details, visiting importers, assembling whatever additional data are needed, and holding disclosure meetings and hearings to finalize the decision.

---

1   *De minimis* is less than 2% of the export price in dumping cases and less than 1% *ad valorem* in subsidy cases; the volume of dumped or subsidized imports is negligible when they represent generally less than 3% of imports of the like product in the importing country.

Exporters should seize
opportunities to ensure that
value calculations are correct

During this period officials usually provide the interested parties with full explanations as to how the preliminary margins of dumping or the amount of the subsidy were established and an assessment of the factors taken into account. While protecting confidentiality, public hearings or disclosure meetings with interested parties usually take place to discuss the details of the case and allow interested parties to contest the facts and methodologies used by the authorities. These meetings also provide an opportunity for parties to present any new information that may have a bearing on the case.

Retroactivity

Retroactivity normally
permitted only during
provisional period

Provisional duties may be applied only during the period between the preliminary and final determinations. If such duties are applied, they may be converted to definitive duties following a final determination of dumping or subsidizing and injury. Provisional duties cannot be increased to match a higher final anti-dumping or countervailing duty.

If provisional duties were set at a level higher than the final anti-dumping duty, the excess must be reimbursed. Retroactivity is not permitted if only a threat of injury is found except when the effect of the dumped imports, in the absence of provisional measures, would have led to a determination of injury. Retroactivity beyond the period during which provisional measures applied is allowed under the agreements only in the very narrowly defined circumstance of massive dumping.

Imposition and collection of duties

An importing country may impose a duty in the full amount of the margin of dumping or the amount of the subsidy or it can levy a lesser amount if that is considered adequate to eliminate the injury. Some WTO member countries have incorporated the lesser duty provision as a requirement in their domestic laws while others use the provision as a means of applying a lower duty where this is considered desirable in the national interest, for instance to promote competition in the market. The duty can never exceed the margin of dumping or the amount of the subsidy. It must, however, be imposed on a non-discriminatory basis on imports from all sources found to be dumping or subsidizing except on imports from sources where a price undertaking is in place.

Duration and review

Anti-dumping and countervailing duties may remain in force only as long as necessary to counteract the dumping or subsidizing that is causing injury. A definitive duty must be terminated not later than five years following the date of its imposition unless a review by the authorities indicates that the duty is still warranted.

Transparency

The Agreements provide for as much disclosure as possible at every stage of anti-dumping and countervailing investigations, while protecting confidential information. A non-confidential summary is usually required in respect of confidential material and decisions are generally supported with statements of reasons outlining the considerations that led to the determination.

Appeal procedures

The Agreements provide that Members shall maintain judicial procedures for the review of administrative actions relating to final determinations. Anti-dumping or countervailing actions are subject to the dispute settlement understanding of the WTO.

FLOWCHART I

Anti-dumping/countervailing procedures

Complaint – initiation

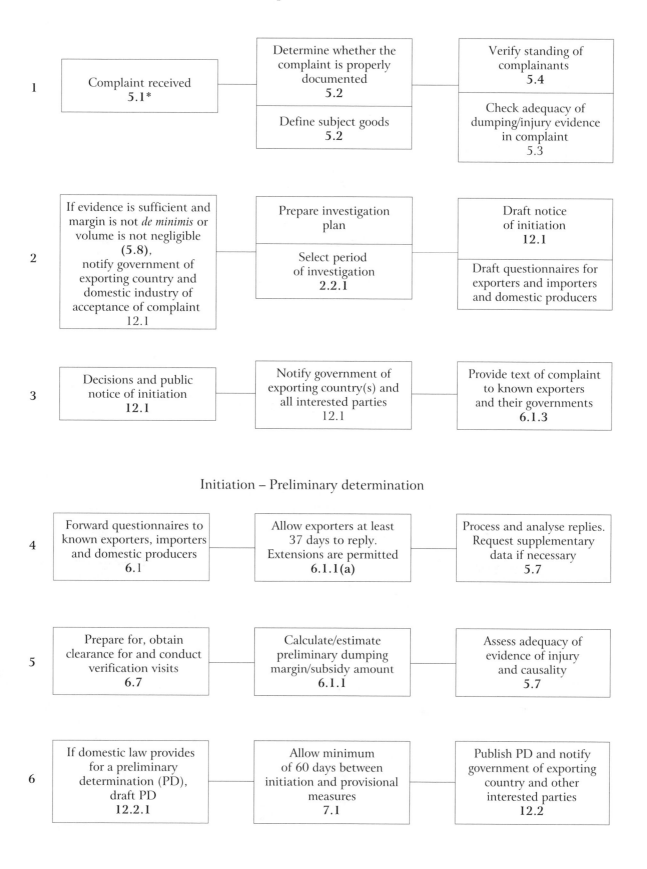

1

| Complaint received 5.1* | Determine whether the complaint is properly documented 5.2 | Verify standing of complainants 5.4 |
| | Define subject goods 5.2 | Check adequacy of dumping/injury evidence in complaint 5.3 |

2

| If evidence is sufficient and margin is not *de minimis* or volume is not negligible (5.8), notify government of exporting country and domestic industry of acceptance of complaint 12.1 | Prepare investigation plan / Select period of investigation 2.2.1 | Draft notice of initiation 12.1 / Draft questionnaires for exporters and importers and domestic producers |

3

| Decisions and public notice of initiation 12.1 | Notify government of exporting country(s) and all interested parties 12.1 | Provide text of complaint to known exporters and their governments 6.1.3 |

Initiation – Preliminary determination

4

| Forward questionnaires to known exporters, importers and domestic producers 6.1 | Allow exporters at least 37 days to reply. Extensions are permitted 6.1.1(a) | Process and analyse replies. Request supplementary data if necessary 5.7 |

5

| Prepare for, obtain clearance for and conduct verification visits 6.7 | Calculate/estimate preliminary dumping margin/subsidy amount 6.1.1 | Assess adequacy of evidence of injury and causality 5.7 |

6

| If domestic law provides for a preliminary determination (PD), draft PD 12.2.1 | Allow minimum of 60 days between initiation and provisional measures 7.1 | Publish PD and notify government of exporting country and other interested parties 12.2 |

Preliminary determination – Final determination

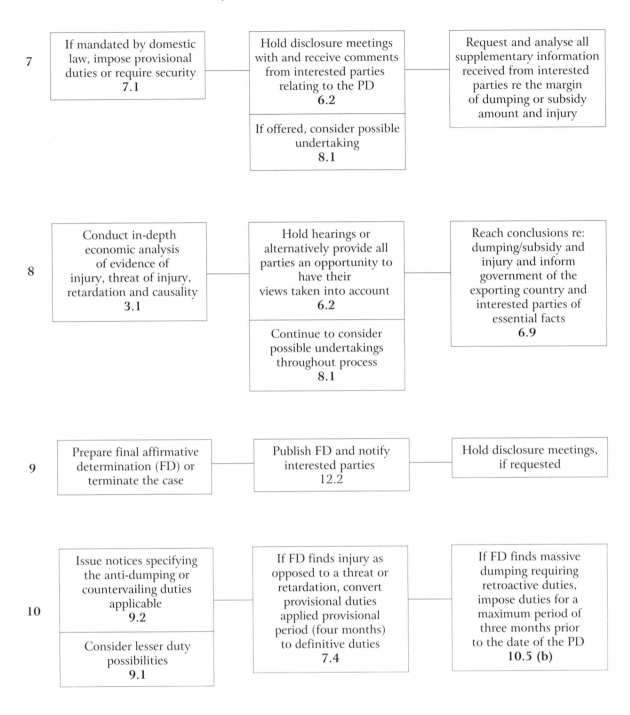

7	If mandated by domestic law, impose provisional duties or require security **7.1**

Hold disclosure meetings with and receive comments from interested parties relating to the PD
6.2

If offered, consider possible undertaking
8.1

Request and analyse all supplementary information received from interested parties re the margin of dumping or subsidy amount and injury

---

8 — Conduct in-depth economic analysis of evidence of injury, threat of injury, retardation and causality
3.1

Hold hearings or alternatively provide all parties an opportunity to have their views taken into account
6.2

Continue to consider possible undertakings throughout process
8.1

Reach conclusions re: dumping/subsidy and injury and inform government of the exporting country and interested parties of essential facts
6.9

---

9 — Prepare final affirmative determination (FD) or terminate the case

Publish FD and notify interested parties
12.2

Hold disclosure meetings, if requested

---

10 — Issue notices specifying the anti-dumping or countervailing duties applicable
9.2

Consider lesser duty possibilities
9.1

If FD finds injury as opposed to a threat or retardation, convert provisional duties applied provisional period (four months) to definitive duties
7.4

If FD finds massive dumping requiring retroactive duties, impose duties for a maximum period of three months prior to the date of the PD
10.5 (b)

---

*   Numbers refer to articles in the Anti-Dumping Agreement.

a   Agreement provides for a 30-day period from the date of receipt of the questionnaire by the exporter which is deemed to be one week after it was sent.

b   If an undertaking is violated, definitive duties may be levied retroactively for 90 days before the application of provisional measures (8.6).

FLOWCHART II

Length of time for investigations

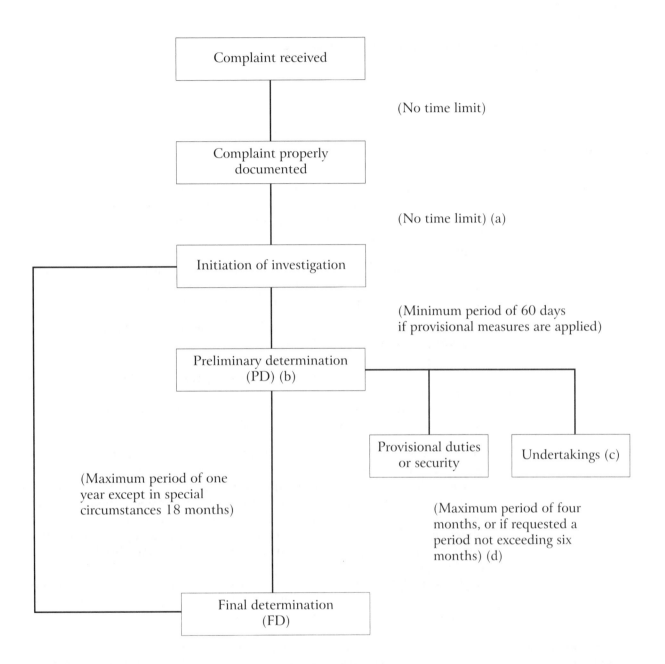

a   Time limits are not triggered until an investigation is initiated.

b   There is no time limit between the PD and the FD if provisional measures are not applied.

c   If an undertaking is violated, provisional measures may be imposed immediately and definitive duties may be levied for a 90-day period before the application of the provisional measures.

d   These time limits may be extended to six and nine months respectively if the authorities are examining whether a duty lower than the margin of dumping would be sufficient to remove injury.

CHAPTER 2

The Canadian trade remedy system

Background

Canada was the first country to use anti-dumping duties

Canada established the world's first anti-dumping system in 1904 as an alternative to a general increase in customs duties. It was designed to protect against predatory disposal of surpluses by large producers from countries much bigger than Canada. These countries themselves operated behind high levels of tariff protection in their domestic markets. Anti-dumping duties were seen as a means of providing protection for Canadian industry against dumped goods, thus avoiding unnecessarily high tariffs on all imports, an action that would have penalized consumers who did not use dumped goods.

Canadian system introduces injury test

The Canadian anti-dumping system remained virtually unchanged from the time of its introduction until 1968. It was strongly supported by Canadian industry because it provided a swift and effective way to deal with dumping. However, the system lacked detailed investigation procedures. It was also regarded by many of Canada's trading partners as an automatic system because it did not incorporate a specific injury test. As such, it was considered to be contrary to the provisions of Article VI of GATT.

During the Kennedy Round of trade negotiations, Canada decided that it was in its long-term interest as a nation heavily dependent on international trade to actively participate in the negotiation of the GATT Anti-Dumping Code. A major consideration that led to this decision was concern about the system that had developed in the United States. The lack of procedural rules in the United States process and the difficulty of terminating anti-dumping orders after dumping had ceased prejudiced Canadian exports. There was also the fear that, given protectionist sentiments in the United States, the anti-dumping law might be used in future in a more restrictive and harassing fashion. There was also the prospect that Europe might imitate United States practices unless measures were taken to correct the situation.

GATT provided a safety net against disruptive anti-dumping practices

If this were to happen, all of Canada's main export markets could be adversely affected. It was concluded that the only way to guard against this development was to secure binding commitments against such practices in an international agreement under GATT. Canadian industry agreed that it stood to gain more than it would lose from an international system involving precise substantive and procedural rules that would be applied in a consistent manner by all countries.

Two-track Canadian system was modelled on the United States system

Canada took a leading role in the negotiation of the original Anti-Dumping Code and, in 1968, put in place a new domestic comprehensive anti-dumping regime. In many respects it was modelled on the United States system and like that process separated the responsibility for determining and measuring dumping from the function of establishing whether the dumped imports were causing or threatening material injury or retardation to the domestic industry. The GATT Code/Agreement went through further changes in the Tokyo and

Uruguay Rounds of negotiations and Canadian law has been amended to reflect these changes.

The Canadian countervailing measures legislation did not become the focus of attention until the Tokyo Round of negotiations when the Subsidies and Countervailing Duties Agreement was negotiated. At that time the Canadian law consisted of a single provision in the Customs Tariff which provided for the imposition of countervailing duties to offset a subsidy granted on imported goods that were causing or threatening injury to Canadian industry. This provision was supported by a set of administrative regulations used to establish the facts in each case. Following the GATT negotiation, substantive revisions were required to bring Canadian law and practice into conformity. This was accomplished through the adoption of the Special Import Measures Act (SIMA) in 1984.

This Act effectively established parallel processes governing the administrative and judicial procedures to be followed in investigating alleged dumping or subsidizing of imported goods.

Prior to the conclusion of the WTO Safeguard Agreement in the Uruguay Round of negotiations, the Canadian Customs Tariff included provisions that enabled the Government to adopt temporary safeguard measures consistent with Article XIX of GATT to protect Canadian producers against 'serious injury' caused or threatened by imports. Canada's safeguard provisions had been in place for a number of years but had not been used to any great extent. This reflects the fact that Canada had always taken the view that these were essentially emergency measures to be used only as a last resort to deal with very serious problems caused by increased volumes of imports. All other possible avenues for coping with the import problem, including anti-dumping or countervailing measures, were explored before safeguard action was considered. An additional factor affecting the use of safeguard measures was the GATT requirement that countries pay compensation for such actions to their most affected trading partners or face the prospect of retaliatory measures. Canadian law was amended to reflect the procedural and transparency requirements of the Safeguards Agreement negotiated in the Uruguay Round.

Canada's use of trade remedy measures

Canada is a major trading country with 37.8% of GDP in 2005 and one in every five jobs accounted for by international trade. The Canadian economy has experienced significant growth over the past decade and international trade has played a major role in the expansion. On average, Canada does $2.5 billion worth of business daily – exports and imports of goods and services – with the rest of the world. In 2005, exports of goods and services increased by 5.2% to reach $516 billion and imports grew by 7.4% to reach $463 billion. The United States was by far Canada's dominant trading partner, representing 81% of Canada's merchandise exports and providing more than half of its imports in 2005. While the United States is clearly the dominant market for exports from Canada, exports to the United States have grown by only 4% over the period 2001–2006 while exports to the other three major export markets have grown by 9% (Japan), 63% (United Kingdom) and 67% (China), and imports from the United States and Japan have remained virtually unchanged from 2001–2006 while imports from China have grown by 132% and imports from Mexico by 20%.

Since 1984, when SIMA was enacted, Canada has initiated a total of 374 measures against individual countries, of which 347 are dumping and 27 are CVD. The current status of these investigations is as follows:

Investigation under way	1
Investigation terminated prior to final determination phase	38
Undertaking accepted, investigation suspended	1
Undertaking accepted, later terminated and investigation resumed	2
Undertaking accepted, now expired	16
Finding by Canadian International Trade Tribunal (CITT): no injury	92
Finding by CITT: injury; duties apply	59
Finding by CITT: injury; now rescinded	167

Dumping actions

The 347 dumping investigations initiated since 1984 have targeted the United States (64 actions), China (22 actions), the Republic of Korea and Taiwan Province (China) (20 actions each), Denmark (19 actions) Great Britain and Japan (15 actions each), Brazil (14 actions) and France (11 actions). The majority of the 347 dumping actions were against steel products (170 actions), with 100 actions against consumer goods, 64 against industrial products and 13 against agricultural goods.

The following chart shows the number of individual dumping actions initiated per year since SIMA's inception in 1984.

Dumping action initiations per year

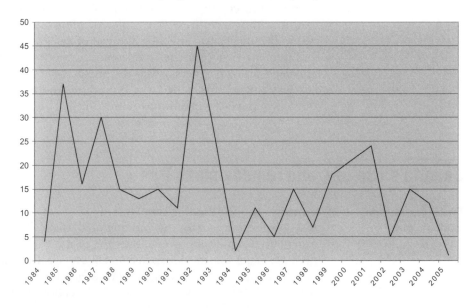

Most recently, between 2000 and 2005 there were 78 actions initiated. Of these actions, 1 was resolved with an undertaking, now expired; 10 were terminated by CBSA prior to making a final determination; 3 resulted in injury findings which have been rescinded; in 28 cases the Tribunal found no injury; and in 36 cases the Tribunal found injury and the duties still remain in place

A total of 55 measures are still in effect against individual countries. The countries still subject to the most dumping investigations are China (11 actions), Taiwan Province (China) (6 actions) and the United States and South Africa (3 actions each). Steel remains the category with the most actions (37); there are 13 actions against consumer goods; 2 against industrial products and 2 against agricultural products. (See annex I.)

Countervailing duty actions

There have been 27 countervailing duty actions initiated since SIMA's inception in 1984. The country named most often was India (6 actions), followed by Brazil (5 actions); there were 4 actions against the United States and 3 against China. The majority of the 27 CVD actions were against steel products (11), 9 involved consumer goods, 2 related to industrial products and 5 dealt with agriculture.

Between 2000 and 2005 there were 11 actions initiated. Of these actions, 2 were terminated by CBSA prior to making a final determination; 2 resulted in injury findings which have since been rescinded; in 3 cases the Tribunal found no injury; and in 4 cases the Tribunal found injury and the duties remain in place. Five measures are still in effect against individual countries. The countries still subject to these CVD actions are China (2 actions), India (2 actions) and the EU (1 action). (See Annex I.)

Existence of trade remedy laws can pose a threat for exporters

More recent data enable us to make a number of observations that should be helpful to the business community, in particular for exporters to Canada, in assessing the sensitivity of Canadian industrial sectors to import competition and the dangers associated with dumping and subsidizing shipments to Canada. It should be noted in this regard that activity under the trade remedy laws is but one indication of the effectiveness of this type of legislation. While one cannot quantify the impact of the mere existence of anti-dumping and countervailing laws and the threat of their use, it is a well-known fact that firms are reluctant to enter into and develop a market if there is a threat of trade remedy actions.

A review of the product coverage of actions taken in recent years does not help to isolate any product areas, other than steel, that have been especially sensitive to imports. Moreover , because of the very heavy demand for steel worldwide in the last few years, steel is no longer particularly sensitive to import competition. The most that can be said is that Canadian anti-dumping and countervailing actions cover a variety of goods and exporters should examine the market carefully before attempting to sell dumped or subsidized goods in the Canadian market.

Canadian firms are not hesitant to use trade remedy measures

Past anti-dumping and countervailing actions moreover signal that Canadian industry, even in relatively small sectors of the economy, is familiar with Canada's trade remedy laws and is not hesitant about using them. This is especially the case in the relatively small Canadian market where a limited number of firms compete in any given sector and imports take on a high profile.

Import sensitivity in the Canadian market is not reflected exclusively by dumping and countervailing actions. Textiles, clothing and footwear have been the subject of many complaints and actions over the years and these continue to be areas of concern. Agricultural products, especially dairy and poultry, are another sector where the normal trade rules do not apply, and exporters should be aware of market constraints before shipping these products to Canada.

Exporters must balance opportunities in the Canadian market against possible costs of trade remedy actions

As indicated above, the Canadian market is growing. Imports are important in ensuring that Canadian producers are in a position to take advantage of the latest technology to enable them to compete on world markets. The Canadian market is one of the most open in the world and it provides an excellent opportunity for exporters to engage in dynamic business activity. Care should, however, be taken to identify whether the product to be exported is likely to lead to trade remedy actions and, if so, whether the market potential is worth the high costs generally associated with these measures.

Present Canadian anti-dumping and countervailing measures system

Canada's anti-dumping and countervailing measures legislation is set out in the Special Import Measures Act (SIMA) and the Canadian International Trade Tribunal Act and their rules and regulations. This package of legislation and the practices and procedures involved comply in all respects with GATT 1994 and the WTO Agreements.

CBSA calculates the margin of dumping or the amount of the subsidy

CITT determines injury

The Canadian anti-dumping and countervailing regime employs a dual track process similar to that used in the United States. The determination of dumping or subsidizing and the calculation of the margin of dumping or the amount of the subsidy are the responsibility of the Canada Border Services Agency (CBSA). CITT conducts inquiries to determine whether the importation of the dumped or subsidized goods is causing or threatening to cause material injury or retardation to production in Canada. CITT is composed of nine people appointed by the Government for a period of up to five years. To assist in its inquiries, CITT has a staff composed of economists, industry specialists and legal experts who bring the latest analytical techniques to examining injury-related considerations.

Their reports are a critical element in the decision that must be made by CITT. This work requires a very different set of skills from those needed by officials of CBSA.

Considerations affecting decision-making are different for injury and dumping or subsidies

A number of considerations entered into the decision to adopt a bifurcated system. One of the most important was the nature of the injury/causality decision as opposed to the decision on whether dumping or subsidizing was taking place. In this connection the terms 'injury', 'threat of injury' and 'retardation' are ill-defined in the WTO Agreements and at best are vague concepts. Indeed it would be difficult for it to be otherwise since the elements involved in deciding injury do not lend themselves to precise definitions, but rather require a reasoned, subjective judgement as to their impact. The calculation of the amount of dumping or subsidy carried out by CBSA requires the ability to analyse and consolidate large volumes of corporate sales, costing and financial information from numerous sources and countries all over the world. Although the calculation of dumping or subsidy is mathematically straightforward, the process is onerous and the officers of CBSA have significant discretion in the application of the law.

CBSA structure and investigation process

CBSA organization

The Trade Programs Directorate of the Admissibility Branch of CBSA administers SIMA. The directorate is made up of a relatively large number of people directly involved in the administration and investigation of anti-dumping and countervailing complaints and case verifications. The directorate is organized along product lines that enable officers to develop a certain expertise in these areas, some of which involve highly technical products. The four main groupings are:

❑ Industrial products;

❑ Consumer products;

❑ Operational policy; and

❑ Fundamental review team.

Overview of CBSA investigation process

Canadian procedures closely follow those provided for in the WTO Agreements

The SIMA procedures covering the investigation of dumping or subsidizing are essentially the same and follow closely the provisions of the WTO Agreements. As indicated above, the agreements recognize that dumping and subsidizing practices *per se* are not to be condemned. Rather, it is only when dumped or subsidized imports cause or threaten to cause material injury or retardation that remedial trade measures are permitted in the form of anti-dumping or countervailing measures.

In general the activities of CBSA in investigating anti-dumping or countervailing cases are as follows.

Procedures generally followed by CBSA in investigations

❑ Guidelines are provided to Canadian producers to assist in the preparation of a properly documented complaint and in completing the 'complainant's questionnaire'. The initiation of an investigation is based on a written 'properly documented complaint received from Canadian producers who together produce more than 25% of total Canadian production of the goods. CBSA may initiate an investigation on its own when it has evidence to support such action. It will also initiate an investigation at the direction of CITT when that body (a) becomes aware of a dumping or subsidizing situation in the course of examining another case or (b) gives advice on request that, in its opinion, there is evidence of a reasonable indication of injury or threat of injury. In all three situations, CBSA will only initiate an investigation where:

 – There is evidence that the goods have been or are being subsidized or dumped;

 – The evidence provides a reasonable indication that the subsidizing or dumping is causing or threatening material injury or retardation; and

 – If a subsidy is involved, that subsidy is actionable under the SCMA.

❑ A notice of the initiation of an investigation is provided to the exporter(s), the importer(s), the government(s) of the country(ies) of export, CITT and the complainant. It is also published in the *Canada Gazette*. Public notices are given thereafter at each stage of the investigation process.

❑ Immediately following the initiation, a detailed questionnaire is sent to the manufacturers, exporters, and importers of the goods. The manufacturer's/exporter's questionnaire is intended to establish the normal value of the goods in the country of export. It covers such things as volumes and values of domestic sales, costs of production, marketing and administration costs, transportation and handling costs, compensatory or special financial arrangements between the parties, etc. The importer's questionnaire seeks information relating to the export price and on matters such as the terms and conditions of purchase, export charges assumed by the exporter, and any special contractual relations between the parties. More detailed questions are involved if the exporter and importer are related.

❑ CBSA establishes a public record listing all information gathered in the investigation. The record is published on the Internet and is updated regularly as new documentation and data are collected by CBSA or filed by interested parties (*www.cbsa-asfc.gc.ca/sima*). Public information that is placed on the record is available to any interested party upon request to the registry.

❑ The accumulation of data takes place within a relatively tight time frame. The exporter is normally given 37 days to respond to the questionnaire. CBSA officials usually visit the manufacturer/exporter to verify the accuracy of the responses provided in the questionnaire and at the same time seek answers to any additional questions they may have concerning the case. This verification forms the basis of a report and recommendations to the CBSA President to enable a preliminary determination (PD) of dumping or subsidizing.

– Information provided to CBSA may be designated as confidential if it is accompanied by an explanation as to why it is to be treated as confidential and a non-confidential summary is also submitted.

– Before making a PD, an investigation may be terminated if CITT advises that the evidence does not disclose a reasonable indication of injury or retardation, CBSA is satisfied that there is insufficient evidence of dumping or subsidizing, or the amounts involved are negligible.

– The PD of dumping or subsidizing is normally made within 90 days of the initiation of an investigation but this period can be extended in complex cases for a further 45 days. The PD must provide an estimate of the margin of dumping or the amount of the subsidy involved and specify the goods to which the ruling applies. It must also indicate if it applies to goods on which there is a prohibited subsidy, specify the amount of the prohibited subsidy and provide the name of the importer of the goods.

– When an affirmative PD of dumping or subsidizing is made, CITT formally begins its inquiry into whether the imported goods are causing or threatening to cause injury or retardation. CBSA also continues its investigation of dumping or subsidizing in preparation for the issuance of a final determination. During this period, provisional duties are levied or the posting of a bond is required in respect of any subject goods entering Canada.

– In the course of an investigation, CBSA may accept an undertaking from an exporter if it is judged to eliminate the subsidy, the margin of dumping or the material injury involved. In a subsidy case, the government of the country of export may also provide an undertaking. An investigation will be completed after an undertaking has been given if the exporter or government of the country of export so requests at the time the undertaking is offered.

– At approximately day 130 of the investigation, parties are invited to submit briefs to CBSA. Parties have access to all of the information in the CBSA record of a case (subject to confidentiality guidelines). Parties are invited to use the preliminary determination and any information on CBSA's record of the case to make submissions to CBSA regarding the methodology to be used to determine normal values, export prices and the amount of the subsidy for the final determination. These briefs are circulated to other parties to the investigation and reply briefs may be submitted.

– A final determination must be issued by CBSA within 90 days after making a PD when it is satisfied that the goods have been or are being dumped or subsidized and that the amounts involved are not negligible.

Canadian law, regulations and practices are very detailed and precise. The legal requirements impose a major burden on the parties involved as well as on CBSA and CITT. Moreover, while the same general procedures apply to both anti-dumping and countervailing investigations, the latter are considerably more sensitive because they involve one country questioning the trade effects of a programme instituted by the government of another country. As such, countervailing actions are not taken lightly and indeed consultations between the parties are a prerequisite to adopting protective measures. Anti-dumping measures, while also serious, are in a somewhat different category since they involve activities between private parties.

Table1: Timing and steps in Canadian anti-dumping and countervailing investigations

Day	Event	Organization
0	Complaint filed.	CBSA
21	CBSA determines whether the complaint is properly documented.	CBSA
51	CBSA initiates an investigation.	CBSA
CBSA initiation		
1	CBSA distributes exporter's and importer's questionnaires.	CBSA
1	CITT publishes a notice of commencement of preliminary injury inquiry.	CITT
4	CBSA compiles and makes available a listing of exhibits.	CBSA
22	CITT distributes information received from CBSA to interested parties for its preliminary injury inquiry.	CITT
32	CITT receives submissions by parties opposed to the complaint (importers, exporters and others) for its preliminary injury inquiry.	CITT
38	CBSA receives responses to its exporter's questionnaire.	CBSA
39–90	CBSA verifies exporter's questionnaire and analyses data.	CBSA
39	CITT receives reply submissions from the complainant and submissions in support of the complaint for its preliminary injury inquiry.	CITT
60	CITT makes a preliminary injury determination or terminates the inquiry.	CITT
75	CITT issues its reasons regarding the preliminary injury determination.	CITT
90	CBSA makes a preliminary determination of dumping or terminates the investigation.	CBSA
91–180	CBSA imposes provisional duties and continues anti-dumping/countervailing duties investigation.	CBSA
91	CITT issues a notice of inquiry and the inquiry schedule, and sends questionnaires to importers, exporters, purchasers and the domestic industry.	CITT
111	Questionnaires completed by importers, exporters, purchasers, and the domestic industry.	CITT
120	CBSA record is closed.	CBSA
130	Case arguments to CBSA due from all parties.	CBSA
140	Reply submissions to CBSA due from all parties in respect of case arguments.	CBSA
140	CITT distributes its staff report and tribunal exhibits.	CITT

Day	Event	Organization
150	Domestic producers file their case.	CITT
160	Importers and exporters file their cases.	CITT
180	Domestic producers file reply submission.	CITT
180	CBSA makes a final determination of dumping or terminates the investigation.	CBSA
180–195	CITT holds its injury hearing.	CITT
210	CITT issues its final injury finding.	CITT
225	CITT issues its reasons.	CITT

The investigation – complaint to preliminary determination

The complaint

There are six basic steps in the preparation of a dumping and/or subsidizing complaint.

❑ Step 1 – Contacting the Trade Programs Directorate;

❑ Step 2 – Completing the statement of complaint;

❑ Step 3 – Answering the questionnaire;

❑ Step 4 – Identifying all confidential information in your complaint;

❑ Step 5 – Preparing a non-confidential version of your complaint;

❑ Step 6 – Filing your complaint.

Step 1 – Contacting the Trade Programs Directorate

The Trade Programs Directorate of CBSA is the administering authority in Canada that conducts investigations into dumping or subsidies. Although the Government may initiate a complaint, in practice most investigations begin with a written complaint from the Canadian producers of the subject goods. The Trade Programs Directorate will assist a complainant by providing advice on preparing the complaint and explaining the complexities of the dumping and subsidizing process.

Step 2 – Completing the statement of complaint

The complainant must complete a 'statement of complaint' which identifies the dumped and/or subsidized imports causing injury to Canadian industry. This statement is also a pledge that the information in the complaint is true and complete.

Step 3 – Answering the questionnaire

The complainant must respond to a detailed questionnaire and provide supporting documentation explaining and supporting the allegations in the complaint. The complaint is dealt with in greater detail below.

Step 4 – Identifying all confidential information in your complaint

CBSA will protect all confidential information submitted by all parties to an investigation but it is required to make non-confidential information available to interested persons so they can understand the reasons for any decisions taken.

Step 5 – Preparing a non-confidential version of the complaint

The complainant must produce a non-confidential version of the complaint. The non-confidential version must be sufficiently detailed to allow a person reading it to have a reasonable understanding of the substance of the confidential information removed.

Step 6 – Filing your complaint

CBSA will evaluate the complaint and decide whether it is properly documented. CBSA will make its decision within 21 days and initiate an investigation or advise the complainant that further information is required.

Complainant's questionnaire

The most important and onerous part of the process is the response to the questionnaire There are eight parts to an anti-dumping or subsidy complaints questionnaire:

❑ Identification of the complainant;

❑ Imported goods;

❑ Goods produced in Canada;

❑ Classes of goods;

❑ Canadian industry;

❑ Dumping;

❑ Subsidizing;

❑ Demonstrating injury.

Identification of the complainant

The complainant can be a Canadian producer or association. An anti-dumping or countervailing measures action is normally launched by the Canadian industry that produces goods like the imports.

Imported goods

The complainant must describe the imported goods allegedly being dumped and/or subsidized, including the tariff classification and the country where the goods are produced and exported from. The complainant must also identify known exporters and importers of the goods, and how they are marketed, priced, and distributed, in Canada.

Goods produced in Canada

A dumping or subsidy investigation can be initiated only if the Canadian industry produces goods in Canada that are identical or similar to the imported goods ('like goods'). The complainant must describe the goods it produces. If the imported goods are not identical to the domestically produced goods the complainant must describe the goods in terms of their characteristics and uses. For example, if a complaint is made against ballpoint pens with blue ink then this is the only product against which possible future protection will be provided. However, if ballpoint pens with black ink are deemed to have the same characteristics and uses then they are like goods and would be included in the subject goods definition.

Anti-dumping or countervailing measures can be imposed only on goods that meet the like goods criteria. Exporters to Canada must examine the product they are exporting and determine if it is 'like' the domestically produced goods. If the exported product has unique features which suggest that the goods defined in the complaint are not like, exporters may seek a specific exclusion for their goods from CITT at either the preliminary or final injury stage of the investigation.

For example, in CITT case 'NQ-93-007 Certain corrosion-resistant steel' the domestic industry complaint defined the subject goods as follows:

> *The products that are the subjects of this inquiry are commonly referred to as galvanized (free zinc coating) or galvannealed (zinc-iron alloy coating) steel sheet. The subject products include corrosion-resistant steel sheet in cut lengths and coils (wound successively in superimposed layers or in spirally oscillated coils) whether the coating or plating is applied by the hot-dipped or electrogalvanizing process.* **SOR at page 2.**

There was no Canadian production of electrogalvanized steel. The domestic industry alleged and CBSA and CITT agreed that the products of the two processes were like goods. At the injury inquiry CITT found that the imports of the subject steel were causing injury to Canadian production of like goods. CITT included electrogalvanized steel in the finding even though it was not made in Canada because, notwithstanding different production methods, the uses and characteristics of the products were similar. However, CITT excluded electrogalvanized steel for use in the automotive industry as the evidence showed that the Canadian hot-dipped steel was not substitutable for that purpose.

Classes of goods

Both the imported goods and the like goods produced in Canada, taken as a whole, may sometimes be divided into smaller 'classes' or 'sub-groupings' of goods.

In CITT case 'NQ-89-003 Women's leather boots and shoes', the complainants claimed:

> *that the inquiry at hand involved only one product class because the uses and characteristics of leather and non-leather boots and shoes all closely resembled one another.* **SOR at page 17.**

CITT determined that ladies' leather shoes and non-leather shoes were one class of goods and that ladies' leather boots and non-leather boots were another class of goods.[2] This division of the like goods meant that the complainants had to meet the 'domestic industry' definition requirements for each class of goods and that CITT would make separate injury determinations for each class of goods.

Canadian industry

The complaint must have the support of Canadian industry before an investigation can be started. In brief, Canadian producer support for the complaint should be greater then opposition and represent not less than 25% of all Canadian production.

---

2   On balance, the Tribunal concludes that boots and shoes are not like goods because they are
     fundamentally different in physical characteristics, design, manufacturing and uses. Because
     of this, the Tribunal is of the view that they are not like goods the uses and characteristics of
     which closely resemble one another. **SOR at page 18.**

The complaint must identify all known Canadian producers and associations of producers of like goods in Canada and provide or estimate the total volume and value of the like goods produced in Canada by each producer for the last three fiscal years and the current year to date. The complaint must also identify any Canadian producer who is related to an exporter or an importer of the goods or who imports the goods in question.

Dumping

The complaint must allege and provide evidence of dumping. In general terms, dumping is occurring if goods are being sold to Canada:

❑ At prices that are less than the price for comparable products in the exporter's home market.

❑ At prices which are unprofitable.

To support the allegation that the imported goods are dumped into Canada the complainant must estimate and compare normal values and export prices to determine a possible amount of dumping.

Generally, two different methods can be used to estimate normal values.

First method

The preferred method of estimating normal values is to use the selling price to unrelated purchasers in the exporter's home market where those goods are sold at a profit. This is based on any evidence of the selling price such as price lists, market surveys, sales invoices, bids, sales correspondence or quotes.

Second method

The second method of estimating normal value is based on all costs relating to the production and sale of the goods, plus an amount for profit.

This second method is used when:

❑ The complainant has difficulty getting price information on sales of the comparable goods in the exporter's home market;

❑ There are no sales of comparable goods in the exporter's home market;

❑ Information indicates that the exporter's sales in the home market are generally unprofitable; or

❑ The sales in the exporter's home market are made to related customers.

Export price

Generally, the export price is the price of the exported goods paid by the importer in Canada.

It is usually estimated using one of two methods:

❑ The first method of estimating the export price is based on the selling price offered by the exporter to the importer in Canada. The complainant will provide evidence regarding the selling price to the importer in Canada, such as price lists; sales invoices; bids, written offers or price quotations; sales correspondence; sales reports; or even Statistics Canada reports (which may provide import prices for the country concerned).

❑ The second method uses the selling price at which the imported goods are resold in Canada as a starting point and deducts all costs and profits to bring the price back to the ex-factory level in the country of export.

Subsidizing

If the complaint alleges subsidies, the complainant must provide evidence that the subsidy exists and such information about the subsidy as is available to the complainant including:

❑ The name of the foreign authority granting the subsidy;

❑ An explanation of how the subsidy operates;

❑ The type of subsidy benefit; and

❑ The amount of the benefit to the industry or the exporters shipping goods to Canada.

Demonstrating injury

The complainant must explain and provide evidence to show how the dumped or subsidized goods have injured the Canadian industry. Typically, this includes information and evidence which shows that:

❑ The imports are displacing Canadian production of the goods;

❑ The low prices of the imports are forcing the Canadian industry to reduce or restrain prices to meet the dumped or subsidized import prices;

❑ The imports have adversely affected specific sales accounts, profits, employment and wages, capacity utilization rates, productivity inventories, return on investments, cash flow and the ability to raise capital.

Allegation of non-market economy status

In 2004 CBSA defined its policy regarding non-market economies.

In the case of non-market economies, SIMA requires that normal values be calculated using prices and costs of like goods in a third country (a 'surrogate' country).

Section 20 of SIMA states that the President may prescribe a country as an non-market economy:

> 20.(1) Where goods sold to an importer in Canada are shipped directly to Canada
>
> (a) from a prescribed country where, in the opinion of the President, domestic prices are substantially determined by the government of that country and there is sufficient reason to believe that they are not substantially the same as they would be if they were determined in a competitive market, or
>
> (b) from any other country where, in the opinion of the President,
>
>> (I) the government of that country has a monopoly or substantial monopoly of its export trade, and
>>
>> (ii) domestic prices are substantially determined by the government of that country and there is sufficient reason to believe that they are not substantially the same as they would be if they were determined in a competitive market …

China is the only country that has been so prescribed for the purposes of this provision (SIM Regulation 17.1).

Sectoral decision

It is crucial to note that Canada makes the decision as to whether imported goods are from a NME on a sectoral basis rather than on the country as a whole. The fact that CBSA has found that the conditions of section 20 exist in a particular sector in a country will normally not have any relevance to a similar determination being made in respect of another sector that is under investigation in that same country.

For example, in the administrative review of 'Certain flat hot-rolled carbon and alloy steel sheet and strip', concluded 11 August 2005, CBSA determined that it was satisfied that section 20 conditions continued to exist in the Chinese primary steel industry. Six months later, in the administrative review of 'Certain bicycles and frames', the Canadian industry alleged that the Chinese industry met the conditions required of a non-market economy and that normal values should be calculated under section 20 of SIMA. CBSA conducted an internal investigation and determined that the conditions required to meet section 20 of SIMA did not apply to the bike industry in China.

CBSA's policy regarding the interpretation and application of section 20 of SIMA and the related Special Import Measures Regulations (SIM Regulations) states:

> *The key principle of the section 20 policy can be stated as follows:*
>
> *Regardless of the country, sector or product under investigation, anti-dumping investigations and re-investigations (administrative reviews) are to be initiated on the presumption that section 20 of the Act is not applicable to the sector under investigation unless there is evidence that suggests otherwise.*

In a new investigation the complainant must allege that the goods exported to Canada meet the conditions for section 20 to apply and must provide information to support the allegation. If the complainant cannot provide sufficient evidence regarding the conditions of section 20, the evidence of dumping provided in the written complaint must allege dumping based on the typical normal value calculation and not on prices and costs in a third country.

Re-investigations are also initiated under the presumption that section 20 is not applicable to the sector under investigation. The Canadian industry must allege that section 20 is applicable and provide facts and supporting information to CBSA if it believes that the conditions of section 20 exist in the sector under investigation.

In either an investigation or a re-investigation, if the section 20 allegation has been made and there is sufficient evidence CBSA will initiate a section 20 inquiry. This will generally be conducted in parallel with the usual dumping investigation.

In order for CBSA to determine whether to conduct a section 20 inquiry, the evidence supporting the allegation must be relevant and reasonably reliable and be capable of supporting a positive determination regarding section 20. If the President of CBSA forms the opinion that the conditions of section 20 exist in the sector under investigation, normal values will usually be determined in accordance with one of the following methods:

❏ The price of like goods sold by producers in any country designated for that purpose by the President, adjusted for price comparability;

❏ The full cost of producing and selling like goods plus a reasonable amount for profit, as determined in a designated country; or

❏ The selling price in Canada of like goods imported from a designated country, adjusted for price comparability.

Properly documented complaint

When the Canadian industry files a complaint, CBSA will take 21 days to ensure that it meets the criteria set out above. If there are deficiencies, CBSA will request additional information from the complainant.

Notification of properly documented complaint

When a complaint is deemed properly documented the complainant and the governments of the exporting countries are notified. CBSA will continue to analyse the complaint and will supplement the data in the complaint with independent research. An investigation will be initiated within 30 days of the date that the properly documented complaint was accepted.

It is important to note that CBSA has access to actual import data on a transaction-by-transaction basis. This information is confidential and will not be released to the complainant. However, it will be used by CBSA to confirm allegations made in the complaint to determine the actual volume and value of imports of subject goods. At this stage of the process, exporters, importers and foreign governments have not been formally advised that an investigation is being considered.

The initiation of an investigation

CBSA initiates investigation

When an investigation is initiated by CBSA it will publish a *statement of reasons*, which summarizes the case and the reasons for the initiation. Notice is sent to CITT, published in the *Canada Gazette*, and sent to the complainant, all known importers and exporters and the foreign governments concerned. A typical initiation notice is attached as appendix II.

Once the President of CBSA has initiated an investigation, CITT must conduct a preliminary injury inquiry and CBSA sends questionnaires to all known exporters in order to begin the formal investigation process.

Preliminary injury inquiry

CITT conducts preliminary injury inquiry

Upon initiation, CITT conducts a preliminary injury inquiry to determine whether there is a reasonable indication 'that the dumping or subsidizing of the goods described in the complaint has caused or is threatening to cause material injury or retardation'. CITT also examines the goods that are the subject of the complaint to determine whether there are multiple classes of goods and which producers make up the domestic industry.

CITT bases its determination on the CBSA file and submissions of interested parties. The CBSA file includes:

❑ A copy of the initiation statement of reasons;

❑ A copy of both the public and confidential versions of the complaint; and

❑ Any other information that has been taken into consideration by CBSA.

CBSA data made available to interested parties for preliminary injury inquiry

The CBSA data will be distributed to interested parties approximately 22 days after initiation. CITT will request submissions from parties opposed to the complaint, such as importers and exporters. Interested parties have the right to examine the evidence upon which CBSA initiated its investigation and respond to it at this stage. If an exporter retains independent counsel who has signed a confidentiality undertaking, counsel will have the right to examine the confidential information.

Submissions to CITT should deal with:

❑ Whether the goods as defined in the complaint (the 'subject goods') cover all like goods produced in Canada;

❑ Whether the goods as described should be treated as more than one class of subject goods;

❑ Whether the domestic producers make up the domestic industry; and

❑ Whether the evidence shows a reasonable indication that the dumping or subsidizing of the subject goods has caused or is threatening material injury or retardation.

These submissions are due approximately 32 days after initiation. The complainant is then given an opportunity to respond to the submissions of parties opposed to the complaint.

The first three items above are related because they deal with the definition of the goods under investigation and whether the complainants have standing; that is, whether the complainants represent the industry as defined above. While CBSA will have checked to make sure that the complainants meet the standing tests, CITT may decide that there is more than one class of goods within the like goods category as defined by CBSA. If so, the complainant will have to meet the standing criteria for each class of like goods and CITT injury decisions will be based on these new definition.

Submissions to CITT due one week after documents distributed

The preliminary injury inquiry process is very short, particularly for exporters who do not have a reliable presence in the Canadian market. CITT distributes the case documents 14 days after it initiates an inquiry and expects submissions one week later. For exporters, this leaves very little time to analyse the case, hire counsel, and respond to the evidence. This is particularly true for exporters who are geographically distant from Canada and those who speak neither English nor French.

CITT decision communicated to interested parties

By the 60th day after the initiation by CBSA, CITT must make its preliminary determination of injury. If CITT determines that there is a reasonable indication that the dumping or subsidizing has caused or threatens to cause material injury, it will notify CBSA, the exporter, the importer, the government of the country of export and the complainant. CITT will publish a notice in the *Canada Gazette*. CBSA will than continue its dumping or subsidizing investigation and CITT will begin its final injury inquiry.

If CITT finds no evidence of a reasonable indication that the dumping or subsidizing has caused or threatens to cause material injury, it will terminate the preliminary injury inquiry, and CBSA will terminate the investigation. CITT will notify CBSA, the exporter, the importer, the government of the country of export and the complainant of its decision. CITT will also publish a notice in the *Canada Gazette*.

The CBSA investigation

The dumping investigation

The CBSA dumping investigation compiles the information required to determine whether dumping exists and, if so, to calculate the margin of dumping.

To determine whether dumping exists CBSA must calculate:

❑ The normal value;

❑ The export price; and

❑ The cost of production of the goods.

Normal value

Methods of calculating normal value

In Canada, the law sets out four methods that can be applied to establish the normal value. These are:

❑ The selling price of the like goods in the country of export;

❑ The selling price to importers in third countries;

❑ The cost of production of the actual imported goods plus a mark-up for profit; or

❑ Ministerial specifications.

These methods are generally applied sequentially although in practice the second method is rarely used, and the last method is brought into play only if all other approaches fail.

Normal values based on sales in the country of export

The object of a normal value exercise is to establish the price charged to customers comparable to the Canadian importer under similar conditions in the exporter's domestic market. In determining the normal value via the domestic selling price approach, officials examine invoices covering home market sales made in the ordinary course of trade under competitive conditions during a 60-day period prior to the sale to Canada. The invoices used reflect sales, in approximately the same volumes as were shipped to Canada, made to purchasers with whom the exporter was not associated but who are at substantially the same trade level as the importer. The normal value thus established is adjusted to reflect differences affecting price comparability between the domestic and export sales. The price used as the basis for normal value is, at the option of the President of CBSA, (a) the weighted average of the prices of like goods sold during the period, or (b) a representative price in any sale by the exporter during that period. Each of these conditions is explained in detail in chapter 3.

Cost of production

Normal values based on cost of production

The cost of production approach provides that the normal value is to be the aggregate of the cost of production of the exported goods, a reasonable amount for administrative, selling and all other costs, and a reasonable amount for profit. The cost of production figure includes all costs attributable in any manner to the production of the goods including costs of design or engineering. The expression 'reasonable amount for profit' generally means an amount that reflects the weighted average profit made on domestic sales that were sold at a profit.

The expression 'reasonable amount for administration, selling and all other costs' is defined as meaning an amount that equals the average of all such costs including warranty, design, engineering etc. that were not included in the cost of production.

SIMA also incorporates special provisions for establishing normal values in situations where special credit terms apply, where the imported goods originate in countries where the price is determined by government, or where there is an export monopoly.

Normal values based on ministerial specification

The ministerial specification method is used only when the President of CBSA is of the opinion that sufficient information has not been furnished or is not available to enable the determination of normal value or export price by one of the other methods outlined in SIMA.

Where an exporter, producer, importer or foreign government chooses not to supply information requested by CBSA to determine normal value, export price or the amount of subsidy, or does not permit its verification or does not provide information in a timely manner, CBSA will use a ministerial specification. A ministerial specification will result in a duty less beneficial than if the party had provided the requested information in a timely way and will be less favourable than the results for exporters who did provide full and timely information. In practice the ministerial specification has usually been the single highest dumping margin found during the investigation.

If the requested information is simply not available and CBSA believes that the party has made its best efforts to provide the information, the ministerial specification may be based on the weighted average margin of dumping determined for other exporters or importers of the goods in question.

Export price

The export price is an amount equal to the lesser of the amount received by the exporter for the goods or the amount paid by the importer. The exporter's sales price is adjusted to arrive at the final export price by deducting:

Export price defined

❑ The costs, charges and expenses incurred in preparing the goods for shipment to Canada that are additional to those generally incurred on domestic sales of like goods;

❑ Any duty or tax imposed on the goods that is paid by the exporter; and

❑ All other costs, charges and expenses resulting from the shipment of the goods from their place of direct shipment to Canada that are incurred by the exporter.

In certain circumstances, the export price may be established on the basis of the resale price of the goods in Canada. This occurs when there is no export price or where the President is of the opinion that the export price is unreliable because the sale of the goods to Canada was a sale between associated persons or involves a compensatory arrangement that affects the price and sale of the goods. In these situations, the export price is established by taking the price at which the goods are resold to an unassociated person by the importer in Canada and adjusting it by deducting an amount equal to the total of all costs incurred on or after the importation of the goods including costs of sales and an amount for profit.

Special rules are also set out in SIMA and the regulations to ensure that the valuation captures differences in credit terms and any indemnity, payment or reimbursement made under agreements by which the exporter undertakes to pay the dumping duties or to provide compensation to the importer indirectly by way of rebate, service or otherwise.

The subsidy investigation

Subsidizing results from a foreign government's programme that has the effect of stimulating export sales either by lowering prices or by making them more profitable at existing price levels. The key differences between subsidizing and dumping cases are the involvement of governments in the former, and the determination of the amount of subsidy on a per unit basis. The subsidy calculations are based primarily on information provided by the foreign government authorities concerning the nature of the subsidy programme and the benefits provided to producers or exporters. Information may also be obtained from the exporters and it may be necessary to visit exporters' premises to verify data.

The term *countervailing duty* is defined as a special duty levied for the purpose of offsetting any bounty or subsidy bestowed, directly or indirectly, upon the manufacture, production or export of any merchandise. In order to establish whether a countervailing duty should be applied, it is necessary (a) for CBSA to determine whether, in fact, actionable imports have benefited from a subsidy, and the amount of the subsidy, and (b) for CITT to determine whether the subsidized imports have caused or threaten to cause injury or retardation to Canadian industry.

The regulations set out rules to be followed in calculating the amount of a subsidy. Generally, the objective of the process, regardless of what form the subsidy takes (e.g. grant, loan, loan guarantee, the provision of goods and services by governments, tax concession, procurement preference) is to establish a value that can be attributed on a per unit production basis to the imported goods. In other words, for the purpose of the application of countervailing duties, the authorities must determine the amount of the benefit to the imported goods that resulted from the subsidy.

Although subsidies are classified into certain types such as grants, loans and tax deferrals, the intricacies of subsidies vary between programmes and from one country to another. Further, because they can take various forms and may be directed to particular activities (e.g. plant construction, acquisition of machinery or other fixed assets, infrastructure, certain types of research or direct production subsidies), establishing the per unit value of subsidy benefits can be an extremely complicated exercise.

It may involve, among other things, estimates of the useful life of assets, the calculation of present value of future benefits, and forecasts of future production activities.

What constitutes a subsidy?

The SCMA contains an internationally agreed definition of *subsidy* that may be summarized as a benefit conferred as a result of a financial contribution by a government or public body involving:

WTO definition of subsidy

❑ A direct or potential direct transfer of funds or liabilities;

❑ Foregoing of government revenues otherwise due;

❑ Provision of goods or services by government other than general infrastructure; or

❑ Any form of income or price support as provided for in GATT Article XVI.

The scope of the definition of *subsidy* is quite broad in that:

❑ The benefit need not take the form of a direct financial contribution;

❑ The benefit from the subsidy may be to a person, firm or industry involved not only in the production or manufacture of goods, but also in the growth, processing, purchase, distribution, transportation, sale, export or import of goods; and

❑ The benefit may be received directly or indirectly.

Subsidies may be direct or indirect

A direct financial or other commercial benefit is one that accrues directly to the person, firm or industry, such as an outright grant of funds to a producer of goods. An indirect benefit is one which does not accrue directly, but which can alter the economic environment and level of costs within which firms operate. For example, the subsidy may have been applied to materials purchased by a manufacturer who thus obtains indirectly the advantage of the (upstream) subsidy given to the producer of the subsidized materials.

In order to determine whether a government programme confers a benefit and thereby constitutes a subsidy, CBSA examines the details of the programme involved and seeks answers to questions such as the following:

❑ Does the subsidy programme involve a financial contribution by the government? Possible forms of such subsidy programmes and practices include:

– Government financing of commercial enterprises, including grants, loans or guarantees;

– Government provision or government-financed provision of utility, supply distribution and other operational or support services or facilities;

– Government financing of research and development;

– Fiscal incentives; and

– Government subscription to, or provision of, equity capital.

CBSA needs to be aware of circumstances governing subsidy programme

❑ Is the subsidy programme specifically targeted by the government so as to favour one part of the economy over another, or one activity, such as export sales, over another? The concept of 'specificity' versus 'general availability' (discussed below) is particularly relevant in establishing whether a subsidy can be countervailed.

❑ Is a commercial benefit bestowed by the subsidy programme or practice on the imports in question?

This type of inquiry is necessary to enable CBSA to identify *pass through* subsidies. For example, a government subsidizes a steel mill that enables it to sell steel to a domestic fabricator. The fabricator in turn sells the fabricated steel to an importer in Canada, at a lower price than would be possible if he had used unsubsidized steel. The fact that the fabricator could buy unsubsidized steel at the same price elsewhere does not change the fact that a commercial benefit from the subsidy results for the imports in question, which are therefore countervailable. In this connection, care is exercised by CBSA since there may be circumstances where the subsidy is not passed through to the importer in terms of lower prices, in which case there would be no apparent negative impact on the domestic producers in Canada.

Specificity

Subsidies referred to in the definition above can be countervailed if they are found to be specific. Basically this means that the subsidies are countervailable when they are directed to certain persons, firms or industries and are not 'generally available' under established public objective criteria and conditions. The theory behind specificity is that government financial assistance measures should be considered as *countervailable* subsidies only if they are specifically targeted by the government to favour one part of an economy over another. There are specific conditions that govern whether a subsidy is specific or not. A subsidy is not specific if the criteria for eligibility and the amount of the subsidy are:

❑ Objective;

❑ Set out in a legislative, regulatory or administrative instrument or other public document; and

❑ Applied in a manner that does not favour or is not limited to a particular enterprise.

A subsidy is specific if it is:

❑ Limited to a particular enterprise within the jurisdiction of the exporting country that is granting the subsidy; or

❑ A prohibited subsidy.

Even where a subsidy is not limited as described above, CBSA may determine the subsidy to be specific if:

❑ There is exclusive use of the subsidy by a limited number of enterprises;

❑ There is predominant use of the subsidy by a particular enterprise;

❑ Disproportionately large amounts of the subsidy are granted to a limited number of enterprises; and

❑ The manner in which discretion is exercised by the granting authority indicates that the subsidy is not generally available.

Actionable and non-actionable subsidies

The WTO Agreement and Canadian law establish three categories of subsidy programmes. **Export subsidies** are described in the following section. The second category are the '**non-actionable**' subsidies that must either be non-specific or be directed to research activities, regional development initiatives or to the adaptation of existing facilities to new environmental requirements. The provisions governing **non-actionable** subsidy programmes were to be reviewed not later than 180 days before the end of the first five-year period to determine whether to extend or modify them for a further period. This did not happen. As a result the non-actionable subsidy category no longer has status under the WTO Agreement and subsidies in this category are now judged on the criteria applicable to all actionable subsidies.

The third or '**actionable**' category of subsidies covers practices which may cause *injury or retardation* to an industry in Canada. These are countervailable.

Export subsidies

Export subsidies on products, other than certain primary products, are prohibited under the WTO Agreement. Furthermore, export subsidies that are directly linked to export performance are considered to be *specific* and thus countervailable. However, all subsidy programmes, even those not specifically linked to exports, need to be examined by CBSA in terms of their specificity to determine whether they are in fact export subsidies. The WTO Agreement also prohibits subsidies contingent on the use of domestic over imported goods.

A distinction is made between a domestic subsidy and an export subsidy because of the special considerations for export subsidies set out in the SCMA. Export subsidies are subsidies that are either directly or indirectly contingent on the product being exported. Annex I to the SCMA provides an extensive illustrative list of possible forms of such subsidies targeted to favour exports, including:

❑ Government financing of commercial export enterprises, including grants, loans or guarantees;

❑ Government provision or government-financed provision of utilities, supply distribution facilities and other operational or support services or facilities conditional on export performance;

❑ Currency retention schemes that involve a bonus on exports;

❑ The remission or drawback of import charges in excess of those levied on imported inputs that are consumed in the production of exported products;

❑ The exemption or remission, in respect of the production and distribution of exported products, of indirect taxes in excess of those levied in respect of the production and distribution of like products when sold for domestic production; and

❑ Fiscal incentives contingent upon export performance.

Export subsidies are characterized by being linked to or contingent upon export performance. Usually the linkage to exports is clear-cut. For example, a grant or tax credit is provided directly by the government on the basis of export sales performance, or loans are given at preferential rates to finance export transactions.

Because these subsidies can be obtained only as a result of export sales, this activity clearly identifies them as export subsidies. The mere fact that a subsidy is granted to an enterprise which exports does not by itself result in the subsidy being classified as an export subsidy.

Moreover, while a subsidy may not be explicitly contingent on export performance, it may have the same effect. For example, where a grant or concessional loan is provided to aid the establishment of an industry producing largely for export markets, the subsidy may be a *de facto* export subsidy.

There are two other important SCMA annexes that provide guidelines relating to the determination of export subsidies.

Annex II deals with guidelines for the treatment of consumption inputs in the production process. These guidelines refer to indirect tax rebate schemes that allow for exemption, remission or deferral of prior-stage cumulative indirect taxes levied on inputs that are consumed in the production of exported goods.

Essentially the process provided for requires CBSA to first determine whether the government of the exporting country has a procedure in place to confirm which inputs are consumed in the production process, in what amounts (making due allowance for normal waste) and whether the system is applied effectively. If there is no such procedure or if the procedure is considered not to be effective, the government of the exporting country is requested to carry out a further examination of the actual inputs to determine whether an excess payment occurred.

Annex III outlines the treatment of substitution drawback systems which allow for the refund of import charges on inputs consumed in the production process of another product and where the latter product contains domestic inputs having the same quality and characteristics as those substituted for the imported inputs. Such drawback schemes can constitute an export subsidy if an excess drawback is involved. As with annex II, CBSA can examine the verification system used by the government of the exporting country to ensure and demonstrate that the quantity of inputs for which drawback is claimed does not exceed the quantity exported and there is no excess drawback involved.

CBSA verification

CBSA will conduct a verification of questionnaire responses. The verification will be done via supplementary questionnaires, 'desk audit' or at the exporter's premises. It is common practice for CBSA officers to visit exporters and the manufacturer(s) to carry out this task. These visits are usually from three to five days.

In certain cases where there are large numbers of exporters or products, CBSA may investigate only a sample of exporters from each country (normally the larger exporters). If an exporter is included in the sample, they must complete the questionnaire or their products will be valued on the basis of the best information available. An exporter who is not part of the chosen sample may voluntarily complete the questionnaire and, if time permits, CBSA will use these data in the calculation of provisional duties. Otherwise exporters not included in the sample will have their provisional duty rate calculated as the weighted average dumping margin found for exporters in the same country who were required to provide information and who fully complied with CBSA's investigation.

During the verification meeting, CBSA will ask for clarification of responses, source documents, working papers and any other supporting documentation relating to any part of the questionnaire. Although a rough agenda is usually provided prior to the verification visit all personnel involved in preparing the questionnaire response should be prepared and available for the duration of the meetings.

CBSA officers will expect that company officials present in the meetings will have the capacity to respond to all of their questions and requests for documentation. The verification process is very paper-intensive and the officers will request source documents in order to create a 'paper trail'. Exporters are required to provide two photocopies of all requested documents and to provide a non-confidential version of every document.

Typical areas of interest in verification exercises include:

❑ *Reconciliation of sales listings.* CBSA will ask exporters to prove that the sales data provided are complete.

❑ *Review of payables.* Accounts payable records will be reviewed to identify whether any payments were made to the Canadian importer that may indicate the possible reimbursement of dumping duties.

❑ *Review of export sales listing.* Several sales will be chosen at random and CBSA will ask for original sales documents. The officers will then go through the sales step by step verifying that all costs and expenses have been properly allocated.

❑ *Review of domestic sales listing.* As with the export sales listing, several sales will be chosen at random and CBSA will ask for original sales documents. The officers will then go through the sales step by step verifying that all costs and expenses have been properly addressed.

❑ *Cost of production.* The officers will review the cost data provided. The company will be required to tie costing information to audited financials.

❑ *Transfer pricing.* If any input goods or services are purchased from associated parties the officers will examine the purchase price of these transactions in order to ensure that they reflect the market value of the goods or the full cost plus profit.

Preliminary determination of dumping or subsidy

If CITT makes an affirmative preliminary determination of injury, the President of CBSA will impose provisional duties as calculated for the preliminary determination. If the CITT preliminary determination of injury is negative, or if CBSA determines that the dumping or subsidy is found to be insignificant, or if the volume of dumped or subsidized goods is negligible, the investigation will also be terminated.

Termination of the investigation

CBSA will have received questionnaire responses from exporters and completed verification visits, allowing them to estimate margins of dumping or subsidizing for exporters. If this preliminary investigation shows that the goods are not being dumped or subsidized, CBSA must terminate the investigation. The investigation is normally terminated only against countries, not individual exporters. Accordingly, if a country has two exporters, one who complies with the investigation and is found not to be dumping and a second who does not respond to the questionnaire, the investigation will be continued.

If CBSA terminates its investigation, all action by CBSA and CITT is ceased. Written notice of the decision is sent to all parties involved in the investigation and is published in the *Canada Gazette*.

De minimis

An investigation may be terminated against one or more countries if:

❑ The margin of dumping is less than 2% of the export price;

❑ The amount of subsidy is less than 1% of the export price;

❑ The volume of dumped goods is less than 3% of the total volume of like goods exported to Canada from all countries, except where the total volume of dumped goods from at least three countries, each of whose exports is less than 3% of all imports, is more than 7% of the total volume of exports to Canada from all countries.

In order for CBSA to terminate in this fashion all exporters from a country must have complied with the investigation and been verified.

Provisional duties

Following an affirmative PD by CBSA all subject goods imported into Canada are subject to provisional duties. The provisional period ends on the date of the CITT injury finding.

CBSA provides normal values to exporters

Provisional duty is based on the estimated margin of dumping or the estimated amount of subsidy on the imported subject goods. If an exporter has completed the questionnaire and verification process to CBSA's satisfaction, CBSA will calculate the normal value and export price based on this information. The provisional duty will be the amount by which the normal value exceeds the export price for goods exported during the period of investigation and this duty will apply to goods imported during the provisional period. In the case of subsidizing, the amount of the subsidy will be added to the export price on either a per unit or percentage basis.

The provisional duty is refunded to the importer if CITT finds no injury. If CITT finds injury the goods imported during the provisional period are reviewed to determine whether they were dumped. If the duty imposed during the provisional period is found to have been too high the difference is refunded to the importer. If the provisional duty is found to have been too low no additional duties are collected.

Exporters should seek disclosure meetings with CBSA re calculations

Once a PD is made, each exporter may request a disclosure meeting with CBSA in order to obtain an explanation of how export price, normal value, the margin of dumping or the amount of subsidy were calculated. This information is essential so that exporters can know how the calculations were made and whether the data that they provided were adequately taken into account. Based on these discussions, exporters will be in a position to decide if further submissions are warranted or if there are grounds for appealing the CBSA findings.

Payment of duties

Importer pays the duty

Anti-dumping and countervailing duties must be paid by the importer. The exporter cannot reimburse or in any way compensate the importer for these duties. If the importer is related to the exporter, the duties must be passed on to their customers.

If the importer is reimbursed or compensated for the payment of anti-dumping or countervailing duties, the export price of the goods then becomes the export price minus the amount reimbursed. This has the effect of doubling the duty. For example, if a product has an export price of $10 and a normal value of $12, the dumping duty is $2. However, if the exporter reimburses the importer the $2 dumping duty, a new export price results which is the original export price minus the amount reimbursed; in this case $10 – $2 = $8. In the Canadian system, the importer would be liable for the payment of $4 in anti-dumping duties.

Final investigation

Following an affirmative PD (except where the investigation is suspended because an undertaking has been accepted), CBSA has 90 days to complete its final investigation and make a final decision regarding the dumping or subsidizing. The purpose of the final investigation is to review and finalize the normal values or subsidy calculations. CBSA may seek additional information or clarification from exporters and may visit those exporters who could not be verified prior to the PD.

If the final investigation reveals that there is no dumping or subsidizing or that the margin of dumping or the amount of subsidy is insignificant, CBSA will terminate the investigation. If the investigation is terminated the CITT inquiry is halted, all parties involved are notified in writing and all provisional duties are refunded.

Approximately 30 days after the preliminary determination CBSA closes the record in the case and will not accept additional data from interested parties. Interested parties then have approximately 10 days (40 days after the preliminary determination) to file briefs and subsequently reply to the briefs filed by opposing parties. Interested parties have access to the preliminary determination data including the detailed methodology used to calculate normal values and export price for each exporter (subject to confidentiality rules); also available to interested parties is the complete record kept by CBSA upon which its final determination will be made (again subject to confidentiality rules). The briefs to CBSA will include arguments as to how normal values and export prices should be calculated, which information should be relied upon or ignored, and how issues such as *de minimis* and non-market economy should be treated.

If CBSA determines that the goods are dumped or subsidized and that the margin of dumping or the amount of subsidy is not insignificant, a final determination is made. In the final determination the precise margin of dumping or amount of subsidy is specified for each exporter, each country and for all parties. All parties involved are notified of the decision in writing and CITT proceeds with its final injury inquiry. Appendix III is an abbreviated example of a final determination.

Undertakings

Exporters may offer
undertakings to raise prices
to eliminate injury

An undertaking is an agreement between exporters and CBSA to sell the allegedly dumped goods at a price that is not dumped or is not injurious to the Canadian industry. If exporters who account for at least 85% of the volume of dumped or subsidized imports into Canada offer to make such an undertaking, the Canadian producers who filed the complaint are consulted for their views including the price levels they feel are necessary to eliminate injury. Appendix IV is an example of a typical undertaking.

The advantage of undertakings is that if they are accepted the investigation is terminated and the time and cost of the CITT final injury hearing is avoided.

Undertakings may be accepted only after the preliminary determination. The offer of an undertaking should be made as soon as possible after the PD to allow CBSA time to consult with the complainants and determine the feasibility of an undertaking.

There are several types of undertakings:

❑ The exporter increases the selling price of goods to importers in Canada sufficiently to eliminate the injury to Canadian production;

❑ The exporter increases the selling price of goods to importers in Canada sufficiently to eliminate the dumping;

❑ The exporter increases the selling price of goods to importers in Canada sufficiently to offset the subsidy (this requires the agreement of the foreign government);

❑ The foreign government undertakes to eliminate the injury caused by a subsidy (by, for example, eliminating the subsidy on the goods exported to Canada).

In dumping cases undertakings eliminate either the dumping or the injury. In a dumping undertaking, CBSA will conduct a regular normal value investigation and the undertaking prices will be based on the exporter's home market price for like goods or their cost of production and an amount for profit.

An injury undertaking increases prices to eliminate injury (in theory the price increase should be less than the price increase in a dumping undertaking) and the exporter and CBSA do not incur the time and expense of a full dumping investigation.

Acceptance of an undertaking

Conditions relating to an acceptable undertaking

Exporters themselves must make undertakings. Undertakings are not acceptable if offered by an association or trade group. The undertaking must increase the price of the goods sold to importers in Canada sufficiently to offset the dumping or subsidy or the injury to Canadian producers, but the undertaking cannot increase prices by more than the amount required to offset the estimated dumping or subsidy.

An undertaking must be practical to administer. CBSA acts as an arbitrator in the undertaking process and is charged with monitoring the behaviour of the participants to ensure they are complying with the agreed terms.

CBSA may not accept an undertaking if:

❑ The number of exporters involved is too large;

❑ A large number of countries are involved;

❑ There is unusual complexity relating to the goods;

❑ The frequency of price changes for the subject goods is too high; or

❑ There are other factors which might lead to difficulties in monitoring the undertaking.

If an undertaking is accepted, written notice of this decision is sent to all parties involved in the investigation. Acceptance of an undertaking causes the investigation to be suspended for all exporters, regardless of whether they are covered by the undertaking. When an investigation is suspended, exporters who have not made an undertaking may do so.

Rejection of an undertaking

When the offer of an undertaking is not accepted the exporter is advised and given reasons for the rejection. If the reason for rejection is that CBSA does not feel it is administrable, exporters may propose alternative solutions that, if acceptable to CBSA, may cause the undertaking to be accepted.

Completion of investigation following acceptance of an undertaking

Exporters may request CBSA to complete the dumping or subsidizing investigation and CITT to complete its injury inquiry at the time when the undertaking is offered. If CBSA terminates the investigation or if CITT finds no injury due to the dumping or subsidizing, all undertakings are terminated. Should an injury finding result, the undertakings that were accepted continue in effect.

However, under these circumstances, no additional undertakings can be accepted from new exporters.

Termination of an undertaking

CBSA may terminate an undertaking at the request of any concerned person (exporter, importer, complainant, and the foreign government in a subsidy case) within 30 days of the date of acceptance of the undertaking and prior to CITT's finding.

CBSA may also terminate an undertaking at any time for the following reasons:

❑ If new information becomes available which makes it difficult for CBSA to effectively monitor the undertaking;

❑ If circumstances change significantly from those prevailing at the time the undertaking was accepted, e.g. a new exporter begins selling large quantities of dumped goods to Canada and is not willing to provide an undertaking agreement;

❑ If there is a serious violation of the undertaking.

The termination of any single exporter's undertaking usually terminates the undertaking for all exporters. If an undertaking is terminated, all parties are informed in writing and CBSA investigation and the CITT inquiry are resumed.

Enforcement of undertakings

Once an undertaking is accepted, CBSA will periodically request information from exporters (domestic sales, export sales, production and pricing data) in order to ensure the price levels in the undertaking are up to date.

Reviews of undertakings

Undertakings, like injury findings, normally stay in place for five years. If there is a CITT injury finding in place, the undertaking stays in force until the CITT decision is rescinded or is allowed to expire. If CITT reviews the need for a possible continuation of the undertaking, exporters and importers are requested to provide information on market shares and trends in the Canadian and world market. All parties may make representations regarding whether the undertaking should continue or be allowed to expire.

CBSA must make its decision regarding the continuation of the undertaking before the end of the five-year period for which it was originally accepted. Written notice of the decision is sent to all parties involved in the investigation and notice is published in the *Canada Gazette*. If CBSA decides that the undertaking will not be renewed, it expires immediately and all action under SIMA ceases. If continued, the undertaking is typically renewed for five years after which it will be reviewed again.

Role of CBSA following CITT injury decision

A CITT finding of injury usually remains in place for five years. There are three possible CITT findings, namely, that the imports in question:

❑ Have not caused and are not threatening to cause injury;

❑ Have caused injury;

❑ Have not caused injury but are threatening to cause injury.

A finding of no injury

A finding of no injury by the Tribunal ends all proceedings in the investigation. In such a case, CBSA refunds to the importer all provisional duties collected and returns any security that was posted with CBSA in lieu of duty payment.

A finding of injury

Where the Tribunal concludes that injury has occurred, anti-dumping or countervailing duty is payable on all dumped or subsidized goods imported during the provisional period, i.e. from the date of the preliminary determination to the date of the Tribunal's finding, and on all shipments of the subject goods released after the date of the Tribunal's finding, until such time as the finding is rescinded. Duties are not payable, however, if the goods are covered by a valid undertaking.

For goods imported during the provisional period (the period between the preliminary determination and the Tribunal's finding) SIMA requires CBSA to make a determination within six months of the date of a Tribunal finding. The effect of this determination is to finalize the amount of duty payable for the goods already imported. This determination may use the information calculated for final determination or, if there is reason to believe that the information used to determine normal value and export price or the amount of subsidy for the final determination is outdated, CBSA may conduct an investigation to update the information.

A finding of threat of injury

If the Tribunal makes a finding of threat of injury only, no anti-dumping duty or countervailing duty is payable on goods released before the date of the Tribunal's finding. Duty is payable on all dumped or subsidized imports released after the date of the finding except where the goods are covered by a valid undertaking.

Re-investigations

Re-investigations to update normal values, export prices or amounts of subsidy and to establish values for new exporters or new models are conducted periodically, generally on an annual basis. Procedures followed during a re-investigation are similar to those in a new investigation. An exporter that is requested to participate in a re-investigation but chooses not to will be subject to a punitive dumping margin.

Appeals from CBSA decisions

A determination of normal value and export price or the amount of the subsidy by CBSA officials may be appealed through various levels of responsibility within CBSA until the President takes a decision. This decision is usually final. However, further appeals are possible. For non-NAFTA (North American Free Trade Agreement) countries, an importer can request that CITT review the President's decision. The CITT decision, in turn, may be appealed to the Federal Court on any question of law. For NAFTA countries, the decisions may be appealed to a bi-national panel under that agreement.

Annex

List of anti-dumping and countervailing duty cases in place in Canada as at 1 July 2006

Goods	Category	Anti-dumping/ Countervailing duty	Country	Initiation date
Whole potatoes	Agricultural	A	United States	1985.10.18
Carbon steel welded pipe	Steel	A	Brazil	1987.09.16
Carbon steel welded pipe	Steel	A	Argentina	1990.11.16
Carbon steel welded pipe	Steel	A	India	1990.11.16
Carbon steel welded pipe	Steel	A	Romania	1990.11.16
Carbon steel welded pipe	Steel	A	Thailand	1990.11.16
Carbon steel welded pipe	Steel	A	Taiwan Province (China)	1990.11.16
Bicycles & frames	Consumer	A	China	1992.05.15
Bicycles & frames	Consumer	A	Taiwan Province (China)	1992.05.15
Refined sugar	Consumer	A	Germany	1995.03.17
Refined sugar	Consumer	A	Denmark	1995.03.17
Refined sugar	Consumer	A	United Kingdom	1995.03.17
Refined sugar	Consumer	A	Netherlands	1995.03.17
Refined sugar	Consumer	A	United States	1995.03.17
Refined sugar	Consumer	C	EU	1995.03.17
Garlic	Agricultural	A	China	1996.08.23
Hot-rolled carbon steel plate	Steel	A	China	1997.02.13
Hot-rolled carbon steel plate	Steel	A	Russian Federation	1997.02.13
Hot-rolled carbon steel plate	Steel	A	South Africa	1997.02.13
Filter tipped cigarette tubes	Industrial	A	France	1998.10.19
Waterproof footwear	Consumer	A	China	2000.05.12
Concrete reinforcing bar	Steel	A	Indonesia	2000.11.03
Concrete reinforcing bar	Steel	A	Japan	2000.11.03
Concrete reinforcing bar	Steel	A	Latvia	2000.11.03
Concrete reinforcing bar	Steel	A	Rep. of Moldova	2000.11.03
Concrete reinforcing bar	Steel	A	Poland	2000.11.03
Concrete reinforcing bar	Steel	A	Taiwan Province (China)	2000.11.03
Concrete reinforcing bar	Steel	A	Ukraine	2000.11.03
Hot-rolled carbon steel sheet	Steel	A	Bulgaria	2001.01.19

Goods	Category	Anti-dumping/ Countervailing duty	Country	Initiation date
Hot-rolled carbon steel sheet	Steel	A	Brazil	2001.01.19
Hot-rolled carbon steel sheet	Steel	A	China	2001.01.19
Hot-rolled carbon steel sheet	Steel	A	Serbia & Montenegro	2001.01.19
Hot-rolled carbon steel sheet	Steel	A	India	2001.01.19
Hot-rolled carbon steel sheet	Steel	A	The former Yugoslav Republic of Macedonia	2001.01.19
Hot-rolled carbon steel sheet	Steel	A	Taiwan Province (China)	2001.01.19
Hot-rolled carbon steel sheet	Steel	A	Ukraine	2001.01.19
Hot-rolled carbon steel sheet	Steel	A	South Africa	2001.01.19
Hot-rolled carbon steel sheet	Steel	C	India	2001.01.19
Leather safety footwear	Consumer	A	China	2001.06.15
Xanthates	Industrial	A	China	2002.06.21
Carbon steel pipe fittings	Industrial	A	China	2002.12.18
Steel, structural tubing	Steel	A	Rep. of Korea	2003.06.05
Steel, structural tubing	Steel	A	Turkey	2003.06.05
Steel, structural tubing	Steel	A	South Africa	2003.06.05
Certain hot-rolled carbon steel plate	Steel	A	Bulgaria	2003.06.13
Certain hot-rolled carbon steel plate	Steel	A	Czech Republic	2003.06.13
Certain hot-rolled carbon steel plate	Steel	A	Romania	2003.06.13
Wood venetian blinds and slats	Consumer	A	China	2003.11.21
Wood venetian blinds and slats	Consumer	A	Mexico	2003.11.21
Stainless steel wire	Steel	A	Switzerland	2003.11.21
Stainless steel wire	Steel	A	Rep. of Korea	2003.11.21
Stainless steel wire	Steel	A	United States	2003.11.21
Stainless steel wire	Steel	C	India	2003.11.21
Carbon steel and stainless steel fasteners	Steel	A	China	2004.04.28
Carbon steel and stainless steel fasteners	Steel	A	Taiwan Province (China)	2004.04.28
Carbon steel and stainless steel fasteners	Steel	A	Taiwan Province (China)	2004.04.28
Carbon steel and stainless steel fasteners	Steel	C	China	2004.04.28
Laminate flooring	Consumer	A	China	2004.10.04
Laminate flooring	Consumer	A	France	2004.10.04
Laminate flooring	Consumer	C	China	2004.10.04

CHAPTER 3

CBSA questionnaires and the calculation of margins of dumping and subsidies

The decision to participate

CBSA issues exporter's questionnaire

On the date of initiation of an investigation CBSA will send questionnaires to all known exporters that have been identified in the complaint. The data compiled in these questionnaires will be used to determine whether dumping or subsidy exists and, if so, to calculate the margin of dumping or subsidy.

If an exporter does not respond to the questionnaire and does not submit to verification, CBSA will estimate that exporter's dumping margin using 'best information available'. Best information available is a euphemism for the highest dumping margin found for any single transaction in the investigation.

Exporter must decide whether to participate in investigation

Exporters must decide whether continuing to participate in the Canadian market justifies the costs of complying with CBSA and/or participating in the CITT inquiry.

Not participating in the CBSA investigation may guarantee very high dumping margins for exporters, which will adversely affect their interests before the CITT. Not participating in the CITT injury process will virtually guarantee a finding of injury against an exporter unless other exporters make the case against an injury finding. Therefore, an exporter who wishes to continue exporting to Canada must complete the questionnaire and participate in the investigation. Exporters should be aware that once CITT finds injury against their goods, they will be labelled as 'dumpers' – a designation that might be used against them in other dumping inquiries in Canada and in other countries.

If exporters wish to continue to sell in the Canadian market, they must provide the data requested

Exporters should also be aware that a dumping or subsidy investigation might actually benefit them by eliminating unfair competition from the Canadian market. For example:

❑ Some exporters may simply decide to not participate in the investigation and withdraw from the Canadian market.

❑ Exporters who are not themselves the manufacturer of the subject goods will have difficulty answering the cost of production portion of the questionnaire and this may adversely affect their ability to participate in the Canadian market.

❑ Exporters who have high-priced domestic markets and costs of production will have high normal values and may not be able to compete in the Canadian market.

The CBSA dumping questionnaire

CBSA will send questionnaires to all known exporters at the initiation of the investigation. The purpose of these questionnaires is to collect the data necessary to calculate the margin of dumping or the amount of the subsidy.

The questionnaire typically has the following major parts:

> A – General information;
>
> B – Exports to Canada;
>
> C – Domestic sales information;
>
> D – Cost of production; and,
>
> E – Profitability

Exporters have 37 days to respond

Each of these sections serves a purpose in the calculation of dumping margin or subsidy amounts. Exporters are required to respond to the questionnaire 37 days from the date of its mailing. A response is complete only if it is submitted:

❑ In the correct format;

❑ In English or French;

❑ In the required number of copies;

❑ Both in hard copy and electronically; and

❑ In both confidential and non-confidential versions.

Appendix VI is an abbreviated sample CBSA exporter's questionnaire. Following is an explanation of the most important parts of this questionnaire from the perspective of an exporter to Canada.

Questionnaire section A – general information

This section provides CBSA with information about the exporter. Specifically it seeks a description of the company and its organization, and an understanding of the place the subject goods have in the company.

It is important to provide CBSA with complete data relating to company structure and organization

The most important part of this section requests information on the ownership and control relationships between the exporter and associated companies.

Associated persons are defined as:

❑ Persons related to each other; or

❑ Persons not related to each other, but not dealing with each other at arm's length.

For the purposes of SIMA, persons are related to each other if:

❑ They are individuals connected by blood relationship, marriage or adoption;

❑ One is an officer or director of the other;

❑ Each such person is an officer or director of the same two corporations, associations, partnerships or other organizations;

❑ They are partners;

❑ One is the employer of the other;

❑ They directly or indirectly control or are controlled by the same person;

❑ One directly or indirectly controls or is controlled by the other;

❑ Any other person directly or indirectly owns, holds or controls 5% or more of the outstanding voting stock or shares of each such person; or

❑ One directly or indirectly owns, holds or controls 5% or more of the outstanding voting stock or shares of the other.

This information is crucial because the SIMA allows CBSA to treat transactions between associated parties differently from transactions conducted between unassociated parties. For example, domestic sales are not taken into account for normal value calculations if they are between associated parties, and purchases of services and raw materials from associated parties are scrutinized to ensure they are acquired at market price and above fully absorbed cost of production.

If CBSA is investigating an allegation of non-market economy imports, section A of the questionnaire will also request detailed information on government involvement in the exporting company, including information on government participation on the board of directors and in the daily decision-making of the company.

Questionnaire section B – exports to Canada

Exporter's sales listings

This section requires exporters to provide detailed information concerning exports to Canada during the period of investigation (POI). The POI is typically the year ending with the date of initiation of the investigation. CBSA will use the information compiled in this section to determine how the subject goods are sold to Canada and how to calculate the export price of subject goods shipped to Canada.

Information relating to sales and distribution methods is important because export price is usually calculated at the ex-factory point and the other conditions of the export sales may influence the choice of domestic like goods sales that are chosen for comparison.

CBSA requires exporters to provide actual sales data for all exports to Canada during the POI. Each export sale must be listed by invoice and model as shown in the format on page 52) in both hard copy and electronic versions.

For each of the exports listed exporters will be required to provide a copy of the following documents (in either English or French):

❑ The importer's purchase order and the exporter's acknowledgement or acceptance of the order, or the contract of sale;

❑ Commercial invoice and credit or debit notes issued in respect of the sale;

❑ Canada Customs invoice (if applicable);

❑ Bill of lading;

❑ Freight invoices covering any expenses incurred by the exporter for the movement of the goods from the factory to the final destination in Canada;

❑ Letter of credit (if applicable); and

❑ Proof of payment (bank advice statement).

CBSA will examine the documents to ensure that data in the sales listing are complete and correct.

Calculation of export price

The export price is the exporter's sale price for the goods, less charges incurred by the exporter which would not have been incurred had the sale been to domestic customers.

EXPORTS TO CANADA

The report should be sorted by: (1) production facility/factory or warehouse; (2) individual product; and (3) date of sale.

1	2	3	4	5	6	7	8	9	10	11	12
CHARACTERISTIC 1	2	3	4	5	6	7	8	PRODUCT NUMBER (IDENTIFIER)	IMPORTER NAME	PLACE OF DIRECT SHIPMENT	NAME OF THE PRODUCERS

13	14	15	16	17	18	19	20	21	22	23
MILL FACILITY/ FACTORY OR WAREHOUSE	DATE OF SHIPMENT	DATE OF SALE	PURCHASE ORDER NUMBER	PURCHASE ORDER DATE	INVOICE NUMBER	INVOICE DATE	TERMS OF SALE	QUANTITY (WEIGHT)	UNIT SELLING PRICE	CURRENCY

24	25	26	27	28	29	30	31	32	33	34
EXTENDED SELLING PRICE	INLAND FREIGHT	OCEAN FREIGHT & OTHER EXPORT CHARGES	DUTY	PROMPT PAYMENT DISCOUNT	OTHER DISCOUNTS	REBATES	OTHER	NET EXPORT PRICE	UNIT NET SELLING PRICE	DATE OF PAYMENT

SIMA allows for the deduction from the exporter's selling price of:

❑ All costs incurred in preparing the goods for shipment to Canada that are additional to those costs, charges and expenses generally incurred on sales of like goods for use in the country of export (for example export packing);

❑ All duties and taxes (including anti-dumping duty) when they are paid by the exporter; and

❑ All other costs, charges and expenses resulting from the exportation of the goods, or arising from their shipment, from the place of direct shipment of the goods to Canada.

These costs include:

- Transportation cost from the point of direct shipment;
- Insurance from the point of direct shipment;
- Export permit fees;
- Bank charges, e.g. handling charge for letters of credit, documents against acceptance arrangement, interest and negotiation fees.;
- Inland transportation cost from the factory to the point where goods are containerized;
- Weight and measurement fees;
- Containerization fees for loading the goods into the container;
- Insurance on the goods from the factory to the containerization point;
- Freight forwarding charges;
- Wharfage;
- Warehousing fees if the goods are required to be stored prior to shipment;
- Export royalty fees;
- Lighterage charges; and
- Customs brokers fees.

Below is an example of a calculation of export price.

If we assume:

Inland freight costs $0.25 per unit
Ocean freight including all other export charges is $0.40 per unit
Canadian customs duty and taxes are 5%
Packing costs $0.10 per unit

Importer A purchases the exported goods, 'duty paid landed Vancouver'. This means the price of the goods includes all expenses from the factory in the country of export to an agreed point in Canada. In the calculation below, all of the expenses from the point of delivery in Canada back to the ex-factory point in the country of export are deducted from the selling price to get to an ex-factory price. Also deducted are extra packing costs to prepare the goods for export that would not be incurred if the goods were sold domestically.

Importer B purchases the exported goods, FOB port of export. This means the price of the goods includes all expenses from the factory in the country of export to the loaded boat at the port of export. In the example below, only inland freight costs (including all port charges to get the goods on the boat) are deducted from the selling price. Also deducted are extra packing costs to prepare the goods for export that would not be incurred if the goods were sold domestically.

Illustrative export price calculations

Importer	Terms	Quantity	Unit selling price ($)	Extended selling price ($)	Inland freight and port charges ($)	Ocean freight and other export charges ($)	Canadian customs duty and taxes ($)	Packing ($)	Net export price ($)	Unit net export price ($)
A	Duty paid landed Vancouver	12	12.00	144.00	3.00	4.80	7.20	1.20	127.80	10.65
B	FOB port of export	550	9.00	4,950.00	137.50			55.00	4,757.50	8.65

Questionnaire section C – domestic sales information

If there are sufficient domestic sales of like goods that are profitable and sold to more than one unassociated customer, normal values are based on the domestic selling price of these sales. If no domestic sales meet these conditions, cost of production will be used to calculate normal values.

This section of the questionnaire requests information needed to determine whether domestic sales of like goods meet the conditions (other than profitability) required to be used to calculate normal values. It also examines the circumstances of these sales to ensure a fair comparison to the exported goods.

Exporters must compile two listings detailing domestic sales

For each export model that meets the definition of like goods, a domestic sales listing must be compiled for all domestic sales of the same 'like goods' over the profitability analysis period (PAP). This is known as the first domestic sales listing (see format on page 57). The second domestic sales listing is the same as the first except that it is necessary to delete all sales to associated parties, sales to different trade levels and sales to customers who purchase substantially different amounts than the importer in Canada. This second sales listing is the basis upon which normal values will be calculated. Each domestic sale must be listed by invoice and model in both hard copy and electronic versions.

Like goods

The domestic sales used to calculate normal value must be for goods like the goods shipped to Canada

The sales that must be detailed in the domestic sales listing which CBSA will use to calculate normal values (if the like goods are profitable) are 'like goods', that is, goods that are 'identical to the product exported to Canada or if there are no identical goods, goods the uses and other characteristics of which closely resemble those of the product exported to Canada'. The like goods must be produced at the same plant as the product that was exported to Canada.

CBSA will decide which product characteristics define the like goods and which characteristics segregate the like goods into different models. For example, if the subject goods are ladies' footwear CBSA might determine that their defining characteristics are:

1. Material – leather or non-leather;

2. Type – shoe, boot or sandal;

3. Colour.

CBSA might then decide that 'identical goods' are those that match all three product characteristics and 'closely resembling goods' would be domestic sales that meet only characteristics 1 and 2. The characteristics define the different models within the like goods category.

If there are domestic sales in the POI that are identical to the exported goods (i.e. meet all four characteristics), these sales are included in the domestic sales listing and are used to calculate normal values provided they meet the other criteria discussed below. If on the other hand there are no identical domestic sales in the POI but there are sales that meet criteria 1 and 2 (i.e. closely resembling goods), these sales will be included in the domestic sales listing and be used to calculate normal values. Finally, if there are sales which only meet characteristic 1, CBSA will request domestic sales of the most closely resembling goods and normal values will be calculated based on the cost of production plus the profit earned on these goods.

Calculation of normal value

In order for domestic sales to be included in the database used to calculate normal values they must meet certain basic requirements.

❑ Domestic market sales selected for the determination of normal value must be to customers who are not associated with the exporter at the time of the sale;

❑ The sales selected for the determination of normal value must be to customers at the same or substantially the same trade level;

❑ The domestic market sales selected for the determination of normal value must be in the same or substantially the same quantities as the sales of the goods to Canada;

❑ The domestic market sales selected for the determination of normal value must be of goods that are sold in the country of export under competitive conditions;

❑ The domestic market sales must be made in the same (or a subsequent) 60-day period as the date of sale for the exported good;

❑ The domestic market sales used must be made at the place where the goods under investigation were shipped directly to Canada;

❑ There must also be 'such a number of sales' of like goods sold domestically to permit the use of the basic normal value calculation. Neither SIMA nor the SIM Regulations provide any guidance as to the volume of domestic sales needed to meet the requirement 'such a number of sales' but the footnote to Article 2.2 of the Anti-Dumping Agreement states that 'sales of the like product destined for consumption in the domestic market of the exporting country shall normally be considered a sufficient quantity for the determination of the normal value if such sales constitute 5 per cent or more of the sales of the product under consideration to the importing Member';

❑ Domestic sales of like goods by the exporter may not be used in the calculation of normal value if within a period of not less than six months:

– The sale is made at a price that is less than the cost of the goods, or
– Either

(a) the sale is of a volume that, or is one of a number of sales made at a price less than the cost of the goods, the total volume of which is not less than 20% of the total volume of like goods sold during that period, or

(b) the average selling price of like goods sold by the exporter during that period is less than the average cost of those like goods, and

– The sale is made at a price per unit that is not greater than the average cost of all like goods sold during that period.

Following are examples of the calculation of normal value and dumping margin.

SALES OF LIKE GOODS

The report should be sorted by: (1) production facility/factory or warehouse; (2) identical or similar product group (i.e. similar product group includes all products identified as being similar); and (3) date of sale.

1	2	3	4	5	6	7	8	9	10	11	12
CHARACTERISTIC 1	2	3	4	5	6	7	8	PRODUCT NUMBER (IDENTIFIER)	CUSTOMER	PLACE OF DIRECT SHIPMENT	MILL FACILITY OR WAREHOUSE

13	14	15	16	17	18	19	20	21	22	23
TRADE LEVEL	DATE OF SALE	PURCHASE ORDER NUMBER	PURCHASE ORDER DATE	INVOICE NUMBER	INVOICE DATE	TERMS OF SALE	QUANTITY (WEIGHT)	UNIT SELLING PRICE	CURRENCY	EXTENDED SELLING PRICE

24	25	26	27	28	29	30	31	32	33	34
FREIGHT	WAREHOUSE EXPENSES	INSURANCE	PROMPT PAYMENT DISCOUNT	OTHER DISCOUNTS	REBATES	OTHER	TAXES	NET SELLING PRICE	UNIT NET SELLING PRICE	DATE OF PAYMENT

Basic normal value calculation using domestic sales of identical goods

When domestic sales are identical to the exported goods, the normal value is the weighted average domestic selling price of the domestically sold goods. The following example demonstrates the most basic normal value calculation. The exported product is identical to the goods sold in the domestic market, sold to the same level of trade, in similar quantities, with the same payment terms, discounts and rebates, the same sales terms and no other differences which might affect price. The Normal value in this case is simply the weighted average selling price of all of the domestic sales which meet all of the requirements to be considered for inclusion in the calculation of normal value and which meet all of the conditions to be identical.

Characteristic			Customer	Level of trade	Invoice	Invoice date	Terms	Quantity	Unit selling price ($)	Gross selling price ($)	Net selling price ($)	Date of receipt of payment
1	2	3										
								Exported product				
LEATHER	SHOE	BLACK	Importer A	Retailer	A	1/1/06	FOB plant	12	11.00	132.00	132.00	3/2/2006
									Export price	11.00		
								Normal value calculation				
LEATHER	SHOE	BLACK	ABC SHOES	Retailer	1	1/1/06	FOB plant	12	11.00	132.00	132.00	3/3/2006
LEATHER	SHOE	BLACK	ABC SHOES	Retailer	2	1/1/06	FOB plant	22	12.00	264.00	264.00	3/3/2006
LEATHER	SHOE	BLACK	DEF SHOES	Retailer	3	1/5/06	FOB plant	15	11.75	176.25	176.25	3/4/2006
								49			572.25	

Normal value 11.68
Dumping per unit 0.68
Dumping as a percentage of export price 6.17%

In this example, the export price is less than the normal value and therefore the product is dumped. The amount of dumping is the difference between the normal value and the export price, i.e. $0.68. The dumping percentage as a function of export price is 6.17%. This is the percentage that the export price would have to be increased by in order to equal the normal value.

Adjustments to normal value

As noted above, SIMA requires that adjustments to normal value be made in order to recognize differences between the exported product and the domestic like goods to reflect differences that affect price comparability.

Sales in similar quantities

If domestic customers who purchase like goods are generally granted a discount for volume, and if the importer in Canada purchases the same volume, the domestic prices used to calculate normal value are reduced by the amount of the discount. In the following example, more than 50% of domestic sales are to customers who received the discount so the discount is generally available. If the domestic customer received a 5% discount for purchasing 200 units then in this example the importer meets the discount criteria. Therefore all of the domestic prices must be adjusted to reflect this discount.

			Exported product			
Characteristic			Customer	Quantity	Unit selling price ($)	Gross selling price ($)	Discount	Net selling price ($)
1	2	3						
LEATHER	SHOE	BLACK	Importer A	200	11.00	2,200.00	11.00	2,200.00
			Normal value calculation					
LEATHER	SHOE	BLACK	DEF SHOES	200	11.75	2,350.00	–117.50	2,232.50
LEATHER	SHOE	BLACK	GHI SHOES	200	11.75	2,350.00	–117.50	2,232.50
				400		4,700.00		4,465.00

Normal value 11.16
Amount of dumping 0.16

The export price is less than the normal value, and therefore the product is dumped. The amount of dumping is the difference between the normal value and the export price i.e. $0.16. The dumping percentage as a function of export price is 1.48%. This is the percentage that the export price would have to be increased by in order to equal the normal value.

Qualitative differences

Where there are no domestic sales of identical goods but there are sales of goods that closely resemble those exported, the closely resembling goods sales are used to calculate normal value but their price is adjusted to reflect differences between the goods.

SIMA requires that adjustments be made when the domestic goods differ from the exported goods: In their quality, structure, design or material; In their warranty against defect or guarantee of performance; In the time permitted from the date they are ordered to the date of their scheduled shipment; or In other conditions of sale.

In the following example, it is assumed that there are no domestic sales of identical goods but there are sales of closely resembling goods (the domestic goods are the same as the exported goods except that they are red while the exported goods are black). These closely resembling goods may be used to calculate normal value if the domestic price is adjusted to reflect the differences between the two. If it is further assumed for this example that it costs $8 to make a black shoe and $7 to make a red one then we must adjust the price of the domestically sold red shoes upward to reflect the difference in cost plus an amount for profit related to that cost difference.

In this example, therefore the calculation of the adjustment is:

Cost difference/unit = $1.00

Profit = 32% (assumed for this example)

Therefore the qualitative adjustment/unit = $1.32

Exported product

Characteristic			Quantity	Unit selling price ($)	Gross selling price ($)	Qualitative adjustment (1.32 * Units)	Net selling price ($)
1	2	3					
LEATHER	SHOE	BLACK	20	11.00	220.00		220.00
				Export price			11.00
				Normal value calculation			
LEATHER	SHOE	RED	12	11.00	132.00	15.84	147.84
LEATHER	SHOE	RED	22	12.00	264.00	29.04	293.04
LEATHER	SHOE	RED	20	11.75	235.00	26.40	261.40
			54		631.00		702.28

Normal value 13.01
Dumping per unit 2.01
Dumping as a percentage of export price 18.23%

The export price is less than the normal value, and therefore the product is dumped. The amount of dumping is the difference between the normal value and the export price, in this example 2.01. The dumping percentage as a function of export price is 18.23%. This is the percentage that the export price would have to be increased by in order to equal the normal value.

Payment terms, discounts and rebates

The price of like goods sold in the domestic market that are used in determining normal value must be adjusted to reflect any rebate, deferred discount or payment discount that is generally granted if the importer would have qualified for the rebate or discount. Discounts are traditionally granted to customers if they purchase a certain amount of a product in a given period of time or if they pay within a given period of time. SIMA requires that domestic prices used for the calculation of normal value be adjusted downward if the discount is generally granted (this means that more than 50% of the domestic customers of the subject goods actually get the discount; and the importer meets the requirements to qualify for the discount).

For the following example, it is assumed that domestic customers who pay within 50 days receive a 0.5% prompt payment discount. As all of the domestic customers received the cash discount, it meets the generally available criteria, and as the exporter paid within the 50-day limit, domestic sales prices used to calculate normal value are reduced to reflect the cash discount. It is important to note that domestic customer DEF in the example below did not meet the 50-day criterion but was still granted the discount, so the discount still applies to its sales. If this customer had not been granted the discount because it did not meet the 50-day payment requirement, the cash discount would have been considered not generally available, as less than 50% of the sales would have received the discount. In this case the cash discount would have had to be eliminated from all domestic sales in the calculation of normal value.

Basic normal value calculation using domestic sales of identical goods

Characteristic			Customer	Invoice date	Quantity	Unit selling price ($)	Gross selling price ($)	Cash discount	Net selling price ($)	Date of receipt of payment	Payment days
1	2	3									
LEATHER	SHOE	BLACK	Importer A	1/1/2006	20	11.00	220.00		220.00	18/2/2006	48

Exported product

Export price 11.00

Normal value calculation

Characteristic			Customer	Invoice date	Quantity	Unit selling price ($)	Gross selling price ($)	Cash discount	Net selling price ($)	Date of receipt of payment	Payment days
LEATHER	SHOE	BLACK	ABC SHOES	1/1/2006	12	13.00	156.00	–7.80	148.20	2/2/2006	32
LEATHER	SHOE	BLACK	ABC SHOES	1/1/2006	12	12.00	144.00	–7.20	136.80	2/3/2006	33
LEATHER	SHOE	BLACK	DEF SHOES	1/5/2006	20	11.75	235.00	–11.75	223.25	3/4/2006	58
					44		535.00		508.25		

Normal value 11.55
Dumping per unit 0.55
Dumping as a percentage of export price 5.01%

The export price is less than the normal value, and therefore the product is dumped. The amount of dumping is the difference between the normal value and the export price, i.e. $0.16. The dumping percentage as a function of export price is 1.48%. This is the percentage that the export price would have to be increased by in order to equal the normal value.

Sales and delivery terms

The price of domestic sales of like goods used to determine normal value must be adjusted if they include an amount for freight and/or other delivery charges.

In the example below, domestic customer ABC purchases the goods at a delivered price. The delivery costs $1 per unit. This amount is deducted from the selling price used to calculate normal value so that all sales prices reflect an FOB plant selling price.

Characteristic			Customer	Terms	Quantity	Unit selling price ($)	Gross selling price ($)	Delivery cost	Net selling price ($)
1	2	3							
LEATHER	SHOE	BLACK	Importer A	FOB plant	20	11.00	220		220
						Export price	11		
Normal value calculation									
LEATHER	SHOE	BLACK	ABC SHOES	Delivered	12	13.00	156	–12	144
LEATHER	SHOE	BLACK	ABC SHOES	Delivered	12	12.00	144	–12	132
LEATHER	SHOE	BLACK	DEF SHOES	FOB plant	20	11.75	235		235
					44		535		511

Normal value 11.61
Dumping per unit 0.61
Dumping as a percentage of export price 5.58%

The export price is less than the normal value, and therefore the product is dumped. The amount of dumping is the difference between the normal value and the export price, in this example $0.61. The dumping percentage as a function of export price is 5.58%. This is the percentage that the export price would have to be increased by in order to equal the normal value.

Level of trade

As noted above, an exporter's domestic sales to the same level of trade should be used to calculate normal values. If there are insufficient sales to the same trade level that meet all of the requirements to be used in determining normal values CBSA may use sales to the nearest and subsequent level of trade. If domestic sales of like goods are sold to purchasers who are at a lower level of trade than the importer in Canada, the price of the like goods is adjusted by the cost of the additional functions performed on sales at the lower trade level or, if this information is not available, the discount that is generally granted on the sales of like goods by other domestic companies to customers who are at the lower trade level.

In the following example, the importer is a distributor and all domestic sales are to customers who are at a lower trade level, in this case the retail trade level. If we assume that the manufacturer has a domestic sales force to sell to retailers but the importer performs this function in the country of import then the prices of the domestic sales must be adjusted by the cost of the additional functions performed on sales to retailers in the domestic market. Assume for this example that this function (the domestic sales force) costs $0.60 per pair of shoes sold. The prices used to calculate normal values are therefore adjusted by deducting this cost.

Exported product

Characteristic			Customer	Level of trade	Quantity	Unit selling price ($)	Gross selling price ($)	Travel level	Net selling price ($)
1	2	3							
LEATHER	SHOE	BLACK	Importer A	Distributor	20	11.00	220.00		220.00
						Export price	11.00		
					Normal value calculation				
LEATHER	SHOE	BLACK	ABC SHOES	Retailer	12	13.00	156.00	–7.2	148.80
LEATHER	SHOE	BLACK	ABC SHOES	Retailer	12	12.00	144.00	–7.2	136.80
LEATHER	SHOE	BLACK	DEF SHOES	Retailer	20	11.75	235.00	–12.0	223.00
					44		535.00		508.60

Normal value 11.56
Dumping per unit 0.56
Dumping as a percentage of export price 5.08%

The export price is less than the normal value, and therefore the product is dumped. The amount of dumping is the difference between the normal value and the export price, i.e. $0.56. The dumping percentage as a function of export price is 5.08%. This is the percentage that the export price would have to be increased by in order to equal the normal value.

Taxation

If any taxes or duties are charged on domestic sales of like goods, or on any materials or components of the like goods, that are not charged on the goods sold to Canada the price of the like goods sold domestically must be adjusted by deducting the taxes or duties. For example, if the domestic sales price has a value added tax included in the selling price and this tax is not charged on exports, the tax is deducted from the selling prices in the domestic sales listings. Taxes which are not included in such deductions are direct taxes such as property tax or income taxes, as these taxes are incurred on all sales.

In the following example, if we assume that a value added tax of 5% is included in the domestic selling price and that this tax is not charged on exports then this tax must be deducted from the domestic sales of like goods for the normal value calculation. Note that the selling price already includes 5% tax so the deduction is actually 4.7619% (1-(1/1.05)).

Exported product

Characteristic			Customer	Quantity	Unit selling price ($)	Gross selling price ($)	Tax	Net selling price ($)
1	2	3						
LEATHER	SHOE	BLACK	Importer A	20	11.00	220		220.00
					Export price	11		
					Normal value calculation			
LEATHER	SHOE	BLACK	ABC SHOES	12	13.00	156	(7.43)	148.57
LEATHER	SHOE	BLACK	ABC SHOES	12	12.00	144	(6.86)	137.14
LEATHER	SHOE	BLACK	DEF SHOES	20	11.75	235	(11.19)	223.83
				44		535		509.62

Normal value 11.58
Dumping per unit 0.58
Dumping as a percentage of export price 5.27%

The export price is less than the normal value, and therefore the product is dumped. The amount of dumping is the difference between the normal value and the export price, in this example $0.58. The dumping percentage as a function of export price is 5.27%. This is the percentage that the export price would have to be increased by in order to equal the normal value.

Questionnaire section D – cost of production

Exporters must verify that domestic sales used to establish normal value are profitable

Domestic sales may be used to calculate normal value only if they are profitable over a period of time. For models where normal values cannot be determined on the basis of domestic selling prices, normal values will be based on the total cost of the goods plus an amount for profit. It is important to note that the manufacturer of the goods must respond to this section of the questionnaire. If the exporter is an intermediary, it must request its supplier to respond to this section.

The accounting and costing systems of individual firms may be used to calculate the cost of production if they conform to generally accepted accounting principles. Cost of production must be calculated for each model shown on the export and domestic sales listings. The costing system must be fully explained and supported with the appropriate documentation.[3]

Production costs must be fully allocated over output

SIMA requires that all costs and expenses related to the production and sale of a product in your domestic market be fully allocated. Therefore, beyond the actual cost of manufacture of the goods, there must be allocations for general selling and administrative expenses, financing expenses, year-end charges, corporate charges and any other costs that are directly or indirectly attributable to the goods.

Quite simply, all costs and expenses shown in the financial statements must be allocated to production. For example, the settlement of a lawsuit related to the production, sale or consumption of a given product must be allocated to the total production cost of that product. If a cost is unrelated to the production of any specific good, it will be allocated over all production. If, in the lawsuit example, the goods that are the subject of the lawsuit are no longer produced by the company, the cost will be allocated over all current production by the factory.

Questionnaire section E – profitability

As discussed above, normal values are based on selling prices of like goods where there are a sufficient number of profitable domestic sales to unrelated customers.

This section combines the domestic sales data in section C with the cost data in section D of the questionnaire to determine which sales meet the profitability test required for sales to be used in the calculation of normal values.

CBSA does not take into account 'Unprofitable sales where the loss occurred over an extended period of time, the volume of sales at a loss was substantial and the sales at a loss were made at prices below the weighted average per unit cost for the period'.

This section of the questionnaire tests the sales for each model of domestic sales listing and determines whether they should be included in the calculation of normal value. The specific profit tests are described in the sample exporter's questionnaire found in appendix VI.

The CBSA exporter's questionnaire also includes sections which provide definitions and useful information concerning words, terms and phrases used, guidance respecting the selection of like goods for each investigation, and a Certificate of Veracity, Accuracy and Completeness form. This form must be typed or copied onto company letterhead and signed by the company official who is responsible for the response.

---

3   SIMA defines cost thus: 'cost' means, in relation to goods, the cost of production of the goods and the administrative, selling and all other costs with respect to the goods.

The other important area dealt with in the questionnaire relates to the treatment of confidential information. The treatment of confidential information and the requirement for non-confidential submissions are discussed extensively in the questionnaire guidelines.

Margin of dumping

The margin of dumping is the amount by which the normal value exceeds the export price. For each export sale, an export price and a normal value is calculated. The export sales listing defines the products exported, the date of sale. The export price and normal values are determined for each 60-day period in the period of investigation (POI).

Margin of dumping for a product

In the following example, there are five export sales of a given product during the POI. For each sale, the total export price is subtracted from the total normal value.

Exporter A Product 1 Units	Unit normal value ($)	Total normal value ($)	Unit export price ($)	Total export price ($)	Margin of dumping ($)
25	15	375	16	400	–25
40	14	560	15	600	–40
20	15	300	12	240	60
50	15	750	12	600	150
30	14	420	10	300	120
165		**2,405**		**2,140**	265

In this example, the total normal value is $2,405 and the total export price is $2,140. The total normal value is greater than the total export price by $265, which is the margin of dumping for this product for the POI. The margin of dumping as a percentage of export price is 265/2,140 or 12.38%.

Margin of dumping for an exporter

If an exporter has sales of more than one product then the margin of dumping for the exporter is the sum of the total normal values and total export prices of all products exported in the POI.

In this example, Exporter A has exports of product 1 and product 2 during the POI. The margin of dumping for Exporter A's exports of product 1 during the POI as calculated above is 12.38% of export price.

Exporter A's exports of product 2 during the POI are detailed below.

Units	Unit normal value ($)	Total normal value ($)	Unit export price ($)	Total export price ($)	Margin of dumping ($)
30	12	360	13	390	–30
20	13	260	15	300	–40
20	13	260	15	300	–40
15	13	195	16	240	–45
25	13	325	15	375	–50
30	12	360	13	390	–30
140		**1,760**		**1,995**	**–235**

For Product 2, the total export price is greater than the total normal value for the POI so there is no dumping, and in this example there is a margin of overselling of 235.

The weighted average normal value for Exporter A is calculated as follows:

Units	Total normal value ($)	Total export price ($)	Margin of dumping ($)
165	2,405	2,140	265
140	1,760	1,995	–235
305	**4,165**	**4,135**	**30**

The sum of the normal values is $4,165 and the sum of the export prices is $4,135. The margin of dumping is the difference between the two, or 30. The margin of dumping as a percentage of export price is 0.73%.

Zeroing

It must be noted that this method of calculating the margin of dumping reflects a very recent change in administrative practice by CBSA. During the recent investigation of certain laminate flooring, CBSA discontinued its policy of zeroing.

The statement of reasons at the final determination of Certain laminate flooring reads in part:

> *CBSA discontinued its practice of zeroing for purposes of determining a margin of dumping for an exporter. In the past, CBSA would set any negative margins of dumping for a product model or type to zero when determining the margin of dumping for a particular exporter. CBSA's current practice in determining a margin of dumping for an exporter is to subtract the total export price from the total normal value of all goods shipped to Canada during the POI, including any individual sales that were made at undumped prices. As such, any individual sales that were made at undumped prices reduced the overall margin of dumping found for that exporter. CBSA believes our revised practice is consistent with SIMA and with Canada's obligations as a member of the WTO.*[4]

This new method of calculation has a significant impact on the margins of dumping calculated in original investigations. In the above example, the margin of dumping is 0.73%, which is *de minimis* (if this were the sole exporter the country would be excluded from the finding automatically). If the same example were calculated using the previous zeroing methodology the normal value would be as follows.

	Units	Total normal value ($)	Total export price (S)	Margin of dumping ($)
Product 1	165	2,405	2,140	265
Product 2	140	1,760	1,995	0
	305	**4,165**	**4,135**	**265**

In this example, Product 1 has a dumping margin of $265 and Product 2 has a negative margin but the negative margin (overselling) is disregarded and made zero (hence zeroing). The margin of dumping here is $265 and the margin of dumping as a percentage of export price is 6.41%.

In Canada, zeroing has an impact only in the original investigation. This is because after the original investigation CBSA typically calculates normal values for all goods exported to Canada from each exporter. There is typically no

---

4   Statement of reasons concerning the making of a final determination with respect to the dumping of certain laminate flooring originating in or exported from the People's Republic of China and France, paragraph 59.

margin of dumping except where a Ministerial Specification is applied. If an exporter sells a product a below the normal value calculated for that product by CBSA then dumping duties are assessed in the amount of the difference.

Margin of dumping for a country

When there are multiple exporters from a country, the weighted average margin of dumping for country is the sum of the product of the margin of dumping for each exporter multiplied by that exporter's percentage of total exports to Canada during the POI.

Weighted average margin of dumping for Exporter A				
	Units	**Total normal value ($)**	**Total export price ($)**	**Margin of dumping ($)**
Product 1	165	2,405	2,140	265
Product 2	140	1,760	1,995	–235
	305	**4,165**	**4,135**	**30**
Total dumping	**30**			
Dumping as a percentage of export price				0.73%
Weighted average margin of dumping for Exporter B				
	Units	**Total normal value ($)**	**Total export price ($)**	**Margin of dumping ($)**
Product 1	200	2,405	2,300	105
Product 2	150	1,760	2,100	–340
	350	**4,165**	**4,400**	**–235**
Total dumping	**–235**			
Dumping as a percentage of export price				–5.34%
Weighted average margin of dumping for Exporter C				
	Units	**Total normal value ($)**	**Total export price ($)**	**Margin of dumping ($)**
Product 1	190	2,405	2,140	265
Product 2	120	1,760	1,600	160
	310	**4,165**	**3,740**	**425**
Total dumping	**425**			
Dumping as a percentage of export price				11.36%

In the above example, margins of dumping have been calculated for three exporters:

Exporter A has a weighted average dumping margin of 0.73%;

Exporter B has no dumping; and

Exporter C has a dumping margin of 11.36%.

Canada does not typically make dumping findings against companies; findings are against countries. In this case the dumping calculation would be:

	Units	Percentage of total exports	Margin of dumping	Share of country margin
Exporter A	305	32%	0.73%	0.23%
Exporter B	350	36%	0.00%	0.00%
Exporter C	310	32%	11.36%	3.65%
	965			**3.88%**

Notwithstanding that two of the three exporters had zero or *de minimis* margins, this country (and all exporters from this country including those with zero and *de minimis* margins) would be found to be dumping.

Calculating subsidies and the subsidy questionnaires

Government subsidy questionnaire

Detailed information is required from governments regarding the operation and benefits of subsidy programmes

The questionnaire is designed to obtain as much information as possible about the subsidy programme alleged to be benefiting exports to Canada. It is sent to foreign government(s) and will normally be the subject of some discussion between CBSA and the foreign government representatives. Generally it will request:

❑ An explanation of how the programme operates, including detailed explanations of:

– The purpose and objectives of the programme;

– The administration and operation of the programme;

– The role and mandate of the organization responsible for providing and administering the programme;

– The date the programme first came into operation;

– The date of any significant changes including any pending changes to the operation of the programme; and

– The name, address, telephone number and facsimile number of a senior official involved in the programme.

❑ Copies of relevant laws, regulations, contracts, agreements, and other materials establishing the programme and its administration.

❑ Descriptions of the eligibility requirements and criteria for the programme.

❑ A description of the application process.

❑ An explanation of the funding mechanism and the process by which financial assistance or benefits are claimed or granted, including an explanation of the type of records maintained by the administering authority relating to the programme.

❑ The intended duration of the programme.

❑ The *total amount* of benefits provided to all participants for a two-year period.

❑ The total number of firms benefiting from the programme.

❑ A description of any anticipated changes to the programme.

Types of subsidy programmes and the general rules followed in calculating the amount of subsidy

CBSA must determine the subsidy benefit on a per unit basis for the imported goods

As a first step in any subsidy investigation CBSA must establish that a subsidy exists and that it is actionable. If the answer to this question is positive, the process moves to the next stage of determining the amount of the subsidy. Regardless of what form the subsidy takes (grant, loan, loan guarantee, the provision of goods and services by government, tax concession, procurement preference, etc.), the objective is to establish a value that can be attributed on a per unit production basis to the imported goods. In other words, for the purpose of the application of countervailing duties, CBSA must determine the amount of the benefit that applies to the imported goods as a result of the subsidy programme. Because subsidies take various forms and are directed to particular activities, such as plant construction, acquisition of machinery or other fixed assets or infrastructure, the task of establishing the unit value of such benefits can be an extremely complicated exercise involving, among other things, estimates of the useful life of assets, the calculation of present value of future benefits and forecasts of future production activities.

Income tax credits on exports

Income tax reductions or tax holidays may be subsidies

Subsidies may be provided by means of reductions in corporate income tax or tax holidays. For example, in order to encourage exports companies may be allowed a reduction in their tax payable on export income. In such cases the subsidy may not be related to individual goods exported, but to the exporter's overall export performance. This type of subsidy could be regarded as an export subsidy. The subsidy in such cases should be determined as the amount of the income tax that is credited, refunded or exempted, according to the taxation laws of the country of export. The amount of the subsidy per unit of goods is determined by dividing the tax saving by the total number of units exported during the taxation period.

For example, assume that a subsidy programme provides for the exemption from tax of 25% of the taxable profit attributable to exports. An exporter of widgets makes $100,000 in taxable profits on export sales of 40,000 units. Under the subsidy programme, the exporter would be exempted from tax on $25,000. At the normal tax rate of 50%, the exporter would have paid $12,500 in tax on this amount; divided by 40,000 units this saving indicates a subsidy of $0.31 per unit.

Over-refund of indirect taxes

Article VI of GATT provides in paragraph 4 that no product shall be subject to anti-dumping or countervailing duty by reason of the exemption of exported goods from duty or taxes borne by the like product when destined for home consumption in the country of origin or export or by reason of the refund of duties or taxes on such goods.

Exports exempted from indirect domestic taxes do not attract countervailing duties

In general, indirect taxes are levied on commodities rather than on income, and include such taxes as sales tax, value added tax, excise tax and turnover tax. They may be levied at various stages in the production or marketing process and their effect can be cumulative. It is an accepted principle of international trade that, where goods are exported, the amount of such indirect tax levied on the goods in the country of export should not be borne by the exported goods. Therefore exports may be exempted from payment of such tax. If the tax has already been paid, the amount may be remitted on export.

Remission of indirect taxes in excess of those paid may be subject to countervailing duty

However the remission (on the exported goods) of amounts in excess of indirect taxes levied on goods sold for domestic consumption may be considered to be an export subsidy.

In these cases, the amount of the subsidy should be the amount by which the remission exceeds the indirect taxes actually levied on like domestic goods. This would encompass not only indirect taxes paid on the finished product, but also any indirect taxes paid on any materials or components that are physically incorporated into the product. For example, during production a variety of indirect taxes may be levied and paid on a widget and its component materials to a total of $0.86 per unit. The government, however, remits $1.00 for each unit exported in order to relieve the burden of tracking such indirect taxes. The difference of $0.14 per unit would be an export subsidy.

Goods or services provided by a government

A subsidy exists when a government provides goods or services to assist export production or sales on terms more favourable than those on which it would provide those goods or services for domestic consumption. To the extent that such goods or services are provided at a lower price, the difference is considered to be a subsidy. An example is subsidized inland freight rates provided by the government, with a lower rate applicable to export shipments. In calculating the amount of the subsidy for the purposes of countervailing duties, the subsidy is allocated over the total number of units of the subsidized goods exported.

Deductions from countervailable subsidies

Certain deductions are taken into account by CBSA in calculating the amount of a subsidy. Examples of such deductions include:

Costs associated with obtaining a subsidy may be deductible

❑ *The amount of any fee or other expenses incurred by the subsidy recipient in order to apply, qualify for, or receive the benefit of a subsidy.* Costs and fees associated with producing and preparing certified documents or test results before obtaining a grant are deducted from the amount of a countervailable subsidy.

❑ *Any charges levied by the government of the country of export to offset the subsidy benefit.* If a government that has granted a subsidy applies an export tax or other charge specifically to offset in whole or in part the subsidy granted, the determination of the amount of the countervailable subsidy should include a deduction for the amount of the offset. In practice this means that where a government grants a subsidy and then entirely or partially cancels the benefit by levying an offsetting charge, only the net benefit should be subject to countervailing duty. This kind of situation arises where the government granting the subsidy intended to reduce the price of goods in the home market by paying a domestic production subsidy, but did not intend to reduce the price of goods sold for export. In order to do this, an export tax is levied to cancel the subsidy when the goods are exported, thus limiting the effects of the subsidy to domestic sales.

❑ *Any losses in the value of a subsidy caused by the deferred receipt of the benefit.* A deduction could be allowable in the case of deferred receipt of a benefit. If the government programme called for specified benefits to be given to an exporter six months following the exportation of goods and the subsidy recipient did indeed have to wait that interval before receiving the benefit, then the loss in value of the benefit, through inflation or other causes, could be taken into account. If however the subsidy programme did not specifically require a delay, but the recipient only received the benefit after some interval because of administrative or bureaucratic delays, then a deduction would not usually be allowed for the loss in value. The delay should be deliberate, and government-imposed, in order to qualify for a deduction for loss in value of the benefit.

Grants

The benefit from a grant must be spread over output attributable to the grant

Governments may provide grants to assist in the purchase or construction of factories, warehouses and equipment, to encourage the establishment of new industries or the expansion of existing industries, to encourage investment in underdeveloped regions, or to facilitate the modernization of declining industries. The subsidy involved must not be applied directly to the goods exported but to the capital assets that are employed in some phase of the production or sale of the goods.

In calculating the amount of subsidy for grants, the distribution should be made in accordance with generally accepted accounting principles. In some cases the use to which the grant is put may need to be taken into consideration. If a grant is given to assist a company in producing widgets in a given year, the per unit subsidy could be readily calculated by dividing the amount of the grant by the total number of widgets produced.

However, if the grant is given to assist in the production or purchase of a fixed asset, the goods produced will be subsidized indirectly. Normally such a grant should be distributed over the estimated total quantity of the goods produced during the useful life of the asset. For example, if machinery purchased with a grant of $100,000 is estimated to be capable of producing 10,000 units during its normal life, the amount of the subsidy would be determined to be $10 per unit. If a grant cannot be directly attributed to any particular goods, CBSA considers different alternatives. For example, if a grant is given to a company to assist it in restructuring or refinancing its debt, it may be necessary to distribute the grant over the estimated quantity of goods produced during the period representing the average useful life of the assets of the firm.

Deferral of income taxes

Deferral of income taxes may constitute a subsidy

When income tax is deferred, it nevertheless remains payable. The subsidy associated with the deferral is like an interest-free loan to the company in which the term of the loan is equal to the period of the tax deferral. The amount of subsidy should generally be defined as the cost to the government of providing such an interest-free loan. The cost to the government is determined as the present value of the interest payments that the government would itself have to pay if it financed the subsidy by obtaining a loan for the period of the tax deferral. The amount of the subsidy on a per unit basis is obtained by dividing the cost to the government by the total number of units of the goods exported during the period of time for which payment of the tax was deferred.

To contrast the calculation of the amount of the subsidy involving tax deferral, as opposed to tax exemption or remission, consider the following example. Suppose the subsidy programme provides for the deferral for one year of taxes on 25% of the taxable profits attributable to exports. An exporter of widgets makes $100,000 in taxable profits on export sales of 40,000 units. If this amount is taxable at 50%, the amount of the tax deferred would be $12,500. If the prevailing interest rate for loans to the government of that country is 18%, then the cost to the government of providing the tax deferral would be calculated as the present value of one year's interest at 18% on a loan of $12,500. Using a discount rate of 18% in the present value calculation, this is approximately $1,907. The amount of the subsidy would be this amount divided by 40,000 units, or $0.048 per unit.

Loans, loan guarantees and equity

A subsidy may be provided in the form of a loan at a preferential rate of interest. Subsidies made through preferential financing can take a variety of forms such as:

❑ Loans to provide working capital;

❑ Loans to cover start-up costs or to finance expansion;

❑ Loans to assist in the purchase of capital assets; and

❑ Low-cost credit extended to exporters or importers to finance the sale or purchase of goods.

In most cases, the benefit provided is a lower rate of interest than would be available to the enterprise if the government had not been involved either directly or indirectly in providing the loan at preferential rates. It is also possible that a benefit could accrue to an exporter or an importer as a result of a government guarantee that would not necessarily result in a cost to the government. The benefit could be a lower interest rate or a loan at a commercial rate that the company would not get without government guarantees.

Article 14 of the SCMA provides that any method used by CBSA to calculate the benefit of a subsidy to the recipient must be consistent with the following guidelines:

❑ Government provision of equity capital shall not be considered as conferring a benefit unless the investment decision is inconsistent with usual investment practice.

❑ A loan by a government shall not be considered as conferring a benefit unless there is a difference between the amount the firm pays on the government loan and what it would pay for a commercial loan. The benefit would be the difference between the two.

❑ A loan guarantee by a government shall not be considered as conferring a benefit unless there is a difference between the amount that the firm receiving the guarantee pays on the government-guaranteed loan and what it would pay for a comparable commercial loan without government support.

❑ The provision of goods or services or purchase of goods by government shall not be considered as conferring a benefit unless there is inadequate remuneration.

The basic concepts involved in calculating subsidies resulting from loans are as follows:

❑ The benefit provided over the period of the loan is measured by what it costs the government to provide the preferential loan;

❑ The present value of the benefit must be determined using an appropriate discount rate; and

❑ The present value that is obtained must be allocated to the appropriate quantity of goods.

By way of illustration, the framework for calculating the amount of subsidy involved in a preferential loan is set out in the following six steps.

Step 1. By comparing the schedule of principal and interest payments applicable to the preferential loan to a comparable schedule for a loan if the government had to borrow the money, CBSA establishes a series of benefits provided by the government that occur at specified intervals during the term of the loan. This amount is the difference between the interest actually payable on the preferential loan and the amount of interest that the government would have had to pay if it had borrowed the money.

For example, ignoring repayment of principal, the preferential loan may provide for interest payable as follows:

> $8,000 payable on 1 December 1996
> $7,500 payable on 1 June 1997
> $7,000 payable on 1 December 1997
> $6,650 payable on 1 June 1998
> … etc.

The cost to the government of providing this subsidy, measured in terms of the interest the government would pay if it had to borrow the money commercially, might be:

> $9,500 payable on 1 December 1996
> $8,800 payable on 1 June 1997
> $7,900 payable on 1 December 1997
> $7,450 payable on 1 June 1998
> … etc.

The net benefit is determined not as a total, but as a series. It is the difference between the above payment schedules, namely:

> $1,500 benefit received on 1 December 1996
> $1,300 benefit received on 1 June 1997
> $900 benefit received on 1 December 1997
> $800 benefit received on 1 June 1998
> … etc.

Step 2. Add the amount of administrative charges related to the loan. For example, suppose there is an administration fee of $20 applied to each repayment, which the government absorbs. Then the total benefit provided would be:

> $1,520 on 1 December 1996
> $1,320 on 1 June 1997
> $920 on 1 December 1997
> $820 on 1 June 1998
> … etc.

Step 3. Determine the present value of the benefits. The series of total benefits obtained in step 2 forms the numerator FV in the present value formula:

$$PV = S \frac{FV}{(1 + i)^n}$$

where **FV** is the future value of the total benefit for each payment date, **n** represents the number of payment periods, **I** represents the discount rate and S represents a summation of all periods.

Step 4. To select the appropriate discount rate CBSA uses the methods referred to above. Suppose for this example that the interest rate prevailing is 6.0% (semi-annually). Then **I** is 0.06 in the formula.

Step 5. The present value calculation is performed by plugging the numbers into the formula and performing the necessary arithmetic:

$$\frac{\$1,520}{1.06} + \frac{\$1,320}{1.06^2} + \frac{\$920}{1.06^3} + \frac{\$820}{1.06^4} + \dots \text{etc.}$$

which is:

$$\frac{\$1,520}{1.06} + \frac{\$1,320}{1.1236} + \frac{\$920}{1.1910} + \frac{\$820}{1.2625} + ... \text{ etc.}$$

that is:

$$\$1,433.96 + \$1,174.80 + \$772.46 + \$649.50 + ... \text{ etc.}$$

Once all the individual numbers are calculated, the summation must be performed. The final result is a single figure representing the present value. In this example, it would be \$4,030.72 plus whatever amount is represented by the 'etc.' In practice there will most likely be complexities involved in actual long-term financing arrangements that would complicate this part of the process. However, the formula does represent the accepted manner of calculating present value.

Step 6. The final step in the calculation is to determine the subsidy on a quantity basis, by allocating the present value obtained in step 5 over the appropriate number of units of the goods.

Other subsidies

In certain instances CBSA may need to prescribe the manner to be used in determining the amount of subsidy on a per unit or a percentage of export price basis. It may also be necessary to adopt special rules where sufficient information has not been furnished by the exporter or foreign government, or where such information is simply not available.

CHAPTER 4

The Canadian International Trade Tribunal: the injury decision-making process

Introduction

Dumping and subsidizing occur often in international commerce. When they cause injury, the WTO allows remedial action

The WTO Agreements require that dumping or subsidizing and injury be considered simultaneously throughout an investigation. To simplify the following narrative, the term *injury* is generally used in this chapter to refer to material injury to a domestic industry, threat of material injury to a domestic industry, or material retardation to the establishment of a domestic industry. It is important to note that, while dumping and subsidizing are commercial facts of life in international trade, it is only when that dumping or subsidizing actually causes or threatens injury or retardation to the industry in Canada that Canadian law permits the application of measures to offset the injury.

In Canada, the injury decision is taken by CITT

Injury decisions involve an analysis of the economic effects on Canadian industry of the dumped or subsidized imports, and therefore a reasoned value judgement must be made by CITT. This reasoned decision on injury is a precondition and the trigger that leads to the application of countermeasures. Thus, in the overall scheme of an investigation, decisions on injury can require a much more judicious effort than the factual decision on whether or not dumping or subsidizing is occurring.

Countries have adopted different approaches in their anti-dumping and countervailing systems and thus procedures and processes vary between countries. The system in Canada employs a dual track in which the investigation of dumping or subsidizing is carried out by CBSA while the inquiry into injury is conducted by CITT, an independent body.

CITT structure and injury inquiry process

CITT organization

CITT is a quasi-judicial independent body charged with making injury decisions in trade remedy cases

CITT is an administrative tribunal created pursuant to the Canadian International Trade Tribunal Act. It is a quasi-judicial independent body that carries out inquiries in an autonomous and impartial manner

The main legislation governing the work of the Tribunal is the CITT Act, SIMA, the Customs Act, the Excise Tax Act, the Canadian International Trade Tribunal Regulations, the Canadian International Trade Tribunal Procurement Inquiry Regulations and the Canadian International Trade Tribunal Rules. CITT reports to Parliament through the Minister of Finance. It is composed of up to nine full-time members, including a chairperson and two vice-chairpersons, who are appointed by the Government for a term of up to five years.

The chairperson is the chief executive officer responsible for the case assignments of members and for managing the work of the Tribunal and its staff.

Members come from a variety of educational and career backgrounds and various regions of the country. They are supported in their work by a permanent staff of about 90 people. Principal staff officers are the Director General, Research, responsible for economic and financial analysis of firms, industries and other fact-finding for inquiries; the Director, Management Services, responsible for corporate management; the Secretary responsible for relations with the public, government departments and other governments and, the General Counsel, responsible for the provision of legal services;

In the year ending 31 March 2005, the Tribunal issued three preliminary determinations of injury, and five injury findings following inquiries. Annexes I and II contain a list of CITT injury decisions and inquiry initiations during the year ending 31 March 2005. The inquiry on Outdoor barbecues was terminated due to a zero dumping margin decision. The Tribunal issued five Orders following reviews and three Orders following interim reviews. Annexes III and IV list the cases that were reviewed by CITT during the same period. At the end of March 2005, 24 injury findings were in force (annex V) and 5 cases had been appealed to either the Federal Court of Canada or the Federal Court of Appeal (annex VI). In 2004, 0.32% of Canadian imports were affected by anti-dumping and countervailing measures, a decline from 0.54% in 1995.

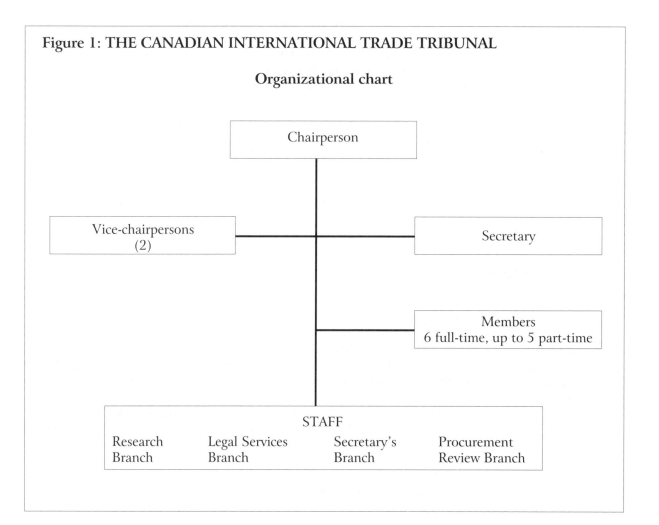

Figure 1: THE CANADIAN INTERNATIONAL TRADE TRIBUNAL

Organizational chart

Chairperson

Vice-chairpersons (2)

Secretary

Members
6 full-time, up to 5 part-time

STAFF

| Research Branch | Legal Services Branch | Secretary's Branch | Procurement Review Branch |

CITT inquiry process in dumping and subsidizing cases

CITT conducts public inquiries relating to injury. Interested parties have a direct role to play in these inquiries

A major role of CITT is to conduct inquiries to establish whether dumping or subsidizing has caused or threatens to cause material injury or material retardation to the production in Canada of like goods. A Canadian producer or an association of Canadian producers begins the process of seeking relief from alleged injurious dumping or subsidizing by making a complaint to CBSA. If CBSA initiates a dumping or subsidizing investigation the Tribunal initiates a preliminary injury inquiry to determine whether the evidence discloses a reasonable indication that the dumping or subsidizing has caused injury, or retardation or is threatening to cause injury. The Tribunal completes its inquiry within 60 days. If its decision is positive, CBSA will continue its investigation; if negative the case is terminated. If CBSA makes a preliminary affirmative dumping or subsidizing determination, CITT begins its final inquiry into whether material injury has, in fact, been caused or threatened by the dumped or subsidized imports.

Definition of 'domestic industry' key issue for consideration

In deciding the question of material injury, CITT must also take decisions on a number of other related matters. Cases can involve issues such as: whether particular firms, such as assemblers, are producers; what constitutes the Canadian industry when there is more than one domestic producer and only some producers wish to support the complaint; and whether the domestically produced goods are 'like' the subject goods. There are also issues relating to whether there is evidence of massive dumping, whether the volume of imports is negligible or the margin is de minimis, and whether to cumulate or cross-cumulate cases. Further, CITT must concern itself with the issue of causality and consider whether there is a direct relationship between the dumping or subsidizing and the material injury. This is not an easy task.

Injury based on objective assessment of indices relating to domestic industry

The term 'material injury' is not defined in the CITT Act. Nor, indeed, is it defined in article VI of GATT or the WTO Agreements. However, the Agreements and Canadian law set out various indices and criteria that are examined in arriving at a judgement as to whether material injury exists or is threatened. They include, among other things, the effects of the dumping or subsidizing on prices, production, sales, market shares, profits, employment and capacity utilization.

All registered parties may have assess to public questionnaire responses

During the investigation, the CITT staff distributes questionnaires to be completed by the Canadian producers, exporters, importers and, in some cases, the Canadian end-users of the goods under examination. The staff may also visit manufacturers' facilities, conduct research into industry and market conditions and collect trade, financial, pricing, sales and other economic data about the goods that are being examined. CITT members may visit plant sites during the inquiry to familiarize themselves with the production processes but not to discuss the merits of the case with the producers.

CITT staff carry out independent studies

The primary research process carried out by the staff depends to a large degree on the cooperation and voluntary compliance of the parties involved. CITT has the power to subpoena witnesses and compel parties to submit documents even when these are commercially confidential.

However, it prefers to rely on voluntary cooperation where possible. Indeed the cooperation of the Canadian industry is vital in deciding whether it is being injured by the imports. Moreover, the process required to properly complete questionnaires can often be time-consuming and difficult. CITT staff are available to assist parties in understanding the questionnaires. In this regard, CITT strictly enforces the confidentiality provisions of the Act and its rules of procedure so that parties have full confidence that their vital business information will be protected.

CITT staff prepare objective analysis and issue staff report to interested parties	Following receipt of the completed questionnaires (usually about three weeks after they were sent out) and the staff research and analysis, confidential and non-confidential pre-hearing staff reports are prepared and distributed. The non-confidential reports are made available to parties who have completed a notice of appearance; the confidential reports are made available only to counsel representing parties and only to those of them who have signed an appearance declaration and confidentiality undertaking pursuant to the CITT Rules of Procedure.

The public hearing process

Exporters use public hearing to make the case that they are not causing injury	The public hearing process provides CITT with an opportunity to gather and test as much information as possible to assist it in arriving at a decision. It also provides the parties and their counsel the opportunity to present their cases and make representations. The hearings are adversarial in nature so that opposing sides are able to examine each other's evidence and cross-examine each other's witnesses. The hearings are governed by the principles of natural justice. This essentially means that the process must be fair and must enable all the parties to know the particulars of the case they have to meet. It also provides them with an opportunity to bring forward any evidence they consider relevant in support of their position.

Material injury criteria

Injury

CITT determines whether there is sufficient evidence of injury to initiate an investigation	When a dumping or subsidizing complaint from Canadian industry is accepted by CBSA, CITT must make a preliminary injury determination. The process involved is described in chapter 2.
	In making this decision, CITT essentially examines the submissions made by the Canadian industry to CBSA, although it may request additional information or hold a hearing. It also receives submissions on the issue from interested parties. If its decision is affirmative, the CITT staff begins to conduct the research needed to support the full inquiry by CITT following a preliminary determination by CBSA.
Injury decision must be based on objective assessment of positive evidence	As noted above, the term 'material injury' is not defined in the WTO Agreements or in Canadian law. However, both set out a non-exhaustive list (no one item of which by itself provides decisive guidance) of criteria that must be examined in rendering a decision on material injury. Specifically, an injury determination must be based on positive evidence involving an objective examination of the impact of the dumped or subsidized imports on producers in Canada of like products. This includes:

❑ An examination of the volume of the dumped or subsidized imports and whether there has been a significant increase in imports either in absolute terms or relative to production or consumption in Canada.

❑ An examination as to whether the effect of the dumped or subsidized imports has resulted in significant price erosion or price depression or has served to suppress price increases in the Canadian market for like products.

Specific requirements that CITT must examine in making injury decisions	These general criteria are supplemented by more specific requirements that CITT takes into account in making its decisions:

❑ The assessment of the impact of the dumped or subsidized imports on the domestic industry must include an evaluation of: all economic factors and indices affecting the industry, including actual and potential declines in sales, profits, output, market share, productivity, return on investment, or utilization of capacity; factors affecting domestic prices; the magnitude of the margin of dumping; and actual and potential negative effects on cash flow, inventories, employment, wages, growth, ability to raise capital or investments.

❑ The examination must demonstrate a causal relationship between the dumped or subsidized imports and the injury to the domestic industry.

❑ The inquiry must examine any known factors other than the dumping or subsidizing that are also injuring the industry to ensure that the injury caused by these factors is not attributed to the dumping or subsidizing.

❑ The effect of the dumped or subsidized imports must be examined in relation to Canadian production of the like product. The respective shares of the market held by Canadian producers and importers are analysed to determine whether imports are displacing domestic production. Loss of market share to dumped or subsidized imports can be an important indicator of injury to domestic production. If the separate identification of that production is not possible, the examination must be in relation to the narrowest group or range of products that includes the like product and for which information is available.

Threat of material injury

A threat of injury decision must relate to a situation that is clearly foreseen and is imminent

Canadian law recognizes that there are circumstances in which anti-dumping or countervailing action is justified even before injury has actually materialized. The circumstances contemplated are those where the conditions of trade clearly indicate that material injury will occur imminently if demonstrable trends in trade adverse to domestic industry continue, or if clearly foreseeable adverse events occur. Thus when considering complaints seeking action based on the threat of injury, the predicted future injury must be *clearly foreseen* and must be *imminent*.

CITT may conclude, in some cases, that while the evidence of past injury is not compelling, the trend of increasing imports and their increasing impact on domestic producers may pose a threat of future injury. This is particularly so if the domestic industry is already in a weakened position and therefore more vulnerable to increased import competition.

Trends taken into account by CITT

In evaluating a complaint that is lacking in evidence of past injury, CITT determines whether there are clear trends in respect to the alleged dumped or subsidized imports that support the allegation of a threat of injury. The threat of injury may exist when there is a significant rate of increase of dumped imports combined with evidence that these dumped imports will undercut prices of domestic goods or will have a significant depressing or suppressing effect on domestic prices. Another element considered is whether the exporters of the subject goods have excess capacity such that they could increase their exports substantially. High inventory levels abroad may also represent potential for future exports at dumped prices.

Factors examined in judging threat of injury complaints

The determination of threat of injury must be based on facts and not mere 'allegation, conjecture or remote possibility'. In making a determination regarding a threat of injury CITT considers factors such as:

❑ Whether there has been a significant rate of increase of dumped or subsidized imports indicating a likelihood of further substantial increased imports;

❑ Whether there are freely disposable like goods or an imminent increase in capacity of the exporter indicating the possibility of substantially increased dumped or subsidized imports;

❑ Whether imports are entering at prices that will have a significant depressing effect on domestic prices and increase demand for imports; and

❑ Whether there have been significant product inventory changes.

Retardation

Action may be taken to deal with imports that retard the establishment of Canadian production

Retardation occurs when imports materially hinder or retard the establishment of an industry. This form of injury can be alleged only in cases where production has not yet started. Specific facts must be presented to substantiate allegations of retardation. The potential domestic producer must document plans for the establishment of the industry such as the purchase of a factory, machinery or equipment, or demonstrate the cancellation or deferral of a planned project. In order to ensure that the complainants have substantive grounds for claiming retardation attributable to the imports, when confronted with a case of alleged retardation, exporters and their counsel should pay particular attention to the timing of the following.

Exporters must be vigilant to ensure that complainants have established their case

❑ When the production plans were first arranged and confirmed;

❑ When importation of the subject goods first began;

❑ When the dumping or the subsidizing of the imported subject goods started; and

❑ When the production plans were cancelled or formally postponed.

Cumulation

Dumped and subsidized imports from all countries can be cumulated in deciding injury

In cases involving both dumping and subsidizing and exports from more than one country, CITT must decide whether the effects of all of these imports on domestic production should be assessed cumulatively. That is, the injury decision may reflect the impact of all of the dumped or subsidized imports taken together and may take into account all such imports from all sources. The WTO Agreements and the Act make clear that this can be done only if:

❑ The margin of dumping or the amount of the subsidy in relation to imports from each country is more than *de minimis* (i.e. more than 2% expressed as a percentage of the export price in dumping cases and 1% *ad valorem* in subsidy cases) and the volume of imports from each country is not negligible.

❑ The cumulative assessment of the effects of the imports is appropriate in light of the conditions of competition between the imports and domestic production.

Exporters to Canada must examine all factors being assessed by CITT in making their representation

CITT makes a decision on cumulation only after it has been able to acquire all or almost all of the data on volumes and sources of the imports alleged to be causing injury. In preparing representations to CITT, exporters, importers and their counsel need to explore these issues in depth in relation to the statistical data and other facts before CITT. Particular attention should be focused on these issues when developing country exports are the subject of the investigation.

Domestic industry

Exporters must be alert to changes in the structure of the Canadian industry throughout the investigation

Early in the complaint stage of a case, the domestic industry must be defined in order to be able to assess whether or not it is suffering injury because of the dumped or subsidized imports. This is not treated as a one-time event. Indeed, CITT and CBSA continually monitor industry changes that might influence the initial decision. Counsel for exporters should likewise be alert to changes in the domestic industry that might affect the position of their clients before both CBSA and CITT. In this connection, issues such as which firms are regarded as producers (assemblers, growers, etc.), the treatment of new entrants into the industry, and the disappearance of firms or the domestic industry during the inquiry must be monitored and taken into account throughout the investigation.

Data accumulation and analysis

Questionnaires and information requests

Exports should cooperate and assist their Canadian customers to complete questionnaires

The CITT staff structure their questionnaires and other requests for information in a manner which will elicit in the shortest possible time all or almost all of the data required to make a decision relating to material injury. Much of these data have to come from and be about the domestic industry. Thus, the injury questionnaire is directed primarily to the complainants, importers and other interested parties (end-users) who can provide information focusing on domestic industry and the domestic market. While CITT has a generic list of the questions that must be answered by all respondents, separate questionnaires are usually developed for each case to capture the unique features of the situation.

Analysis process

Exporters must bring forward all the evidence available to support the position that their exports are not causing injury

The complainants' written responses to questionnaires and other submissions on injury must fully develop their position and support their allegations with evidence concerning how they have been or might be materially injured by the imported dumped or subsidized goods. At the same time, exporters, importers and foreign governments in subsidy cases respond to questionnaires and make submissions outlining their position on the issues.

The primary research process relating to injury depends to a large degree on the cooperation and voluntary compliance of the parties involved, especially the complainant domestic industry. The initial task of the research team is to ensure that the design of the questionnaire is specific to the industry involved. The questionnaire is sent to the domestic producers, importers and, in some cases, to end-users of the imported goods in Canada in order to obtain all the information that may be needed in deciding whether the industry is injured or threatened by injury. CITT staff may visit the production facilities of the domestic industry, carry out research into industry and market conditions, and assemble statistics on trade, financing, pricing, sales and other data that may be relevant to the case. Because completing the questionnaire can be a costly and time-consuming exercise, especially for small firms, CITT staff assist firms in this regard where possible. On receipt of the completed questionnaires, they are analysed and the data are brought together in usable form.

Analysis report

The CITT staff report is a key document for exporters in the injury analysis

The culmination of the CITT staff work is the preparation of a report in two versions, confidential and non-confidential. The report consists of a comprehensive examination of all relevant economic information available on the product and industry in question. It describes the industry, provides a profile of the firms in the industry, examines economic indices such as employment, regional considerations, prices, profits, sales, imports and exports, and reviews the general competitiveness of the domestic industry compared to producers in other countries.

In assembling the report, staff set out, usually in the form of summary tables, basic economic indicator data. For example, the tables usually provide data for a three- to four-year period on the following:

Domestic production Volume % increase(decrease) % used for further manufacture Capacity utilization rate (%)	**Export sales** **Landed imports** List by country source For sale as subject goods Total subject countries Other countries Total imports
Apparent market sales Volume % increase (decrease)	
Shares of market sales (%) Domestic producers Subject import countries Other import countries	**Direct employment** Employees Person-hours worked **Combined domestic industry**
Domestic selling prices Domestic industry Subject imports Landed import prices	**Income statement** Net sales Cost of goods sold Gross margin GS&A Net income (loss)

In most cases, this is the basic information required to enable CITT to render a decision. The actual presentation of the information and its accumulation will, of course, depend on the nature of the product under investigation, the number of complainants, importers and exporters involved and the general complexity of the case. Clearly, a case dealing with 20 grades of a product imported from 15 exporters in 10 different countries will require different processes, data accumulation techniques and summary presentation tables than a case involving a single product imported from one company in one exporting country.

Exporters' counsel must insure that they have access to the confidential version of the report as soon as possible in the process

The report is a compilation of data provided by all interested parties and independent research by the staff. It does not attempt in any way to judge the impact or effect of the imports in question on the domestic industry. In other words, the document basically reports in an unbiased manner on all of the facts assembled and the analysis of these data having a bearing on the situation. The confidential report is made available only to CITT Members and to counsel representing the parties who have given an undertaking to protect confidential information. A non-confidential version is made available to all parties to assist them in protecting their interests either in disclosure meetings or in public hearings.

In this regard, CITT strictly enforces the confidentiality requirements of the Act and regulations so that the parties can have full confidence that their vital business information is protected.

Exporters must study the staff report carefully

Exporters have an important part to play in the public hearing process when they are expected to present a case opposing the claims of injury to the domestic industry. The report is an essential building block that exporters and their counsel must take into account in preparing their submissions to CITT.

Public hearings

A panel of three CITT members usually preside over dumping and subsidizing inquiries

Public hearings in Canadian dumping and subsidizing cases are held before a panel of three members. The hearings are fair, enable the parties to know the particulars of the case they have to address, and provide an opportunity for the parties to examine each other's evidence.

In some instances, CITT may call witnesses of its own in order to obtain independent third party information concerning the case before it.

Pre-hearing conferences enable counsel to judge the amount of time and input required by the exporter

Written submissions must be received by CITT in time to permit their study and examination before the hearing. A pre-hearing conference may be held to consider matters that might assist in the orderly conduct of the public hearing, such as organizing the hearing agenda, resolving procedural and information disputes, or setting hearing schedules. These conferences help to limit the time required to carry out a formal hearing. They also enable the parties to know with some certainty the amount of time that their presence will be required and the costs associated with appearing at a public hearing.

Because CITT hearings are quasi-judicial, a certain amount of formality is necessary. Parties appearing before CITT do not need to be represented by counsel. As a general rule, only CITT staff, persons presenting confidential information and independent counsel representing parties who have filed undertakings of non-disclosure are permitted to be present at an in-camera hearing.

Formality in proceedings is a necessity

The established procedure is for the complainant to present its public evidence as detailed in case briefs followed by cross-examination by counsel for the exporters and importers and questions by the CITT panel. Next importers and exporters present their cases, which are likewise subject to cross-examination by counsel for the complainant.

The final stage of the hearing consists of closing arguments, first by the complainant then by the importers and exporters. The complainant is entitled to have the last word in rebuttal.

In-camera hearings assure that all confidential data will be protected

In-camera hearings may be held during the inquiry when it is necessary to receive confidential information. At these sessions, the process is similar to that outlined above: the complainant makes its submissions first, followed by cross-examination by counsel for the other interested parties. At the appropriate time in the proceedings, further in-camera sessions may be needed so that the importer(s) or exporter(s) can present any confidential evidence or information they wish to submit.

Competitors and Canadian industry do not participate in in-camera hearings relating to exporters' activities

A public summary of the confidential information presented at the in-camera hearing is made available to any party not represented by counsel. In this connection, it is relevant to note that where there is more than one complainant, which is usually the case, each individual complainant (producer) presents its own case at an in-camera hearing in order to protect sensitive data.

Information about cost of production, for example, is not usually shared with the other complainants since they may well be each other's competitors in the marketplace. Likewise, importers and exporters usually have individual in-camera sessions for the presentation of confidential information. The in-camera process is valued highly by all parties in these proceedings and is safeguarded by CITT and its staff. It can and does, however, lengthen the hearing process considerably.

Canada has the most open trade remedy system in the world. It protects the interests of all parties involved

The above procedures described above have resulted in Canada having the most open trade remedy system in the world – a system in which all parties can be confident that their views will be fully taken into account in arriving at decisions. From the perspective of an exporter this process provides reassurance that they will be treated fairly under the law. However, the system also imposes a significant burden on all parties, including exporters and importers, to take an active role in the process in order to defend their own interests. This can be time-consuming, costly and require the attention of exporters from the earliest stages of the investigation. It also means that exporters need to have an in-depth understanding of the dynamics and economic sensitivities of the sector of the Canadian market to which they are exporting. Close cooperation with Canadian importers in identifying possible areas of concern is important in this regard.

The injury determination

In the period immediately following the public hearing, CITT assesses and analyses all of the evidence received in the case. CITT staff prepare briefings if requested by panel members. The CITT Panel meets to discuss, review the evidence and testimony, and analyses the data presented during the hearings. The actual injury decision-making process depends on the quality and thoroughness of the submissions made by the parties and the research work carried out by the CITT staff. Essentially, the job of CITT is to examine the facts, moderate and listen to the positions put forward by all sides, and then to render a decision based on the information presented.

When CITT has all the relevant data, there is no particular weighting that can be assigned to the various factors. Price sensitivity, economic recession, shifts in product preferences and so on may in some cases be more important than global overcapacity in arriving at a decision. Changing market trends, the introduction of new products, movements in the relative levels of import and domestic prices, availability of subject goods from domestic producers in the styles, quantities and sizes required, the role of major purchasers in the marketplace (single distribution/retail chain outlet for subject goods), specific evidence of lost sales, changes in technology, and reduced financial performance all affect to varying degrees the ultimate decision on injury or threat of injury.

The CITT analysis is comprehensive, taking into account all the data available

In this context, CITT weighs and balances the dumping/subsidizing and non-dumping/non-subsidizing factors and takes into account the relative importance of each of them in the time periods involved. In some cases it is necessary to completely reconstruct the chronology of events that have affected the domestic industry in order to fully understand the impact of the dumping or subsidizing in relation to the other factors and to establish causality. The allegations put forward by interested parties may require substantiation by contemporaneous internal company memos or field reports as well as actual written quotations, purchase orders and invoices. Verification may also be made by analysing information provided by the opposing parties and the responses received to the importers', producers' and purchasers' questionnaires, other sales data and parties' testimony during the hearing.

In some instances the price paid for the imported product may be revealed to have undercut the price paid for the domestic product. Rather than trying to maintain prices and continuing to lose sales, the domestic producers may have matched these low-priced imports in order to maintain plant loadings and market share. In this regard, importers may argue that they are only matching domestic prices and accordingly cannot be causing injury to the domestic industry.

In cases involving a threat of injury, the focus may be directed to the size of inventories overhanging the global market, foreign investment intentions for the subject goods, evidence of serious dumping or subsidizing in other markets, overcapacity, and evidence of delayed or postponed investments in the domestic market.

A consensus among CITT members is not required. The view of the majority prevails

CITT members seek to achieve a common view on the case. Consensus decision-making is not required (i.e. the individual members are not obliged to find common ground). The decision is based on the view of the majority, but any dissenting opinions are also published, as is a statement of reasons supporting the decision.

Types of injury findings

An injury finding by CITT may take one of four possible forms and the action required by CITT after the finding depends on its nature. The four possible findings are:

❑ No injury;

❑ Affirmative injury or retardation decision;

❑ Threat of injury only; or

❑ A combination of the above.

The last of these occurs if CITT makes different decisions with respect to the injurious effects of dumping or subsidizing. For example, the decision might involve no injury from goods exported by country A, but injury caused by goods from country B; or no injury caused by dumped imports below a certain size, but a threat of injury from imports of dumped goods above this size. Thus a decision can entail one of, or a combination of, three distinct possibilities: no injury, injury or retardation, and threat of injury.

Finding of no injury

A 'no injury' finding by CITT terminates an investigation

A finding of no injury by CITT terminates all proceedings in the investigation provided the finding is not overturned as a result of a review or appeal. CBSA must, when proceedings are terminated, refund any provisional duty that has been paid or cancel security that has been posted. There are usually administrative matters that must be carried out immediately by CITT and CBSA following a decision to terminate. These include notifying all interested parties of the decision and ensuring that all staff are aware that the goods are no longer subject to anti-dumping or countervailing proceedings.

Decision that the dumping or subsidizing has caused injury or retardation

When there is a final determination of dumping or subsidizing and an order or finding by CITT that the dumping or subsidizing has caused injury or retardation, CBSA must within six months of the date of the finding:

❑ Determine whether goods released during the provisional periods prior to CITT's final finding are the goods described in the finding;

❑ Determine the normal value and export price of, or the amount of the subsidy on, the goods released; and

❑ Issue a notice of its decision to all interested parties.

The Canadian system imposes duties on a prospective basis: duties apply to future shipments of goods actually dumped or subsidized

When a positive decision is made, duties are normally collected from the date of the provisional determination to the date of the final CITT finding and for up to five years from the date of the finding. In this connection it is relevant to note that the Canadian system imposes duties on a prospective basis. That is, an anti-dumping or countervailing duty is applied in the amount of the margin of dumping for each individual future shipment (goods imported after the provisional period) where the export price is less than the normal value specified in the final determination. Exporters found to be dumping and causing injury usually raise their export selling prices to Canadian importers so that no dumping margin remains and no duties are collected. The CITT injury finding automatically terminates at the end of the five-year period unless a decision is taken to review and continue it prior to the expiry date.

Decision of threat of injury

When a 'threat of injury' decision is made, duties apply only to future imports

A finding of threat of injury means that anti-dumping or countervailing duty is payable on all future dumped or subsidized importations of goods released from customs after the date of the finding. As noted in the previous section, these duties can be avoided by increasing the selling price to eliminate any margin of dumping or the amount of any subsidy. Provisional duties are no longer applicable. If CITT makes a finding of threat of injury only, then no anti-dumping or countervailing duty is payable on goods released from Customs before the date of the finding and any provisional duty paid or security posted is returned.

Appeals and reviews

Decisions made by CITT are final but are subject to review by the Federal Court, which may set aside a finding where it can be demonstrated that CITT erred in law, violated a principle of natural justice or made its finding in complete disregard of the facts.

CITT decisions may be appealed to the Federal Court or internationally to panels under the WTO or to NAFTA, if applicable

If a finding is set aside, CITT must either re-open the inquiry or terminate the case. In the latter instance, any duties that had been collected must be refunded. A decision involving goods of United States or Mexican origin can be reviewed by a bi-national Panel appointed under the terms of the North American Free Trade Agreement (NAFTA) or by the Federal Court. Under the present legislative scheme, a case involving exporters from both NAFTA and non-NAFTA countries can be appealed to three different bodies, namely the Federal Court, a NAFTA bi-national Panel or the WTO.

A decision may also be reviewed and modified by CITT itself. This can be done on its own initiative, at the request of CBSA President or at the request of any other interested parties including exporters and foreign governments. CITT will usually agree to review a case only if a year has passed since the date of the decision.

Review mechanism incorporated in Canadian legislation

The legislation also incorporates a review mechanism. It provides for a decision of material injury to lapse automatically five years after the date of its issuance, unless a review has been initiated by CITT prior to that date. Accordingly, shortly before the fifth anniversary of an injury finding, CITT must decide whether to conduct a formal review. Based on an assessment from CBSA as to whether dumping is likely to resume or subsidizing is likely to continue, CITT will examine the question of whether an anti-dumping or countervailing duty remains necessary to prevent material injury in future. In such a review, CITT follows procedures similar to those followed in the original injury inquiry. On completion of the review, CITT can either rescind the original finding or continue it with or without amendment as the circumstances require.

Public interest inquiries

Canadian law provides for the elimination or reduction of duties for overriding reasons of national interest

Under Canadian law the Minister of Finance is permitted, subject to the approval of Parliament, to not impose an anti-dumping or countervailing duty, to eliminate the duties, or to limit the amount of the duties for overriding reasons of public interest. This is a major decision since such action effectively denies a segment of Canadian society access to laws normally available to all citizens. For this reason, public interest considerations are usually entertained only where there are reasonable grounds for adopting measures to remove or eliminate the duties. The Minister of Finance acts only following an inquiry and recommendation from CITT.

CITT conducts public interest inquiries on request in anti-dumping and countervailing cases

Under Canadian legislation, CITT may conduct a public interest inquiry following a finding of injury caused by dumped or subsidized imports that results in the imposition of anti-dumping or countervailing duties. CITT may decide, either as a result of a request received from interested parties or on its own initiative, that there are reasonable grounds to consider that the imposition of part of those duties may not be in the public interest. CITT will then conduct an inquiry, which may result in a report to the Minister of Finance recommending that the duties be removed or reduced and by how much. The public interest inquiry is usually carried out shortly after the decision is taken that material injury is present and this new inquiry does not alter in any way the injury finding *per se*. The issue of public interest normally involves a balancing of competing interests within the country that only governments are in a position to decide.

Lesser duty

A duty less than the full margin of dumping or the amount of the subsidy is possible

The concept of *lesser duty* is found in Article 9.1 of the ADA and Article 19.2 of the SCMA, both of which use identical wording: 'It is desirable that the imposition be permissive in the territory of all Members, and that the duty be less than the margin (total amount of the subsidy) if such lesser duty would be adequate to remove the injury to the domestic industry.'

In both agreements this provision is in the article that is concerned primarily with the *imposition and collection of duties* even though its operative condition relates to *injury*. A lesser duty is applied in those situations where such a lesser amount of duty is adequate to eliminate any injury that the domestic industry has been found to be suffering. In other words, the *lesser duty* approach is primarily directed to removing the injury, not to reducing the duties applicable.

A lesser duty is considered only after an affirmative injury decision

In this connection, it is important to note that this issue involves two separate and distinct injury determinations that must be treated as sequential, even though they occur at or about the same time. The *first* determination required is a positive finding that the subject dumped or subsidized imports are causing or threatening to cause injury. The *second* decision relates to whether or not the anti-dumping or countervailing duties should not be applied for reasons of public interest or not be applied in the full amount of the margin of dumping or the amount of the subsidy in order to offset the injury. For the most part, the same basic data are required in making both decisions. However, the *first* decision is a precondition for the *second*, and the latter is discretionary under Canadian law.

The objective of examining *lesser duty* is to ensure that unwarranted protection is not provided to domestic industry. It is also a means of promoting competition in the domestic economy. A decision relating to the application of a lesser duty is in some ways more difficult than the decision as to whether dumped or subsidized imports are causing or threatening to cause injury. This is because the lesser duty decision effectively requires CITT to measure or attribute a value to the injury being caused to the domestic industry, something that it does not have to do when it makes the decision that dumped or subsidized imports are causing injury.

The concept of 'lesser duty' *per se* has not been incorporated in Canadian law. There are no proceedings under which CITT can establish a level of duty lower than the dumping margin or the amount of the subsidy but sufficient to remove the injury caused to the Canadian industry. However, as stated above, a procedure has been put in place which enables CITT to conduct an inquiry and as a result make recommendations to the Minister of Finance that might have a similar effect.

There is no single, simple method of establishing an appropriate level of duty, if any, that should apply. The CITT inquiries take into account issues such as the impact of the removal or non-imposition of a duty on competition, on price levels for the products in question, on the general price level, on users and consumers, on economic gains and losses for the industry, on employees and on the economy in general. It also examines the effects of the imposition of duties on:

❑ The availability of subject goods from alternative sources;

❑ Competition in the domestic market between producers;

❑ The choice and availability of subject goods at competitive prices for consumers;

❑ Importers who use the subject goods as inputs in the production of other goods or services; and

❑ The access of domestic producers to technology.

CITT allows all parties in a case to know the facts on which the decision on lesser duty is made, and in some instances it may require more data than it had available for the injury decision or seek new submissions from interested parties directed specifically to a justification for a duty or the application of a lesser duty. In any event, the process requires CITT to take into account the level of the margin of dumping or the amount of the subsidy and the views of interested parties (especially the domestic industry) as to the appropriate level of the duty, if any, required. also requires CITT to engage in calculations of a factual nature to determine what level of import price would be required to enable the domestic industry to cover costs and realize a normal rate of return.

This fact-driven process tries to avoid attempting to quantify what in many cases is not quantifiable (i.e. who gains and who loses from the imposition of a duty).

A 'public interest' decision can be taken only by the Government on the recommendation of the Minister of Finance. This provides another opportunity for exporters to make their case

If CITT is of the opinion, following its public interest inquiry, that the imposition of all or part of the duty might not be in the public interest, it reports this conclusion to the Minister of Finance who, in turn, may recommend that the Government reduce or eliminate the duties.

Annex I

CITT preliminary determinations of injury issued during year ending 31 March 2005

Preliminary injury Inquiry No.	Product	Country	Date of determination	Determination
PI-2004-001	Outdoor barbecues	China	11 June 2004	Injury
PI-2004-002	Fasteners	China and Taiwan Province (China)	28 June 2004	Injury
PI-2004-003	Laminate flooring	Austria, Belgium, China, France, Germany and Poland	3 December 2004	Injury

Annex II

CITT dumping findings issued and dumping inquiries during year ending 31 March 2005

Inquiry No.	Product	Country	Date of finding	Finding
NQ-2003-003	Wood venetian blinds and slats	China and Mexico	18 June 2004	Injury/No injury
NQ-2004-001	Stainless steel wire	Republic of Korea, Switzerland, United States and India	30 July 2004	Injury
NQ-2004-002	Steel fuel tanks	China and Taiwan Province (China)	31 August 2004	No injury
NQ-2004-003	Frozen self-rising pizza	United States	18 August 2004	No injury
NQ-2004-004	Outdoor barbecues	China	23 December 2004	Inquiry terminated
NQ-2004-005	Fasteners	China and Taiwan Province (China)	7 January 2005	Injury/No injury
NQ-2004-006	Laminate flooring	Austria, Belgium, China, France, Germany and Poland		In progress

Annex III

CITT dumping orders decisions and requests for interim reviews under consideration during year ending 31 March 2005

Review or request No.	Product	Country	Date of order	Order
RD-2004-001	Stainless steel round bar products	Germany, France, India, Italy, Japan, Spain, Sweden, Taiwan Province (China), United Kingdom and Republic of Korea	6 August 2004	Order amended
RD-2004-002	Hot-rolled carbon steel plate	Brazil, Finland, India, Indonesia, Thailand and Ukraine	23 August 2004	Finding amended
RD-2004-003 to RD-2004-007	Stainless steel round bar	Brazil, India, Germany, France, India, Italy, Japan, Spain, Sweden, Taiwan Province (China), United Kingdom and Republic of Korea	18 January 2005	Finding and order rescinded
RD-2004-008	Waterproof rubber footwear	China		Under consideration
RD-2004-009	Fasteners	China and Taiwan Province (China)		Under consideration
RD-2004-010	Dishwashers and dryers	United States		Under consideration

Annex IV

CITT orders issued and expiry reviews in progress during year ending 31 March 2005

Review No.	Product	Country	Date of order	Order
RR-2003-001	Carbon steel plate	Italy, Republic of Korea, Spain and Ukraine	17 May 2004	Order rescinded
RR-2003-002	Flat hot-rolled carbon and alloy steel sheet products	France, Romania, Russian Federation, Slovakia	30 June 2004	Finding rescinded
RR-2003-003	Corrosion-resistant steel sheet products	Brazil, Germany, Japan, Republic of Korea and United States	27 July 2004	Order rescinded
RR-2003-004	Cold-rolled steel sheet products	Belgium, Russian Federation, Slovakia and Turkey	26 August 2004	Finding rescinded
RD-2004-001	Concrete reinforcing bar	Cuba, Republic of Korea and Turkey	11 January 2005	Finding rescinded
LE-2004-008	Stainless steel round bar	Brazil and India	18 January 2005	Review not warranted
RR-2004-002	Women's boots	China		In progress
RR-2004-003	Carbon steel welded pipe	Republic of Korea		In progress
RR-2004-004	Hot-rolled carbon steel plate	Brazil, Finland, India, Indonesia, Thailand and Ukraine		In progress
RR-2004-005	Dishwashers and dryers	United States		In progress
RR-2004-006	Whole potatoes	United States		In progress
RR-2004-007	Refined sugar	United States, Denmark, Germany, Netherlands, United Kingdom and European Union		In progress
RR-2004-008	Waterproof footwear and bottoms	China		In progress

Annex V

CITT findings and orders in force as of 31 March 2005

Review No. or inquiry No.	Date of decision	Product*	Country	Related decision No. and date
NQ-99-003	1 May 2000	Iodinated contrast media	United States (including the Commonwealth of Puerto Rico)	
RR-99-003	1 May 2000	Women's boots	China	RR-94-003 (2 May 1995) NQ-89-003 (3 May 1990)
RR-99-004	5 June 2000	Carbon steel welded pipe	Republic of Korea	RR-94-004 (5 June 1995) RR-89-008 (5 June 1990) ADT-6-83 (28 June 1983)
NQ-99-004	27 June 2000	Carbon steel plate	Brazil, Finland, India, Indonesia, Thailand and Ukraine	
NQ-2000-001	1 August 2000	Dishwashers and dryers	United States (WCI and Whirlpool)	RD-2002-005 (19 March 2003)
RR-99-005	13 September 2000	Whole potatoes	United States	RR-94-007 (14 September 1995) RR-89-010 (14 September 1990) CIT-16-85 (18 April 1986) ADT-4-84 (4 June 1984)
RR-99-006	3 November 2000	Refined sugar	United States, Denmark, Germany, Netherlands, United Kingdom and European Union	NQ-95-002 (6 November 1995)
NQ-2000-004	8 December 2000	Waterproof footwear and bottoms	China	
NQ-2000-006	2 May 2001	Garlic, fresh or frozen	China and Viet Nam	
NQ-2000-007	1 June 2001	Concrete reinforcing bar	Indonesia, Japan, Latvia, Republic of Moldova, Poland, Taiwan Province (China) and Ukraine	

Review No. or inquiry No.	Date of decision	Product*	Country	Related decision No. and date
RR-2000-002	24 July 2001	Carbon steel welded pipe	Argentina, India, Romania, Taiwan Province (China), Thailand and Brazil	RR-95-002 (25 July 1996) NQ-91-003 (23 January 1992) NQ-90-005 (26 July 1991)
NQ-2001-001	17 August 2001	Flat hot-rolled steel sheet and strip	Brazil, Bulgaria, China, Taiwan Province (China), India, The former Yugoslav Republic of Macedonia, South Africa, Ukraine and Yugoslavia	
NQ-2001-003	27 December 2001	Leather footwear with metal toe caps	China	
RR-2001-001	20 March 2002	Fresh garlic	China	NQ-96-002 (21 March 1997)
RR-2001-005	18 October 2002	Waterproof rubber footwear	China	RR-97-001 (20 October 1997) RR-92-001 (21 October 1992) R-7-87 (22 October 1987) ADT-2-82 (23 April 1982) ADT-4-79 (25 May 1979)
RR-2001-006	10 January 2003	Hot-rolled carbon steel plate	Mexico, China, South Africa and Russian Federation	NQ-97-001 (27 October 1997)
RR-2002-001	9 December 2002	Bicycles and frames	Taiwan Province (China) and China	RR-97-003 (10 December 1997) NQ-92-002 (11 December 1992)
NQ-2002-003	4 March 2003	Xanthates	China	
NQ-2002-004	16 July 2003	Carbon steel pipe nipples, threaded couplings and adaptor fittings	China	
NQ-2003-001	23 December 2003	Structural tubing	Republic of Korea, South Africa and Turkey	
NQ-2003-002	9 January 2004	Hot-rolled carbon steel plate and high-strength low-alloy steel plate	Bulgaria, Czech Republic and Romania	
NQ-2003-003	18 June 2004	Wood Venetian Blinds and Slats	China and Mexico	
NQ-2004-001	30 July 2004	Stainless steel wire	Republic of Korea, Switzerland, United States and India	
NQ-2004-005	7 January 2005	Fasteners	China and Taiwan Province (China)	

* For a complete product description, refer to the most recent finding or order.

Annex VI

CITT cases before the Federal Court of Appeal or the Federal Court

Case No.	Product	Country of origin	Forum	File No./Status
RR-2002-002	Prepared baby foods	United States	FCA	A-280-03 Appeal dismissed (26 May 2004)
MP-2003-001	Bicycles	Taiwan Province (China) and China	FC	T-755-04 Appeal discontinued (4 May 2004)
NQ-2003-03	Wood venetian blinds and slats	Mexico and China	FCA	A-382-04 Appeal withdrawn (17 September 2004)
NQ-2004-002	Fuel tanks	China and Taiwan Province (China)	FCA	A-527-04
NQ-2004-005	Fasteners	China and Taiwan Province (China)	FCA	A-46-05 A-47-05 A-48-05 A-49-05 A-50-05

Source: CITT Annual Report, 2004–2005.

Notes: FCA – Federal Court of Appeal
FC – Federal Court
BP – Binational Panel

CHAPTER 5

The Canadian safeguards process

Introduction

Canada provides broad access to its merchandise goods markets and governs this access through legislation and administrative policies to ensure fair trade. One of the pillars of this policy is Canada's safeguards legislation.

Safeguards are emergency measures against injurious imports

Safeguards are temporary trade measures applied on an emergency basis against increased imports of a particular good that is causing or threatening to cause serious injury to a domestic industry that produces a like or directly competitive product. Safeguard measures are applied on a non-discriminatory basis, that is, on all imports of the goods irrespective of source, and can take the form of either tariff increases or quantitative restraints. Special safeguard provisions were introduced in Canadian law in 2002 to give effect to the Protocol on The Accession of the People's Republic of China to WTO. These are discussed below.

Canadian law and CITT

Canadian legislation allows for the application of import safeguard measures to assist domestic producers who are suffering or being threatened by serious injury from increased levels of imports. This legislation implements Canada's rights and obligations under Article XIX of the General Agreement on Tariffs and Trade 1994 as elaborated in the WTO Agreement on Safeguards and bilateral/trilateral free trade agreements. These agreements establish the conditions for applying import safeguard measures as well as notification and consultation procedures for safeguard inquiries.

WTO guidance in safeguards measures

CITT conducts the safeguard investigations

In Canada, the Canadian International Trade Tribunal (CITT) is responsible for investigating safeguard complaints. CITT may initiate import safeguard inquiries following a complaint by domestic producers. Alternatively, the Canadian Government may direct it to conduct an inquiry. If CITT determines in its inquiry that increased imports of the goods have caused or are threatening to cause serious injury to Canadian producers of like or directly competitive goods, the Canadian Government can apply safeguard measures.

The legislation

The safeguard law

CITT conducts safeguard inquiries, exclusion inquiries, mid-term reviews and extension inquiries pursuant to the *Canadian International Trade Tribunal Act* (the CITT Act), its regulations and the Canadian International Trade Tribunal Rules. The Government applies import safeguard measures in the form of surtaxes pursuant to the *Customs Tariff* administered by the Canada Border

Services Agency or in the form of quantitative restrictions pursuant to the *Export and Import Permits Act*, administered by the Department of Foreign Affairs and International Trade.

Establishing serious injury is the key

'Serious injury' is defined in the legislation as 'a significant overall impairment in the position of domestic producers' and 'threat of serious injury' is defined as 'serious injury that, on the basis of facts, and not merely of allegation, conjecture or remote possibility, is clearly imminent'. These definitions attempt to spell out that a higher standard of injury applies when serious injury is involved rather than material injury, which applies in the anti-dumping and subsidies/countervailing agreements. Because the safeguards legislation is concerned only with the injurious impact of imports on domestic producers, CBSA officials are not involved in the inquiry process.

A causal link must be established between the imports and the injury

The main consideration in a safeguard inquiry is whether imports are causing or threatening to cause serious injury to the domestic industry. In examining this issue, CITT explores whether there has been a significant increase in imports or significant price undercutting, depression or suppression. Other important factors examined include the impact of the imported goods on domestic producers with respect to their output, sales, market share, profits, capacity utilization, inventories and employment. The CITT Act also provides that the increased imports should be in such quantities as to be a principal cause of serious injury, that is, there must be a causal link between the increased imports and the serious injury or threat thereof. A principal cause is an important cause that is no less important than any other cause of injury. In a bilateral safeguard inquiry, the increased imports must alone constitute a principal cause of serious injury.

Duration of safeguard measures

Measures may be applied for a maximum of eight years and are subject to progressive liberalization

The WTO Safeguards Agreement and Canadian law permit the application of global import safeguard measures for an initial period of up to four years. They also provide that such measures are to be progressively liberalized during their period of application. The measures can be extended if CITT determines that they continue to be necessary to remedy serious injury and there is evidence that domestic producers are adjusting to the import competition. The maximum period of application of measures, including the period of initial application, cannot exceed eight years (10 years for developing countries). If an initial import safeguard measure is to be applied for a period exceeding three years, or is extended, the WTO Safeguards Agreement provides for the maintenance of the level of trade concessions and obligations between Canada and countries whose exports are affected by the measures.

Compensation or retaliation may come into play after three years

In the absence of agreement on trade concessions, the governments of the exporting countries may, subject to the notification and consultation provisions of the Safeguards Agreement, suspend the application of substantially equivalent trade concessions or obligations.

Provisional measures

Interim duties until inquiry process is complete

In critical circumstances, where delay might result in damage that would be difficult to repair, Canadian law permits the Minister of Finance to apply provisional measures before there has been a final determination regarding serious injury. These measures cannot exceed 200 days unless, before that time, CITT reports that the goods in question are being imported under such conditions as to cause serious injury to Canadian producers. Provisional measures must be in the form of tariffs on imports that are refundable if the final determination establishes that increased imports are not causing or threatening to cause serious injury. This period counts as part of the initial period of application of any safeguard measure. Any action taken on an agricultural product must conform to the conditions of the WTO Agreement on Agriculture.

Global versus bilateral

Free trade areas and
safeguard inquiries

The application of safeguard measures by Canada is directly affected by the free trade agreements to which Canada is a party. As a result of these free trade agreements, two streams of safeguard inquiries have emerged – global and bilateral inquiries. Global safeguard inquiries are subject to the WTO Agreement provisions. Bilateral safeguard inquiries are governed by the free trade agreements.

Under Article 1102 of the Canada–United States Free Trade Agreement (FTA) the two signatories agreed to exclude each other from global safeguard actions under GATT Article XIX unless imports from the other party (a) are substantial in comparison to the quantity imported from other countries (i.e. the party must normally be among the top five suppliers concerned in terms of import share, during the most recent three-year period); and (b) are 'contributing importantly' to the serious injury or threat thereof caused by increased imports. The FTA standards in respect of safeguards or emergency measures were essentially carried over into the North American Free Trade Agreement (NAFTA), which brought Mexico under the same free trade umbrella as Canada and the United States. In this regard, Article 802 of NAFTA provides for the exclusion of one party's goods from the other party's global safeguard action. These same safeguard-limiting principles are also contained in the Canada–Chile Free Trade Agreement and the Canada–Israel Free Trade Agreement.

No surcharge can be imposed in respect of any fresh fruit or vegetable from a NAFTA country that may be subject to a temporary duty under NAFTA.

Separate findings concerning imports from NAFTA countries are also required if an extension order is sought. If, after a surcharge is imposed against imports from sources other than NAFTA countries, a surge in imports occurs from NAFTA countries, a surcharge may be imposed to prevent such imports from undermining the purpose of the original global order.

Countries included in
safeguard inquiries

In a global safeguard inquiry, CITT considers the effects of imports from all sources on domestic producers. If CITT determines that increased imports are causing or threatening to cause serious injury, it must also determine whether the like goods being imported from a country with which Canada has a bilateral free trade agreement are substantial and contribute importantly to the serious injury. If CITT does not so determine, the government must exclude imports from that country from any global safeguard measures that it applies.

Mid-term review

Safeguard actions are
re-examined halfway through
their term

If an import safeguard measure is to remain in place for more than three years, CITT must conduct a review of the measure before its mid-point. CITT notifies interested parties and governments of a mid-term review five months before the mid-point of a measure. The CITT notice is published and interested parties are asked to make written submissions on why a measure should remain in effect, be revoked or be amended. Based on these submissions and other information, CITT prepares a report to the Government on developments since the measure was applied and advises on whether the measure should remain in effect, be revoked or be amended. Notice of the report is published and given to interested parties and governments.

Extension inquiry

Safeguard measures may be extended

CITT may, after a request from domestic producers, conduct extension inquiries to determine whether safeguard measures that are due to expire continue to be necessary. The extension inquiry is similar to an initial safeguard inquiry. CITT issues a notice, informs interested parties, governments and the Minister of Finance, obtains information through questionnaires, calls for submissions, and holds a public hearing. CITT must submit its report to the Government no later than 45 days before the date of expiry of the measure.

During its extension inquiry, CITT must also determine whether there is evidence that the domestic producers are adjusting to the competition from imports of like goods.

As in safeguard inquiries, the Government may ask CITT to examine and report on any other matter relating to the request for an extension inquiry.

The report of CITT is published and is made available to interested parties and governments. If CITT has determined that the measures remain necessary to prevent or remedy serious injury and that there is evidence that the domestic producers are adjusting to import competition, the Government may extend the safeguard measures.

Safeguard inquiries: Imports from China

In 2002, amendments were made to the CITT Act to implement the safeguard provisions of the WTO Chinese accession protocol. These provisions will be available until 2013. Under these provisions, if CITT determines that increased imports of goods from China have caused or are threatening to cause market disruption to Canadian producers of like goods, the Government may apply measures to remedy the market disruption. Further, if CITT determines that an action under the protocol affecting imports of Chinese goods into another market has caused or is threatening to cause a significant diversion of trade from that country to Canada, the Government may apply measures to remedy the trade diversion. Measures adopted may be import surtaxes, quotas or tariff rate quotas.

Following receipt of a written complaint from domestic producers, CITT will decide, normally within 21 days, whether or not to accept the complaint. It will begin an inquiry only if the complaint is made by or on behalf of producers that produce a major proportion of domestic production of like goods and all of the CITT's information requirements have been met. If an inquiry is launched, the Tribunal must submit its report to the Government and the Minister of Finance within 90 days (70 days in the case of trade diversion inquiries). The Government may also direct CITT to conduct a market disruption inquiry and report by a specified date.

For the purposes of these provisions, 'market disruption' means 'a rapid increase in the importation of goods that are like the goods produced by the domestic industry, in absolute terms or relative to the production of like goods, so as to be a significant cause of material injury, or threat of material injury, to the domestic industry'. 'Significant cause' means 'an important cause that need not be as important as, or more important than, any other cause of the material injury or threat.'

In making its decision in market disruption cases, the Tribunal will examine among other things:

❑ The actual volume of goods imported into Canada from China;

❑ The effect of the imported goods on prices of like goods in Canada; and

❑ The impact of the imported goods on domestic producers of like goods in Canada.

In making its decision in trade diversion cases, the Tribunal will examine, among other factors:

❑ The actual and imminent increase in Canadian market share of goods originating in China;

❑ The nature or extent of the diversion action;

❑ The actual or imminent increase in the importation of goods originating in China that is due to the action;

❑ The conditions of supply and demand in the domestic market for the like goods; and

❑ The volume of goods originating in China that are imported into Canada and into any WTO Member taking an action.

As in a regular safeguards case, the complainants are required to provide detailed data to support their allegations concerning increased imports from China and the CITT staff prepares a pre-hearing report based primarily on replies to questionnaires previously issued to domestic producers and importers seeking information on economic indicators relevant to the inquiry. All interested parties are given an opportunity to make their views known to the Tribunal and, if the Tribunal deems it appropriate, a short public hearing may be held. The Tribunal will submit its Report to the government and the Minister of Finance for appropriate action. The Report is also published and made available to the complainant and other parties that have made representations during the inquiry.

WTO safeguard actions and Canada

Safeguard measures worldwide

By 1 May 2006, 148 safeguard investigations had been notified to WTO since the coming into force of the WTO Safeguards Agreement. These actions have so far resulted in the implementation of 72 definitive safeguard measures around the world. None were applied by Canada.

Developing countries are increasing their use of safeguard actions

Traditionally, developed countries have generally exercised recourse under GATT Article XIX. A significant change since the coming into force of the Safeguards Agreement is that developing countries (including Argentina, Brazil, Chile, Czech Republic, Ecuador, Egypt, India, Indonesia, Jordan, the Philippines, Latvia, the Republic of Korea and Venezuela) are increasingly utilizing safeguard measures and have actually accounted for a significant portion of safeguard actions covering a broader spectrum of goods taken under the new WTO framework. Chile, India and the United States have been the largest users of safeguards.

Canada in safeguard actions

CITT has conducted three major safeguards inquiries since the coming into force of the WTO Agreement. These covered steel in 2001, bicycles in 2004, and most recently barbecues from China in 2005. However, Canada has not taken any safeguard measures following these inquiries and WTO safeguard actions have, so far, had a minimal impact on Canadian exports. The Canadian Government has exercised its rights under the Agreement to intervene on behalf of Canadian exporters in certain safeguards investigations in other WTO countries.

The CITT inquiry process

Overview

Safeguard inquiries launched at the request of Canadian industry

The procedures and processes followed by CITT in investigating whether a safeguard measure should be applied usually begin with a request filed by one or more Canadian producers or an association of Canadian producers. If the request is properly documented, CITT must decide whether or not to initiate an investigation within 30 days . If its decision is positive, appropriate notices are given and the investigation is completed within six months from the date of initiation. In special circumstances, the length of time taken to investigate may be extended to nine months.

Minister of Finance may initiate a safeguard inquiry

Safeguard inquiries may be initiated by CITT at the request of the government through the Minister of Finance, or domestic producers can file complaints of serious injury with CITT. Under the CITT Act, the Tribunal will commence an inquiry if it is satisfied, following receipt of a properly documented complaint, (a) that the information available discloses a reasonable indication that the subject goods are being imported in such increased quantities and under such conditions as to cause or threaten serious injury to domestic production of like or directly competitive goods, (b) that the complaint is made by or on behalf of domestic producers who produce a major proportion of domestic production, and (c) that, if the complaint relates to goods examined by CITT in the previous 24 months, the new circumstances are sufficiently different to warrant a new inquiry.

The complaint process is identical for Canadian producers who claim that because of tariff reductions under a bilateral free trade agreement they are being injured by an increase in imports from the country that is a party to the agreement.

When it initiates an inquiry, CITT publishes a notice of inquiry and forwards it to all known interested parties and the governments of countries whose exports will be the object of the inquiry. The notice identifies the product and outlines the general rules for parties wishing to participate in the inquiry. It also gives information on the dates for the submission of briefs and the filing of information requested by CITT, as well as the date and location of the public hearing.

In any safeguard inquiry, CITT typically requests information from interested parties, receives representations and holds a public hearing. Parties may cite evidence and make argument in support of their position. While parties may choose to be represented by counsel, they are not required to do so.

How CITT builds a case

The CITT staff obtains information through questionnaires and other sources and may visit manufacturers, importers and purchasers of the goods in question. The CITT staff prepare a report that sets out the data relating to the factors that CITT is to examine in arriving at its decision. This report becomes part of the record and is made available to counsel and parties in the inquiry.

Your confidential information is protected

Where confidential information is provided to CITT, it is protected under the confidentiality provisions of the CITT Act. CITT will distribute confidential information only to counsel, acting on behalf of a party, who have signed a declaration and undertaking agreeing not to disclose confidential information.

Provisional safeguard measures may be applied for a maximum of 200 days if a preliminary determination is made by the Minister of Finance that critical circumstances exist which in the absence of immediate action would result in damage that would be difficult to repair and that there is clear evidence that the increased imports have caused or threatened to cause serious injury to domestic producers.

How the safeguard measures are applied

Safeguard actions can take the form of either quantitative restrictions or surcharges on imports. Surcharges cannot, at the maximum, exceed the rate that is sufficient to prevent or remedy the injury. They can be only be imposed by the Government as a result of (a) a report of the Minister of Finance or (b) an inquiry made by CITT which finds that goods are being imported into Canada under conditions that threaten serious injury to Canadian producers of like or directly competitive goods. Actions based on a report from CITT remain in effect for a period of four years but may be extended, amended or revoked prior to that time.

A provisional safeguards measure may be applied if the Minister of Finance makes a preliminary determination and decides (a) that there are critical circumstances (i.e. that delay in taking safeguards actions would cause damage which would be difficult to repair), (b) that there is clear evidence that increased imports of the investigated product have caused or are threatening to cause serious injury, and (c) that there is a clear causal link between the two. A provisional safeguard measure may only be in the form of an increase in customs duties. Definitive safeguard measures may take the form of either tariff increases or quotas.

Under normal circumstances, safeguard investigations do not involve inquiries in the country of export or the country of production of the imported goods since the subject goods are being imported under fair trading conditions.

CITT usually makes its decision regarding the impact of the imports on the health of the domestic industry and its producers based on data from submissions made by interested parties in Canada and from other domestic sources such as national statistics.

Canada works for resolution even after safeguard measures are imposed

The application of safeguard measures by Canada effectively alters the balance of rights and obligations between it and the WTO member countries that are exporting the goods likely to be affected by the measures.

Because of this, Canada is required to consult affected trading partners with a view to arriving at a mutually satisfactory solution. If the measure is to be in force for more than three years it is essential that the parties enter into compensation discussions.

Canadian law requires the progressive liberalization of safeguard measures. As a result, it is essential that domestic producers put in place an adjustment plan that will enable them to compete with the import competition within a reasonable period of time. Any person directly affected by the report of CITT may seek judicial review in the Federal Court of Canada.

Launching the process

Like anti-dumping and countervailing measures investigations, safeguard inquiries begin with a notice of inquiry that is forwarded to all interested parties and is published in the *Canada Gazette*. The notice indicates the complaint's origin, its terms of reference, and the time limits for the submission of briefs, documents, questionnaires and so on. It also advises the place and time fixed for the public hearing. Confidential information is examined in closed sessions and is protected. In addition, the Tribunal carries out economic research, and obtains other information and data from various sources to assist it in making its finding. CITT reports are always made public.

A properly documented written request for a safeguard measure will include information that is reasonably available to the applicant on:

In addition to providing the information set out in subsections 23(2) and (3) of the Act, a complaint filed with the Tribunal shall be signed by the complainant or by the complainant's counsel, if any, and shall be accompanied by the following information:

Substantive elements covered in a properly documented complaint

❏ The name, address for service, telephone number and fax number, if any, of the complainant and of the complainant's counsel, if any;

❏ The name and description of the imported goods concerned, their tariff classification, their current tariff treatment, and the name and description of the like or directly competitive domestic goods concerned;

❏ The locations of the establishments in which the complainant produces the domestic goods;

❏ The percentage of domestic production of the like or directly competitive goods that the complainant accounts for and the basis for claiming that the complainant is representative of an industry;

❏ The names and locations of all other domestic establishments in which the like or directly competitive goods are produced;

❏ Data on total domestic production of the like or directly competitive goods for each of the five most recent full years;

❏ A list of any documents that may be useful in explaining or supporting the complaint;

❏ A list of any other interested parties;

❏ The actual volume of the goods imported into Canada for each of the five most recent full years that form the basis of the complaint and the effect of the imported goods on the prices of like or directly competitive goods in Canada, including

  – Whether there has been a significant increase in the importation into Canada of the goods, either absolutely or relative to the production in Canada of like or directly competitive goods,

  – Whether the prices of the goods imported into Canada have significantly undercut the prices of like or directly competitive goods produced and sold in Canada, and

  – Whether the effect of the importation into Canada of the goods has been

    ● To depress significantly the prices of like or directly competitive goods produced and sold in Canada, or

    ● To limit to a significant degree increases in the prices of like or directly competitive goods produced and sold in Canada; and

❏ The impact of the imported goods on domestic producers of like or directly competitive goods in Canada and all relevant economic factors and indices that have a bearing on the industry that comprises or includes the like or directly competitive goods, including, without limiting the generality of the foregoing,

  – Actual and potential changes in the level of production, employment, sales, market share, profits and losses, productivity, return on investments, utilization of production capacity, cash flow, inventories, wages, growth or ability to raise capital or investments, and

  – Factors affecting domestic prices.

When a request has been received, CITT and its staff may seek such additional information as is deemed necessary, before deciding whether to initiate an investigation. A request will be considered properly documented when the complainants have provided all reasonably available information sought by CITT and its staff and they have concluded their analysis of the relevant data. When a request is properly documented, CITT must decide whether or not to initiate an investigation within 30 days of its receipt.

Notice of decision to initiate

Exporters are encouraged to cooperate with CITT

All known exporters are informed of the safeguard investigation

When a decision has been taken to initiate an inquiry, the CITT staff must prepare appropriate notices and forward them to the exporters, importers, representatives of the governments of the exporting countries, the complainants, and other parties known to have an interest. Subject to the requirement to protect confidential information, CITT will provide the full text of the written application to all interested parties including exporters and their governments. Notification is also given to the WTO committee established under the Safeguards Agreement and the notice is published.

The notification will contain:

❏ The statutory authority for the inquiry;

❏ The name of the complainant;

❏ The imported goods that are the subject of the inquiry, including their tariff classification, together with such details or explanation of the inquiry as the Tribunal directs;

❏ The date on or before which any written submission must be filed with the Tribunal and the number of copies of any written submission that must be filed;

❏ Instructions with respect to the filing of confidential information;

❏ A statement as to whether the Tribunal has or has not directed that a hearing be held;

❏ Where the Tribunal has directed that a hearing be held, the following information, namely,

  – The place and time fixed for commencement of the hearing or, if the place and time have not been fixed, a statement that notice of the place and time fixed for the hearing will be given to any person who files with the Secretary a written request for such a notice,

  – The date on or before which any person interested in the matter must file with the Tribunal a notice of participation, and

  – The date on or before which counsel for a person who files a notice of participation must file with the Tribunal a notice of representation and, if appropriate, a declaration and undertaking referred to in subrule 16(1) or (2);

❏ The address to which written submissions or correspondence may be sent or delivered and at which information in respect of the inquiry may be obtained and non-confidential documents filed in the course of the inquiry may be inspected, as well as the name, address and telephone number of the office to be contacted for more information; and

❏ Such other information as the Tribunal specifies.

Interested parties have a period of 30 days from the date of initiation to indicate to CITT in writing whether they are interested in participating in the inquiry. CITT may allow interested parties to indicate their interest in participating after this date, upon cause shown. If CITT decides not to initiate an inquiry, the requesting producers are notified of the reasons for this decision. Any application for the initiation of an inquiry may be withdrawn prior to initiation, in which case it is considered not to have been made.

Confidentiality[5]

Confidential information is kept secret

CITT must, during and after an investigation, keep confidential any information that is by its nature confidential or is provided on a confidential basis by parties to an investigation. The following types of information are deemed to be by nature confidential, unless CITT determines that disclosure in a particular case would neither be of significant competitive advantage to a competitor, nor have a significantly adverse effect upon a person supplying the information or upon a person from whom the information was acquired:

❑ Business or trade secrets concerning the nature of a product, production processes or operations, production equipment, or machinery;

❑ Information concerning the financial condition of a company which is not publicly available; and

Confidential and non-confidential information must be provided

❑ Information concerning costs, identification of customers, sales, inventories, shipments, or amount or source of any income, profit, loss or expenditure related to the manufacture and sale of a product.

Parties seeking confidential status for information must request such treatment at the time information is submitted, including the reasons confidential treatment is warranted. CITT will consider such requests expeditiously, and inform the party submitting the information if the request for confidential treatment is not warranted.

Parties must furnish non-confidential summaries of all information for which confidential treatment is sought. The non-confidential summaries should permit a reasonable understanding of the substance of the information submitted in confidence and may take the form of indexation of figures provided in the confidential version, or marked deletions in the text. In exceptional circumstances, parties may indicate that information for which confidential treatment is sought cannot be summarized, in which case a statement of the reasons why summarization is not possible is provided.

If CITT finds that a request for confidential treatment is not warranted, and if the supplier of the information is unwilling to make the information public, CITT disregards such information, and returns the information concerned to the party submitting it.

Confidential information is in no case disclosed without the specific permission of the party submitting it. CITT, upon request, provides interested parties whose products are subject to the inquiry access to non-confidential evidence, including the non-confidential data used for initiating or conducting the inquiry.

Reliance on information available

As soon as possible after the initiation of the investigation, CITT specifies in detail the information required from interested parties or other entities having relevant information, the way in which that information should be structured and the time period within which responses are required.

---

5   The same confidentiality conditions apply to anti-dumping, countervailing duty and safeguard inquiries.

CITT research staff is
resourceful

CITT may request that information be provided in a particular medium (e.g. computer tape) or computer language having regard to the ability of the interested party to respond in that medium. If this is not practicable, the information should be supplied in the form of written material or other form acceptable to CITT. CITT will take due account of any difficulties experienced by interested parties, in particular small companies, in supplying information requested, will provide any assistance practicable, and/or may extend any time period prescribed for the submission of a given information whenever applicable.

Assessment of serious injury

CITT members decide
whether there is serious injury
and a causal link to imports

CITT Members assign own
weighting to the factors
considered in the serious injury
decision

CITT is prepared to consider the serious injury issue once it has assessed and analysed all of the evidence received in the case. Decision-making in the injury process is largely dependent on the submissions made by the parties and the research work carried out by the CITT staff. CITT examines the facts, considers the positions advanced by all sides and makes a reasoned decision based on the information presented regarding serious injury and the causal link to the imports. This determination is highly subjective as it reflects the views and perspectives of the individual CITT Members presiding over the inquiry. When CITT has all the relevant data, there is no particular weighting assigned to the various factors.

Indicators of evidence of serious injury

WTO guidance in considering
serious injury

The WTO Safeguards Agreement requires that there be an objective evaluation of the relevant quantifiable factors having a bearing on the situation facing the industry in determining whether increased imports have caused or are threatening to cause serious injury to the Canadian industry. The following factors are indicators of injury to domestic production (this is not an all-inclusive list):

❑ Losses on net sales or reduction of profits;

❑ Lost orders, market share, or declining sales;

❑ Reduced employment;

❑ Reduced capacity utilization;

❑ Price erosion, suppression or degradation;

❑ Failure to achieve realistic projected goals for profits, production, employment, sales, etc.;

❑ Retardation in the implementation of definite plans for production;

❑ Inability to raise capital for investments;

❑ Negative effects on cash flow, inventories and wages;

❑ Domestic producer's sales are increasing at a slower rate than the market is growing; and

❑ Delay or cessation of planned plant expansion or purchase of additional machinery by domestic producers.

Following is a brief review of the elements taken into account in making assessments of some of these indicators.

Changes in market share/lost sales

Quantify domestic market to measure share

The respective shares of the market held by domestic producers and importers must be analysed to determine whether imports are displacing domestic production. The size of the apparent national market can be calculated by totalling domestic production plus imports less exports. Loss of market share to imports is an important indicator of injury to domestic production.

Market share versus market growth

The CITT staff ensure that market share is not confused with increased sales. If the producer's sales are increasing at a slower rate than the market is growing and the imports are gaining a larger proportion of the increase it could point to displacement by imports, even though the producer has increased sales. CITT must also be satisfied that the situation is not caused by other factors. For instance, CITT staff members verify that the domestic industry possesses the production and marketing capability to take advantage of an expanding market.

Other situations may also be encountered. For example, a domestic producer can be injured even though it is holding its market share. This arises when, in order to maintain sales, the domestic producer may be forced to sell at lower prices because of the foreign competition. If the company had not offered a lower price, sales would have been lost to the imports. In this situation, the market share indicator is linked to price erosion or suppression.

Alternatively, where the total domestic market is in a decline, in order to maintain a certain level of sales the imported product may be sold at reduced prices, resulting in an increase in market share for the imports.

Price erosion or suppression

Decrease in or inability to increase price

Price erosion means that historic price levels in a market can no longer be maintained because of an outside influence pressuring prices to decrease. Price erosion may be due to the availability of a large volume of low-priced imports or due to other factors. Price suppression can mean that prices are forced to stay at a certain level even during times of inflation and increasing costs. Price suppression may also be a result of dumped or subsidized goods, which dictate price levels in the market.

Price erosion or suppression may occur when domestic producers are faced with the predicament that if they maintain prices at current levels or implement price increases they will no longer be competitive with the import competition and will suffer lost sales and declining market share. Rather than allow this to happen a domestic producer may match the price of the import competition by lowering its prices or refraining from price increases. In this situation, production and sales may be maintained but the effects of price erosion or suppression are evident in the financial performance of the company and lead to reduced profitability.

Profitability

Only financial data for the product under review are considered

Profitability of a firm is influenced directly by depressed price levels, lost sales and loss of market share. When a complainant identifies profitability problems CITT seeks to distinguish between situations where a firm suffers only a reduction in its normal profits and those situations where the continuing production and sale of the domestic goods have become unprofitable.

Reduced profits on sales of domestic goods may or may not constitute injury. CITT will examine the extent of the reduction in profits and, if a company is earning very large profits, whether these are in line with industry norms. CITT will also determine the impact of a reduced profit on the company's financial position and whether it threatens continued production.

Information detailing the complainant's profitability is generally available by examining financial statements. However, if the complainant is a multi-product producer, a breakdown of the financial data for the individual product under review is required.

In such cases CITT will examine the data submitted to ensure that it agrees with the financial statements relating to the whole operation and to obtain clarification if there appear to be contradictions between the data for the specific product and data for the company as a whole. When examining the financial data of a company a period sufficient to identify trends is reviewed and a link made between this information and other data such as marketing and selling activities, pricing patterns and import competition.

Production, inventories, capacity utilization

Reduced production linked to unfair import competition

Generally, a result of lost sales is a reduction in the level of production, which in turn may lead to reduced capacity utilization. CITT will determine what the standard production levels for the complainant have been historically. A decrease from the norm that is a direct result of the imports may be indicative of injury to domestic production. CITT will also ensure that decreased production and underutilization of capacity are not caused by other factors, such as employee strikes, machinery breakdowns, decreased demand for the goods, or the unavailability of raw materials. An analysis of production levels should be considered together with inventory levels. Some companies may show constant levels of production although their sales are down and accordingly their inventory levels will be rising and will be above normal. The company may be incurring costly expenses to maintain these inventories.

Employment

Decreased employment (layoffs) attributed to import competition

An indicator usually related to reduced production levels is reduced employment. When sales and production levels decrease many companies are forced to lay off employees. Employee levels and hours worked are analysed over a period of time because the particular industry involved may have seasonal layoffs every year. In determining the cause of the reduced levels of employment CITT also evaluates factors such as the automation of labour-intensive procedures, the introduction of new technology, or decrease in the demand for the goods. Increases or decreases in the level of exports must also be considered to determine the effect on employment. Also, when the complainant manufactures other goods not subject to the request, care should be taken to relate the proper level of employment to the subject goods only and not to the entire company.

Indicators of threat of serious injury

Factors considered regarding impending serious injury

The Safeguards Agreement recognizes that there are circumstances in which safeguard action is justified even before injury has actually materialized. The circumstances contemplated by the Safeguards Agreement are those where the conditions of trade clearly indicate that serious injury will occur imminently if demonstrable trends in trade adverse to domestic industry continue, or if clearly foreseeable adverse events occur. Thus, when considering requests for action based on the threat of injury, the predicted future injury must be clearly foreseen and must be imminent.

CITT may conclude, in some cases, that while the evidence of past injury is not compelling, the trend of increasing imports and their increasing impact on domestic producers could cause injury in the future. This is particularly so if the domestic industry is already in a weakened position and therefore more vulnerable to increased import competition. Another element considered is whether the exporters of the subject goods have excess capacity such that they could increase their exports substantially. High inventory levels abroad may also represent potential for future exports at dumped prices.

Establishing the causal link

Serious injury and a causal link to imports must be established

A decision on serious injury or threat thereof can be taken only if there is clear evidence that the increased imports have caused injury or are threatening to cause injury. In evaluating any request, CITT must determine whether the causal link exists and whether other factors such as the following are not possible causes of the complainant's difficulties.

❑ Is the evidence of injury the result of general economic conditions, such as a recession, or an overall contraction in demand for the product in question?

What else might cause serious injury?

❑ Is the injury due to a declining market for the particular product, perhaps due to competition from substitutes, a change in consumer taste or technological changes?

❑ Is the injury attributable to competition from other sources such as competition among domestic producers?

❑ Can the domestic producer's problems be attributed to factors such as inferior quality of the domestic product, inadequate sales network, poor after-sales service, etc.?

Preliminary determination and provisional safeguard measures

The public notice of the Minister of Finance's decision of a preliminary determination and the imposition of provisional measures contains the following data:

Exporter is notified of a safeguard measure

❑ Names of the known exporters and producers of the investigated product;

❑ A description of the investigated product including the Canadian tariff classification;

❑ The factors that have led to the determination of serious injury or threat thereof and causal link; and

❑ The amount of any duty or tariff increase proposed as provisional measures to be applied, the reasons why such provisional measures are necessary to prevent injury caused during the investigation and the intended duration of the provisional measures.

Government of exporting country notified

The public notice is forwarded to the country or countries exporting the product subject to the inquiry, and to other known interested parties. After a decision has been taken to apply a provisional safeguard measure, and before the measure takes effect, the Government of Canada immediately notifies the WTO Safeguards Committee in conformity with the requirements established by the Committee. As soon as the measure has been applied, the consultations referred to in Article 12.4 of the Agreement are initiated.

The public hearing process

Exporters have opportunity to argue case

CITT holds the public hearing phase of its inquiry once the staff report has been distributed and interested parties have made their submissions.

Importers, exporters and users may present arguments

At the public hearing, the domestic industry normally provides evidence relating to the impact of the increased imports. The domestic producers' evidence may cover such factors as loss of sales to imports and price depression or suppression, as well as declines in market share, profitability and employment. Importers, exporters, and sometimes users of the product typically challenge the domestic industry's case. After cross-examination and questions from CITT members, each party has an opportunity to summarize its case and respond to the other parties' cases in final argument.

If exporters don't make their case, the domestic industry will make it for them

The public hearing is an opportunity for exporters to argue the case made against their exports by the domestic industry. Strategic approaches may involve evidence that differentiates the product imported from that produced by the domestic industry or evidence that the imports are not contributing to any serious injury that may be suffered by domestic producers.

This is a critical chance for exporters to defend themselves and present their case in a safeguard inquiry. Up to this point, the entire case has focused on evidence presented by the domestic industry and CITT research. Unless challenged, the evidence submitted by the domestic industry could be accepted.

During or after an inquiry, the Government may direct CITT to examine and report on related matters, such as the effects on domestic producers of possible courses of action to deal with any serious injury.

The CITT Act also requires CITT to refer the matter to the Canada Border Services Agency (CBSA) if, before or after the initiation of an inquiry, it forms the opinion that the alleged injury appears to be caused by dumped or subsidized imports. If CBSA does not act, or terminates its investigation into dumping or subsidizing, CITT may initiate or resume the inquiry if requested to do so by the complainant.

CITT recommendations

Report

Timing, form and responsibility for safeguard measures

CITT submits its report to the Minister of Finance within 180 days (270 days in complex cases) from the date of the initiation of its inquiry. Notice of the submission of the report is sent to all interested parties and governments and is published. The safeguard measures may be in the form of a surtax, quantitative restrictions, or some combination of the two.

Quotas as definitive safeguard measures

Special permits are required for certain goods to be imported

A definitive safeguard measure in the form of a quota on imports of the investigated product will not reduce the quantity of those imports below the average level registered in the most recent three representative years for which statistics are available unless it is clearly demonstrated that a lower level is required to remedy the serious injury.

Dividing up the quota

If more than one country exports the investigated product to Canada, any quota on imports will be allocated among supplying countries. The Department of Foreign Affairs and International Trade attempts to reach agreement with those having a substantial interest in supplying the investigated product as to the allocation of shares of the total quota amount. Where this method is not reasonably practical for allocation of the quota, the quota is allocated among countries having a substantial interest in supplying the investigated product.

The allocation is based on the proportions of the investigated product supplied by such countries during the previous three years. In allocating the quota among supplying countries, due account is taken of any special factors which may have affected or may be affecting trade in the investigated product.

WTO rules on the extension of safeguard quotas

A quota safeguard measure may be extended one time only for a period of not more than four years in accordance with Articles 7.3 and 9.2 of the WTO Agreement. CITT may recommend extending a quantitative safeguards measure only if it is determined that the measure continues to be necessary to prevent or remedy serious injury, and that there is evidence that the domestic industry is adjusting. An extended definitive safeguard measure may not be more restrictive than at the end of the initial period of application. During the extension period, the measure continues to be progressively liberalized in accordance with the notice provided for in the regulations.

WTO guidance in allocating quota

In a case in which serious injury to the domestic industry has been found, the quota may be allocated among supplying countries on a different basis, provided consultations have been held with supplying countries and a clear demonstration is provided to the WTO Safeguards Committee that:

❑ Imports from certain countries have increased in disproportionate percentage in relation to the total increase in imports of the investigated product during the representative period;

❑ There are strong reasons for the departure from the normal methodology for quota allocation envisaged above; and

❑ The conditions of such departure are equitable to all suppliers of the product concerned.

Safeguards exclusions

Free trade agreement exemptions and limitations

Bilateral import safeguard measures may be applied during the transitional period of tariff reductions under the terms of Canada's free trade agreements. The tariff reduction schedule provided for in the free trade agreement with the United States is fully implemented and no longer in transition. However, other negotiated tariff reduction schedules remain in transition (e.g. with Chile) relative to the terms of those free trade agreements. Moreover, Canada is involved in negotiating other new free trade negotiations that are expected to further alter bilateral tariff reduction transitional periods.

Safeguard measures taken during the transitional period of tariff reductions of a free trade agreement are limited to the temporary suspension of tariff reductions or restoration of tariffs to MFN levels.

Measures may be applied for up to three years, followed, in some cases, by a phasing out period of one year. The free trade agreements provide for trade liberalizing compensation or, in the absence of agreement, equivalent tariff action by the government of the country against whose goods the safeguard action is taken.

Free trade exemptions may be overridden

In cases where the Government has excluded from global safeguard measures imports from countries with which Canada has free trade agreements, domestic producers may file a complaint with CITT that a surge in imports from those countries is undermining the effectiveness of the measures. CITT must decide within 30 days of receipt of a complaint whether it will conduct an inquiry.

It must report to the Government within 60 days after initiating an inquiry. If CITT reports that a surge in imports is undermining the effectiveness of the measures, the Government may impose the measures on imports from the relevant countries. Notice of the report is given to interested parties and governments and published.

Final safeguards determination – public notice

Finalize, justify and explain the results of the inquiry

CITT makes its decision within six months from the date of the initiation of the investigation. As soon as it reaches its determination, whether negative or affirmative, a notice of these decisions must be published. Affirmative decisions will include a summary of the injury determination, including the factors considered and their relevance to the decision, the reasons why CITT concluded that the safeguard measure is in the public interest, details concerning the domestic industry's adjustment plan, a timetable for the progressive liberalization of the safeguard measure, the form, level and duration of the proposed safeguard measure, and the proposed date of application of the definitive safeguard measure; if a quantitative restriction is proposed, the notice should specify the allocation of the quota among the supplier countries and identify any developing countries exempted from the measure.

If the decision is not to apply a definitive safeguard measure, the notice will set forth the factual and legal basis for the decision. CITT immediately notifies the Safeguards Committee if it is determined that increased imports have caused or threaten to cause serious injury to the domestic industry.

Safeguard measures cannot be applied continuously

No new safeguard measure can be imposed in respect of any product that has been previously subjected to a definitive safeguard measure unless a period of at least two years has elapsed, and if the previous measure applied for more than four years any new measure must be limited to a period not exceeding one-half of the initial period. However, a safeguard measure with a duration of 180 days or less may be applied in respect of a product which was previously subject to a safeguard measure if at least one year has elapsed since the earlier measure applied and safeguard measures have not been applied to that product more than twice in the five-year period immediately preceding the date on which the new safeguard measure is to take effect.

Termination of investigation

An application for a safeguard investigation may be withdrawn at any time after an investigation has been initiated, in which case CITT will terminate the investigation without measures, unless it is determined that it is in the interest of Canada to continue the investigation.

A safeguard investigation will be terminated at any point during the investigation, with no definitive safeguard measure applied, when CITT decides that there is insufficient evidence of serious injury or threat of serious injury to justify proceeding with the case.

APPENDIX I

Historical listing of dumping and subsidy investigations conducted pursuant to the Special Import Measures Act since its implementation on 1 December 1984

	Goods	A/C	Country	Disposition	Tariff Classification	Initiation date	Preliminary margin	Final margin	Quantity dumped (%)	Date of Tribunal finding
0	Alloy tool steel bars, plates, and forgins	A	AT GB KR SE	FR/CA or FN/CN	N/A	1984.08.22	N/A	N/A	N/A	N/A
1	Charcoal briquettes	A	US	FR/CA	2702.20.00 2704.00.00 4402.00.10 4402.00.90	1985.01.18	22.40	60.50	99.40	1985.08.14
2	Rail car and locomotive axles	A	JP US GB	TT/CC FN/CN FR/CA	8607.19.10	1985.01.24	7.35 10.20 25.60	1.37 10.20 28.50	16.90 100.00 100.00	1985.08.22
3	Polyphase induction motors, 1 to 200 horsepower inclusive	A&C A	BR JP MX PL TW GB	FR/CA	8501.51.90.00 8501.52.90.10 8501.53.19.00 8501.52.90.20 8051.52.90.30	1985.02.07	6.60 20.30 38.20 52.70 24.60 24.90	6.60 13.70 38.20 49.70 15.90 14.20	44.00 93.00 100.00 100.00 79.60 96.20	1985.10.11
4	Modular automated plants	A	US	T/C	N/A	1985.02.14				–
5	Frozen pot pies and compartment dinners	A	US	UX/EX	1602.31.10 1602.39.10 1602.50.10 1602.49.10	1985.04.24				–
6	Barbed wire	A	AR BR PL KR	FR/CA	7313.00.10 7217.33.00	1985.05.01	46.21 32.69 54.71 4.26	49.86 31.50 47.30 5.56	100.00 99.81 100.00 55.72	1985.11.04
7	Surgical adhesive tapes and plasters	A	JP	FR/CA	3005.10.10 3005.10.91 3005.10.99 3005.90.10 3005.90.20 3005.90.30 3005.90.91 3005.90.92 3005.90.99	1985.05.08	57.60	57.60	100.00	1985.12.04
8	Polyphase induction motors, 1 to 200 horsepower inclusive	A	RO	FN/CN	N/A	1985.07.05	35.00	30.10	100.00	1985.11.26
9	Hot-rolled carbon steel plate	A	DE	UX/EX	7208.11.00 7208.12.00 7208.21.00 7208.22.00 7208.31.00 7208.32.00 7208.33.00 7208.41.00 7208.42.00 7208.43.00	1985.07.11		11.90		–

	Goods	A/C	Country	Disposition	Tariff Classification	Initiation date	Preliminary margin	Final margin	Quantity dumped (%)	Date of Tribunal finding
10	Pentaerythritol	A	CL	FN/CN	N/A	1985.08.19	51.87	40.99	100.00	1986.03.13
11	Rubber hockey pucks	A	CZ DE	FR/CA	5607.49.10 5607.49.20 5607.50.10 5607.50.20	1985.08.21	66.50 58.92-59.05	63.32 55.15	100.00 100.00	1986.03.18
12	12-gauge shotshells	A	BE FR IT GB	FR/CA	N/A	1985.09.12	37.00 10.00-21.00 13.00-28.00 14.00-25.00	12.52 35.77 14.31 5.97	84.00 84.00 84.00 84.00	1986.03.27
13	Photo albums with self-adhesive leaves (imported together or separately)	A	CN	FR/CA	4820.50.90.10 4823.90.90.60	1985.09.20	34.00-43.00	68.49	100.00	1986.02.14
14	Colour televisions	A	KR	FN/CN	N/A	1985.09.03	8.22	4.54	37.97	1986.03.27
15	Oil and gas well casing	A	US (Maverick) US (others) KR DE AR AT	FR/CA FR/CA FR/CA FR/CA FR/CA FN/CN	7304.29.00.11 7304.29.00.19 7304.29.00.29 7306.20.90.11 7306.20.90.19 7306.20.90.21 7306.20.90.29	1985.09.20	13.39 13.39 9.76 3.34 47.20 2.44	3.70 14.06 13.03 0.67 35.00- 52.50 0	96.00 100.00 64.60 100.00 0.00	1986.04.17
16	Boneless manufacturing beef	C	EC	FR/CA	0202.30.00	1985.10.18				1986.07.25
17	Whole potatoes	A	US	FI/CD	0701.90.00	1985.10.18	30.70	32.40	84.97	1984.06.04
18	Single-use hypodermic needles and syringes	A	JP US	T/C	N/A	1985.11.08	22-62 25-74			–
19	Drywall screws	A	TW	FR/CA	7318.15.00.32	1985.12.20	23.00	32.35	100.00	1986.07.10
20	Spandex filament yarn	A	KR	T/C	N/A	1986.02.13	10.1-22.6	1.17		–
21	ABS resin	A	KR	FR/CA	3903.30.10 3903.30.90	1986.03.19	29.33	17.00		1986.10.15
22	Artificial graphite electrodes	A	BE JP SE US	FR/CA	8545.11.12 8545.11.22 8545.90.92	1986.04.30	13.62 27.28 9.02 18.25	3.86 23.99 9.02 18.00	100.00 100.00 100.00 100.00	1986.11.26
23	Pressure cleaners	A	US	T/C	N/A	1986.06.16	35.2-46.5	11.71	100.00	–
24	Dry pasta	C	EC	FN/CN	N/A	1986.07.02				1987.01.28
25	Grain corn	C	US	FR/CA	1005.90.10 1005.90.90 2039.90.91 2309.90.92 2309.90.99	1986.07.02	1.04799/ bushel	0.849/ bushel		1987.03.06
26	Drywall screws	A	KR	FR/CA	7318.15.00.32	1986.08.01	31.12	14.88	99.00	1987.02.20
27	Carbon steel seamless pipe	C	BR	FN/CN	7306.30.10.14 7306.30.10.24 7306.30.10.34 7306.30.90.14 7306.30.90.19 7306.30.90.24 7306.30.90.29 7306.30.90.34 7306.30.90.39	1986.08.13	74.22/ton	81.55/ton		1987.03.12
28	Oil and gas well casing	A	DE JP	UX/EX	7304.29.00.11 7304.29.00.19 7304.29.00.21 7304.29.00.29 7306.20.90.11 7306.20.90.19 7306.20.90.21 7306.20.90.29	1986.08.20	0.00-8.00 10.10-22.50	34.12 45.00	100.00 99.00	–
29	Tile backer board	A	US	UX/EX	6810.19.00	1986.10.08		11.40	47.90	–
30	Yellow onions	A	US	FR/CA	0703.10.91 0703.10.99	1986.10.14	35.00-56.00	42.58	96.61	1987.04.30

	Goods	A/C	Country	Disposition	Tariff Classification	Initiation date	Preliminary margin	Final margin	Quantity dumped (%)	Date of Tribunal finding
31	Gasoline powered chain saws	A	DE SE US	FR/CA	8467.81.00	1986.10.24	30.71 20.32 33.35	26.44 16.55 18.42	100.00 100.00 98.36	1987.07.03
32	Absorbent clay	A	US	T/C	N/A	1986.11.14	44.00-75.00	16.00	0.00	–
33	Fertilizer blending equipment	A	US	FN/CN	N/A	1987.03.05	7.97	9.41	99.00	1987.09.30
34	Printing plates	A	JP GB	FN/CN FR/CA	8442.50.90	1987.04.01	45.71 28.60	46.18 31.88	100.00 95.93	1987.10.27
35	High voltage porcelain station post insulators	A	DE JP	UX/EX	8546.20.00	1987.04.08	11.90 60.30		61.10 100.00	–
36	Photo albums with self-adhesive leaves	A	MY SG TW	FR/CA	4820.50.90.10 4823.90.90.60	1987.04.09	45.10 45.60 53.30	49.30 52.90 60.80	100.00 100.00 100.00	1988.02.26
37	Phenol	A	ES	FN/CN	N/A	1987.05.22	40.60	39.16	100.00	1987.12.18
38	Wide flange steel shapes	A	ES	FR/CA	7216.10.00.30 7216.33.00.11 7216.33.00.12 7216.33.00.13 7216.33.00.20 7216.33.00.91 7216.33.00.92	1987.05.22	6.14	7.29	78.84	1987.12.18
39	Hot-rolled carbon steel reinforcing bars	A	MX US	FN/CN	N/A	1987.05.27	20.62 20.66	20.62 21.04	30.74 91.20	1987.12.22
40	Solid urea	A	DE RU	FN/CN	N/A	1987.05.29	66.47 61.35	66.51 57.66	100.00 100.00	1987.12.24
41	Drywall screws	A&C	FR	FR/CA	7318.15.00.32	1987.06.04	38.20	38.20	100.00	1987.12.31
42	Automobiles	A	KR	FN/CN	N/A	1987.07.15	36.30	26.30	100.00	1988.03.23
43	Photo albums with pocket sheets	A	DE HK JP MY CN KR SG TW	FR/CA	4820.50.90.00 4820.90.90.20 4820.90.90.90	1987.08.28	44.80 71.60 23.30 41.60 64.90 69.50 66.60 58.70	44.00 64.00 24.00 40.00 63.00 59.00 66.00 59.00	100.00 100.00 100.00 100.00 100.00 100.00 100.00 100.00	1988.02.26
44	Recreational vehicle doors	A	US	FN/CN	N/A	1987.08.28	12.32	14.86	45.00	1988.03.18
45	Carbon steel welded pipe	A	BR LU CS** PL TR	UT/FE & FI/CD UT/FE & FN/CN FN/CN FN/CN	7306.30.90.14 7306.30.90.19 7306.30.90.24 7306.30.90.29 7306.30.90.34 7306.30.90.39	1987.09.16	26.10 11.70 33.90 29.70 56.30	25.10 11.70 28.10 10.70 51.00	100.00 48.90 97.90 100.00 100.00	1992.01.23
46	Stainless steel butt-weld fittings	A	JP	FR/CA	7307.23.00 7307.29.10	1988.02.08	40.00	40.00	100.00	1988.08.03
47	Steel wool	A	US	T/C	N/A	1988.05.26	13.90	13.90	19.80	–
48	Sour cherries	A	US	FR/CA	0809.20.21.00 0809.20.29.00 0809.20.90.00 0811.90.20.10 0811.90.20.99 0812.10.00.90	1988.06.21	39.04	35.36	74.64	1989.01.30
49	Apples	A	US	FR/CA	0808.10.10.96	1988.07.08	31.90	27.45	98.56	1989.02.03
50	Lead acid batteries	A	KR	T/C	8507.10.00	1988.08.30	4.50-44.60	4.60	25.80	–
51	Padded coat hangers	A	TW US	FN/CN	44.21.10.00	1988.09.16	19.00 20.00	19.00 20.00	100.00 100.00	1989.04.14
52	Grinding balls	A	US	UX/EX	7325.91.90.90	1988.09.23	13.70	13.04		–

	Goods	A/C	Country	Disposition	Tariff Classification	Initiation date	Preliminary margin	Final margin	Quantity dumped (%)	Date of Tribunal finding
53	Motors over 200 horsepower	A&C A	BR FR JP SE TW GB US	FN/CN	8501.53	1988.09.30	19.50 11.70 40.60 34.60 30.60 11.70 19.30	28.70 28.10 38.00 33.80 17.50 9.60 15.30	80.80 73.33 100.00 93.00 81.40 100.00 69.30	1989.04.28
54	Mini refrigerators	A	PL	FN/CN	8418.22.90.90	1989.01.19	75.40	75.60	100.00	1989.08.15
55	Key blanks	A	IT	FR/CA	8301.70.00.10 8301.70.00.20 8301.70.00.90	1989.03.17	42.00	45.75	100.00	1989.10.13
56	Plastisol (dispersion, liquid polyvinyl chloride)	A	US	T/C	N/A	1989.07.07	29.00	5.20	95.00	–
57	Landing nets	A	US	UX/EX	9507.90.90.20	1989.07.17	6.30-45.30	21.00		–
58	Certain transit concrete mixers	A	US	UX/EX	8474.31.00.20 8705.40.00.00	1989.08.04		12.20	97.00	–
59	Women's footwear, boots and shoes, leather and non-leather * Boots only	A&C A	BR PL RO TW CS** CN	FR/CA FR/CA FR/CA FR/CA FR/CA FR/CA	6402.91.00.22 6402.91.00.92 6402.99.00.92 6403.30.00.20 6403.51.00.22 6403.51.00.92 6403.59.90.92 6403.91.00.22 6403.91.00.92 6403.99.20.92 6403.99.30.00 6403.99.90.92 6404.19.90.92 6404.20.90.92 6405.10.90.00	1989.08.25	24.81 34.13 38.00 29.54 23.75 21.69	26.10 38.74 20.00 27.50 26.20 47.30	63.24 100.00 100.00 69.83 100.00 100.00	1990.05.03
60	Textured polyester yarn	A	MX	T/C		1989.10.03	30.12	12.30	92.44	–
61	Refill paper	A C	BR	FR/CA	4823.51.00.00	1989.12.08	32.50	32.50	100.00	1990.07.06
62	Municipal tractors	A	DE	FN/CN		1990.03.21	31.70	28.70	100.00	1990.10.17
63	Dry dog food	A	US	T/C	2309.10.00.99 2309.10.00.20	1990.03.28	34.00-53.00	44.68	100.00	–
64	Certain stainless steel bars	A	IN	FN/CN		1990.05.03	38.05	30.60	100.00	1990.11.13
65	Photo albums	A	ID	FR/CA	4820.50.90.10 4823.90.90.60	1990.06.08	76.50	73.60	100.00	1991.01.02
66	Lint rollers	A	US	FN/CN		1990.07.06	25.20	25.89	94.00	1991.02.01
67	Photo albums	A	PH TH	FR/CA	4820.50.90.10 4823.90.90.60	1990.07.10	78.00 55.50	78.00 55.50	100.00 100.00	1991.01.02
68	Wedge clamps	A	US	UX/EX	8205.70.10.00 8205.70.90.00	1990.11.14	33.50	6.50	45.00	–
69	Carbon steel welded pipe	A	AR IN RO TW TH VE	FI/CD FI/CD FI/CD FI/CD FI/CD FR/CA	7306.30.90.14 7306.30.90.19 7306.30.90.24 7306.30.90.29 7306.30.90.34 7306.30.90.39	1990.11.16	46.50 37.10 18.30 13.90 41.40 33.10	46.50 19.80 17.80 13.60 40.80 33.10	100.00 100.00 100.00 99.20 100.00 100.00	1991.07.26
70	Stainless steel welded pipe	A	TW	FR/CA	7306.40.90.10 7306.40.90.20 7306.40.90.30	1990.12.24	16.90	18.20	78.00	1991.09.05
71	Malt beverages (beer)	A	US	FR/CA	2203.00.00.11 2203.00.00.12 2203.00.00.19 2203.00.00.21 2203.00.00.22 2203.00.00.29 2203.00.00.31 2203.00.00.32 2203.00.00.39	1991.03.06	30.00	29.80	100.00	1991.10.02

	Goods	A/C	Country	Disposition	Tariff Classification	Initiation date	Preliminary margin	Final margin	Quantity dumped (%)	Date of Tribunal finding
72	Carpets	A	US	FR/CA	5703.20.10.90 5703.30.10.91 5703.30.10.92 5703.30.10.99 5703.90.10.00	1991.08.06	21.05	12.02	61.00	1992.04.21
73	Toothpicks	A	US	FR/CA	4421.90.90.30 4421.90.90.99	1991.08.19	18.50	16.90	56.00	1992.03.13
74	Graphite electrodes and connecting pins	A	AT FR ES DE GB	T/C	8545.11.12 8545.11.22 8545.90.92	1991.09.20	8.60-69.10 7.60-16.60 14.00-31.50 8.50-38.60 7.10	33.60 11.20 15.30 25.90 19.80	88.50 88.50 88.50 88.50 88.50	–
75	Aluminum coil stock	A	SE	FR/CA	7606.11.20.11 7606.11.20.13 7606.12.29.11 7606.12.29.13 7616.90.90.90	1991.07.12	47.00	42.40	99.90	N/A
76	Christmas trees	A	US	T/C	0604.91.30.00	1991.11.15	31.00	14.90	1.10	–
77	Roller bearings	A	JP	FN/CN	8482.20.10.00 8482.99.10.21 8482.99.10.29	1991.12.12	44.72	36.17	97.00	1992.07.09
78	Bicycles & frames	A	CN TW	FI/CD	8712.00.00.12 8712.00.00.20 8712.00.00.30 8712.00.00.40 8712.00.00.50 8712.00.00.90 8714.91.00.00	1992.05.15	45.00 25.00	34.00 13.00	98.00 92.00	1992.12.11
79	Lettuce	A	US	FR/CA	0705.11.11.00 0705.11.12.00 0705.11.90.00 2005.90.99.69	1992.06.08	31.60	31.00	87.50	1992.11.30
80	Wedge clamps	A	US	UX/EX	7616.90.90.90	1992.05.08		31.60	65.32	–
81	Gypsum board	A	US	FR/CA	6809.11.10.00 6809.11.90.00	1992.06.24	28.00	27.28	94.58	1993.01.20
82	Cauliflower	A	US	FN/CN	0704.10.11.00 0704.10.12.00 0704.10.90.00	1992.06.30	46.10	50.00	99.60	1993.01.04
83	Hanging file folders	A	US	UX/EX	4820.30.00.90	1992.07.22		23.10	98.60	–
84	Waterproof footwear	A	CZ SK CN KR TW	FN/CN	6401.91.20.00 6401.92.12.00 6401.92.92.00 6401.92.92.00 6402.91.00.91 6404.19.90.20	1992.07.09	36.60 36.60 18.70 47.20 5.50	47.20 47.20 47.20 47.20 5.50	100.00 100.00 100.00 100.00 22.30	1993.02.04
85	Hot-rolled carbon steel plate	A	US BR CZ DK DE RO GB MK BE SK SI	FN/CN FR/CA FR/CA FR/CA FR/CA FR/CA FR/CA FR/CA FR/CA T/C T/C	7208	1992.08.24	10.20 51.30 39.80 65.00 12.80 45.00 40.80 40.90 23.70 0.00 0.00	10.20 43.20 53.80 53.80 12.30 53.80 32.90 40.90 23.60 0.00 0.00	81.30 100.00 100.00 100.00 85.90 100.00 100.00 100.00 98.00 0.00 0.00	1993.05.06
86	Tomato paste	A	US	FN/CN	2002.90.00.19 2002.90.00.11	1992.09.01	13.10	11.20	46.01	1993.03.20
87	Hot-rolled carbon steel plate – heat treated (joined with # 85 above at PD)	A	US BR CZ DK DE RO GB MK SK SI	FN/CN FR/CA	7208	1992.09.08	10.20 51.30 39.80 65.00 12.80 45.00 40.80 40.90 0.00 0.00	10.20 43.20 53.80 53.80 12.30 53.80 32.90 40.90 0.00 0.00	81.30 100.00 100.00 100.00 85.90 100.00 100.00 100.00 0.00 0.00	1993.05.06

	Goods	A/C	Country	Disposition	Tariff Classification	Initiation date	Preliminary margin	Final margin	Quantity dumped (%)	Date of Tribunal finding
88	Hot-rolled carbon steel sheet	A	DE FR NZ IT GB US	FN/CN	7208	1992.09.16	55.40 17.30 39.20 55.40 36.30 10.90	56.54 18.92 39.23 56.54 40.82 11.60	100.00 99.88 100.00 100.00 100.00 95.72	1993.05.31
89	Cold-rolled carbon steel sheet	A	FR DE IT GB US	FR/CA	7209.15.10 7209.15.90 7209.16.10 7209.16.90 7209.17.10 7209.17.90 7209.18.10 7209.18.90 7209.25.10 7209.25.90 7209.27.00 7209.28.00 7209.90.00 7211.23.10 7211.23.90 7211.29.10 7211.29.90	1992.11.16	27.60 23.80 46.60 35.80 22.33	24.80 27.70 46.60 35.80 16.05	100.00 100.00 100.00 100.00 94.46	1993.07.29
90	Fibreglass pipe coverings	A	US	FR/CA	7019.39.90.13	1993.02.04	51.00	38.00	99.00	1993.11.19
91	Copper pipe fittings	A	US	FR/CA	7412.10.00.11 7412.10.00.19 7412.10.00.20 7412.10.00.90 7412.20.00.11 7412.20.00.12 7412.20.00.19 7412.20.00.20 7412.20.00.90	1993.02.05	52.00	47.00	94.00	1993.10.18
92	Synthetic baler twine	A A&C	US PT	FR/CA T/C	5607.41.00.10	1993.07.30	17.40 0.00	13.00 0.00	57.00 0.00	1994.04.22
93	Hot-rolled carbon steel plate	A	IT ES UA KR	FR/CA	7208.51.10.00 7208.51.99.10 7208.51.99.91 7208.51.99.92 7208.51.99.93 7208.51.99.94 7208.51.99.95 7208.52.19.00 7208.52.90.10 7208.52.90.91 7208.52.90.92 7208.52.90.93 7208.52.90.94 7208.52.90.95	1993.10.18	45.60 27.50 43.20 45.60	44.50 38.20 39.10 44.50	100.00 100.00 100.00 100.00	1994.05.17
94	Corrosion resistant steel sheet	A	US AU BR FR DE ES SE GB JP KR NZ	FR/CA	7210.30.00 7210.49.00 7212.20.00 7212.30.00 7225.91.00 7225.92.00 7225.99.00.90 7226.93.00 7226.94.00	1993.11.17	24.10 (9.8) 32.70 55.90 34.10 62.40 28.40 24.00 24.30 62.40 13.10 30.00	6.89 32.70 51.40 32.80 60.80 28.40 23.50 23.50 60.80 11.30 32.10	86.40 100.00 100.00 100.00 100.00 100.00 100.00 100.00 100.00 100.00 100.00	1994.07.29
95	Plastic shrinkable bags	A	US	UX/EX	3917.32.90.20 3923.21.90.41 3923.21.90.42	1993.11.19				–
96	12-gauge shotshells	A	HU CZ PL	FR/CA FR/CA T/C	9306.21.00.00	1993.11.24	44.00 35.00 0.00	37.00 32.00 0.00	99.00 97.00 0.00	1994.06.22
97	Memorials	A&C	IN	FR/CA	6802.23.00.20 6802.93.00.20	1993.12.22	47.00	29.00	10.10	1994.07.20

	Goods	A/C	Country	Disposition	Tariff Classification	Initiation date	Preliminary margin	Final margin	Quantity dumped (%)	Date of Tribunal finding
98	Apples – red Delicious apples – Golden Delicious	A	US	FR/CA	0808.10.10.96	1994.07.14	30.00	28.00	61.00	1995.02.09
							12.00	18.00	59.00	
99	Residential steel storage buildings	A	US	UX/EX	9406.00.99.20 9406.00.99.90	1994.09.13	19.10	21.90	99.20	–
100	Refined sugar	A	US	FI/CD	1701.91.00.11	1995.03.17	44.00	44.00	99.90	1995.11.06
		C	US	T/C	1701.91.00.19		N/A		N/A	
		A	KR	FN/CN	1701.91.00.21		64.00	64.00	100.00	
		A	DK	FI/CD	1701.91.00.29		64.00	64.00	100.00	
			DE		1701.91.00.91		50.00	50.00	100.00	
			NL		1701.91.00.99		64.00	64.00	100.00	
			GB		1701.99.00.10		64.00	64.00	100.00	
		C	EU	FI/CD	1701.99.00.21		GB	All EC/	100.00	
					1701.99.00.29		€56.34/100 kg	€50.79/		
					1701.99.00.90		Others	100 kg		
					1702.90.11.00		€51.41/100 kg			
					1702.90.12.00					
					1702.90.13.00					
					1702.90.14.00					
					1702.90.15.00					
					1702.90.16.00					
					1702.90.17.00					
					1702.90.18.00					
					1702.90.30.10					
					1702.90.60.00					
101	Jars and jar caps	A	US	FR/CA	7010.91.00.21 7010.91.00.29 7010.92.00.21 7010.92.00.29 7010.93.00.94 7010.94.00.94 8309.90.90.91	1995.03.24	35.00	35.80	100.00	1995.10.20
102	Pasta	A&C	IT	FN/CN	1902.10.10.30 1902.19.91.30 1902.19.12.30 1902.19.92.30	1995.08.30	27.00	18.80	91.00	1996.05.13
103	Portable file cases	A	CN	FN/CN	4820.30.00.90	1995.09.21	70.70	70.70	100.00	1996.06.04
104	Culture media	A	US GB	FN/CN	3821.00.00.00 3822.00.00.10 3822.00.00.20	1995.09.29	40.80	41.10	97.10	1996.05.31
105	Refill paper	A	ID	FN/CN	4823.51.00.00 4820.10.00.00	1996.03.01	4.20	3.30	63.20	1996.09.27
	Spiral books									
			ID				3.20	2.40	67.00	
			BR				53.10	57.50	100.00	
106	Garlic	A	CN	FI/CD	0703.20.00.00	1996.08.23	72.00	70.00	96.00	1997.03.21
107	Polyiso insulation board	A	US	FR/CA	3921.13.91.00 3921.13.99.10 3921.13.99.91 3921.13.99.99	1996.09.13	40.70	36.00	91.00	1997.04.11
108	Concrete panels	A	US	FR/CA	6810.11.00.00 6810.19.00.00 6811.10.00.00 6811.20.00.00	1996.11.29	43.00	35.00	100.00	1997.06.27
109	Hot-rolled carbon steel plate	A	CN	FI/CD	7208.51.10.00	1997.02.13	23.90	27.30	100.00	1997.10.27
			MX	FR/CA	7208.51.99.10		26.20	26.20	100.00	
			RU	FI/CD	7208.51.99.91		25.30	25.20	100.00	
			ZA	FI/CD	7208.51.99.92		18.10	18.10	100.00	
			PL	T/C	7208.51.99.93		- - - -	- - - -		
					7208.51.99.94					
					7208.51.99.95					
					7208.52.19.00					
					7208.52.90.10					
					7208.52.90.91					
					7208.52.90.92					
					7208.52.90.93					
					7208.52.90.94					
					7208.52.90.95					

	Goods	A/C	Country	Disposition	Tariff Classification	Initiation date	Preliminary margin	Final margin	Quantity dumped (%)	Date of Tribunal finding
110	Baby food	A	US	FR/CA	1602.10.90.00 1901.90.59.00 1902.20.00.10 1902.30.11.10 1902.30.12.10 1902.30.20.10 1904.10.10.90 1904.10.21.90 1904.10.29.90 1904.10.90.90 1905.90.39.19 2005.10.00.00 2007.10.00.00 2009.19.90.21 2009.70.90.10 2009.80.19.94 2009.80.19.95 2009.80.20.10 2009.90.30.31 2104.20.00.00 2106.90.99.99	1997.10.03	68.71	59.76	100.00	1998.04.29
111	Stainless steel round bar (Investigations joined)	A	DE FR IT JP ES SE TW GB IN	FR/CA	7222.11.00.11 7222.11.00.21 7222.20.10.00 7222.20.90.11 7222.20.90.21 7222.30.00.11 7222.30.00.21	1997.12.23 1998.03.06	49.5 49.5 9.8 49.5 49.5 37.8 49.5 49.5 3.7 19.3	52.4 52.4 8.2 52.4 52.4 42.8 52.4 52.4 0.6 52.4 18.8	100.00 100.00 94.73 100.00 100.00 100.00 100.00 100.00 50.00 100.00 75.81	1998.09.04
112	Filter tipped cigarette tubes	A	FR DE	U/E T/C	4813.10.00.00	1998.10.19	25.1 - - - -		99.30 - - - -	–
113	Stainless steel round bar	A	KR	FR/CA	7222.11.00.11 7222.11.00.21 7222.20.10.11 7222.20.10.21 7222.20.90.11 7222.20.90.21 7222.30.00.11 7222.30.00.21	1998.12.03	52.4	52.4	100.00	1999.06.18
114	Hot-rolled carbon and alloy steel sheet	A	FR RO RU SK	FR/CA	7208.25 7208.26 7208.27 7208.36 7208.37 7208.38 7208.39 7208.53 7208.54 7208.90 7211.13 7211.14 7211.19 7211.90 7225.20 7225.30 7225.40 7225.99 7226.20 7226.91 7226.99	1998.12.03	24.0 43.0 43.0 43.0	11.8 42.1 41.6 35.4	98.66 100.00 100.00 100.00	1999.07.02

	Goods	A/C	Country	Disposition	Tariff Classification	Initiation date	Preliminary margin	Final margin	Quantity dumped (%)	Date of Tribunal finding
115	Cold-rolled steel sheet	A	AR BE NZ RU SK ES TR	FN/CN FR/CA FN/CN FR/CA FR/CA FN/CN FR/CA	7209.15 7209.16 7209.17 7209.18 7209.25 7209.26 7209.27 7209.28 7209.90 7211.23 7211.29 7211.90	1999.01.29	42.0 42.0 42.0 26.0 18.0 12.0 26.0	29.0 7.0 29.0 29.0 24.0 13.0 20.0	100.00 67.00 100.00 100.00 100.00 93.00 100.00	1999.08.27
116	Concrete reinforcing steel bars	A	CU KR TR	FR/CA	7213.10.00.00 7214.20.00.00	1999.06.16	21.0 20.6 15.4	4.9 20.8 9.0	88.00 92.60 100.00	2000.01.12
117	Iodinated Radiographic (X-RAY) contrast media	A	US (incl PR)	FR/CA	3006.30.00.10	1999.08.20	82.0	69.0	100.00	2000.05.01
118	Hot-rolled carbon steel plate	A A A C A C A C A	BR FI IN IN ID ID TH TH UA	FR/CA	7208.51.10.00 7208.51.99.10 7208.51.99.91 7208.51.99.92 7208.51.99.93 7208.51.99.94 7208.51.99.95 7208.52.19.00 7208.52.90.10 7208.52.90.91 7208.52.90.92 7208.52.90.93 7208.52.90.94 7208.52.90.95	1999.10.15	57.6 57.6 13.6 NA/SO 57.6 NA/SO 56.3 NA/SO 57.6	35.5 57.6 14.9 NA/SO 21.3 NA/SO 49.0 NA/SO 57.6	100.00 100.00 86.00 NA/SO 100.00 NA/SO 100.00 NA/SO 100.00	2000.06.27
119	Top-mount electric refrigerators, electric household dishwashers and gas or electric laundry dryers	A	US	FR/CA	8418.10.90.21 8418.10.90.22 8422.10.90.10 8422.10.90.90 8451.21.00.11 8451.21.00.19 8451.21.00.91 8451.21.00.99	1999.11.30	15.0	12.0	88.00	2000.08.01
120	Bingo paper	A	US	UX/EX	4504.90.90.90 4823.51.00.00	2000.03.20	43.5		92.00	–
121	Stainless steel round bar	A C C	BR BR IN	FR/CA	7222.11.00.11 7222.11.00.21 7222.20.10.11 7222.20.10.21 7222.20.90.11 7222.20.90.21 7222.30.00.11 7222.30.00.21	2000.03.31	37.3	37.3	100.00	2000.10.27

	Goods	A/C	Country	Disposition	Tariff Classification	Initiation date	Preliminary margin	Final margin	Quantity dumped (%)	Date of Tribunal finding
122	Waterproof footwear	A	CN	FI/CD	6401.10.19.00 6401.10.20.00 6401.91.20.00 6401.92.11.00 6401.92.12.00 6401.92.92.90 6401.99.21.00 6401.99.29.00 6401.99.30.10 6401.99.30.90 6402.19.90.90 6402.91.00.10 6402.91.00.91 6402.91.00.92 6402.91.00.93 6403.19.90.90 6403.40.00.10 6403.91.00.10 6403.91.00.91 6403.91.00.92 6403.91.00.93 6404.11.99.90 6404.19.90.20 6404.19.90.91 6404.19.90.92 6404.19.90.93	2000.05.12	40.0	33.0	96.00	2000.12.08
123	Grain corn	A&C	US	FN/CN	1005.90.00.11 1005.90.00.12 1005.90.00.13 1005.90.00.14 1005.90.00.19 1005.90.00.99	2000.08.09	57.00	38.00	98.00	2001.03.07
124	Fresh or frozen garlic	A	CN VN	FR/CA	0710.80.90.90	2000.10.31	70.10 65.20	68.10 55.70	99.50 100.00	2001.05.02
125	Concrete reinforcing bar	A	ID JP LV MD PL TW UA	FI/CD	7213.10.00.00 7214.20.00.00	2000.11.03	30.00 30.00 20.00 30.00 30.00 30.00 27.00	40.90 39.90 3.90 40.90 40.90 40.90 15.70	100.00 100.00 79.40 100.00 100.00 100.00 100.00	2001.06.01
126	Pulp-dewatering screw presses	A	NO	T/C	8439.10.10.19 8439.10.10.50 8439.10.90.99	2000.11.27				–
127	Corrosion-resistant steel sheet	A A&C A A A A A	CN IN MY PT RU TW ZA	FN/CN FN/CN FN/CN T/C FN/CN FN/CN FN/CN	7210.30.00.00 7212.20.00.00 7226.93.00.00 7210.49.00.10 7212.30.00.00 7226.94.00.00 7210.49.00.20 7225.91.00.00 7210.49.00.30 7225.92.00.00	2000.12.04	40.50 24.80 40.50 40.50 26.70 40.50	37.20 22.70 4.10 16.70 8.00 22.40	100.00 100.00 78.50 100.00 45.80 100.00	2001.07.03
128	Hot-rolled carbon steel sheet	A A A A A&C A A A A A A A	BR BG CN CS IN KR MK NZ SA TW UA ZA	FI/CD FI/CD FI/CD FI/CD FI/CD FN/CN FI/CD FN/CN FN/CN FI/CD FI/CD FI/CD	7208.25.10.10 7208.25.10.20 7208.25.10.30 7208.25.10.40 7208.25.90.10 7208.25.90.20 7208.25.90.30 7208.25.90.40 7208.26.10.10 7208.26.10.20 7208.26.10.30 7208.26.10.40 7208.26.90.10 7208.26.90.20 7208.26.90.30 7208.26.90.40 7208.27.10.10 7208.27.10.20 7208.27.10.30	2001.01.19	35.70 49.00 25.40 46.30 26.30 34.20 49.00 28.60 49.00 26.40 49.00 49.00	11.20 92.90 7.70 56.40 34.20 24.70 62.90 17.30 62.90 30.20 62.90 62.90	96.50 100.00 72.50 99.00 100.00 100.00 100.00 90.20 100.00 97.20 100.00 100.00	2001.08.17

Goods	A/C	Country	Disposition	Tariff Classification	Initiation date	Preliminary margin	Final margin	Quantity dumped (%)	Date of Tribunal finding
Hot-rolled carbon steel sheet (cont'd)				7208.27.10.40					
				7208.27.90.10					
				7208.27.90.20					
				7208.27.90.30					
				7208.27.90.40					
				7208.36.00.10					
				7208.36.00.20					
				7208.36.00.30					
				7208.36.00.40					
				7208.37.10.10					
				7208.37.10.20					
				7208.37.10.30					
				7208.37.10.40					
				7208.37.90.10					
				7208.37.90.20					
				7208.37.90.30					
				7208.37.90.40					
				7208.38.10.10					
				7208.38.10.20					
				7208.38.10.30					
				7208.38.10.40					
				7208.38.90.10					
				7208.38.90.20					
				7208.38.90.30					
				7208.38.90.40					
				7208.39.00.10					
				7208.39.00.20					
				7208.39.00.30					
				7208.39.00.40					
				7208.53.00.10					
				7208.53.00.20					
				7208.53.00.30					
				7208.53.00.40					
				7208.54.00.10					
				7208.54.00.20					
				7208.54.00.30					
				7208.54.00.40					
				7208.90.00.00					
				7211.13.00.00					
				7211.14.00.90					
				7211.19.10.00					
				7211.19.90.10					
				7211.19.90.90					
				7211.90.10.00					
				7211.90.90.90					
				7225.20.00.91					
				7225.20.00.92					
				7225.30.10.00					
				7225.30.90.00					
				7225.40.10.10					
				7225.40.10.20					
				7225.40.10.30					
				7225.40.10.40					
				7225.40.20.10					
				7225.40.20.20					
				7225.40.20.30					
				7225.40.20.40					
				7225.40.90.11					
				7225.40.90.19					
				7225.40.90.21					
				7225.40.90.91					
				7225.40.90.92					
				7225.40.90.93					
				7225.40.90.94					
				7225.99.00.90					
				7226.20.00.91					
				7226.20.00.92					
				7226.91.10.00					
				7226.91.90.20					
				7226.91.90.30					
				7226.91.90.40					
				7226.91.90.90					
				7226.99.90.00					

	Goods	A/C	Country	Disposition	Tariff Classification	Initiation date	Preliminary margin	Final margin	Quantity dumped (%)	Date of Tribunal finding
129	Cold-rolled steel sheet	A	BR	FN/CN	7209.15.00.10	2001.03.12	14.34	10.71	18.53	2001.10.09
			TW		7209.17.10.20		31.10	28.71	12.10	
			CN		7209.18.91.30		9.98	17.99	13.04	
			IT		7209.28.00.10		31.10	69.14	1.81	
			KR		7209.15.00.20		30.95	68.64	18.48	
			LU		7209.17.10.30		8.95	2.47	0.63	
			MK		7209.18.99.10		12.86	14.67	0.65	
			MY		7209.28.00.20		23.12	69.14	0.87	
			ZA		7209.15.00.30		31.10	33.97	3.05	
					7209.17.91.10					
					7209.18.99.20					
					7209.28.00.30					
					7209.16.10.10					
					7209.17.91.20					
					7209.18.99.30					
					7209.90.00.90					
					7209.16.10.20					
					7209.17.91.30					
					7209.25.00.10					
					7211.23.10.00					
					7209.16.10.30					
					7209.17.99.10					
					7209.25.00.20					
					7211.23.90.00					
					7209.16.91.10					
					7209.17.99.20					
					7209.25.00.30					
					7211.29.10.00					
					7209.16.91.20					
					7209.17.99.30					
					7209.26.00.10					
					7211.29.90.00					
					7209.16.91.30					
					7209.18.10.10					
					7209.26.00.20					
					7211.90.10.00					
					7209.16.99.10					
					7209.18.10.20					
					7209.26.00.30					
					7211.90.90.90					
					7209.16.99.20					
					7209.18.10.30					
					7209.27.00.10					
					9959.00.00					
					7209.16.99.30					
					7209.18.91.10					
					7209.27.00.20					
					7209.17.10.10					
					7209.18.91.20					
					7209.27.00.30					
130	Leather safety footwear	A	CN	FI/CD	6403.40.00.10	2001.06.15	31.40	39.4	90.90	2001.12.27
					6403.40.00.20					
					6403.40.00.90					
131	Fresh tomatoes	A	US	FN/CN	0702.00.99.10	2001.11.09	37.0	26.0	87.00	2002.06.26
					0702.00.99.20					
					0702.00.99.90					
132	Automotive laminated windshields	A	CN	FN/CN	7007.21.00.21	2001.12.18	35.0	21.44	45.66	2002.08.30

	Goods	A/C	Country	Disposition	Tariff Classification	Initiation date	Preliminary margin	Final margin	Quantity dumped (%)	Date of Tribunal finding
133	Waterproof footwear and waterproof footwear bottoms	A	HK MC VN	FN/CN	6401.10.19.00 6401.10.20.00 6401.91.19.00 6401.91.20.00 6401.92.91.10 6401.92.91.90 6401.92.92.90 6401.99.21.00 6401.99.29.00 6401.99.30.10 6401.99.30.90 6402.19.90.90 6402.91.00.10 6402.91.00.91 6402.91.00.92 6402.91.00.93 6403.40.00.10 6403.91.00.10 6403.91.00.91 6403.91.00.92 6403.91.00.93 6404.11.99.90 6404.19.90.20 6404.19.90.91 6404.19.90.92 6404.19.90.93	2002.04.16				2003.01.07
134	Xanthates	A	CN	FI/CD	2930.10.10.10 2930.10.10.20 2930.10.10.90 2930.10.90.00	2002.06.21	45	44.7	100.00	2003.03.04
135	Carbon steel pipe fittings	A	CN	FI/CD	7307.99.99.11 7307.99.99.19	2002.12.18	79	147	100.00	2003.07.16
136	Steel, structural tubing	A	KR TR ZA	FI/CD	7306.30.10.23 7306.30.10.33 7306.30.90.23 7306.30.90.29 7306.30.90.33 7306.50.00.30 7306.60.90.12 7306.60.90.22 7306.60.90.29	2003.06.05	44.0 7.8 22.6	89.0 17.5 55.4	100.00 67.90 100.00	2003.12.23
137	Certain hot-rolled carbon steel plate	A	BG CZ RO	FI/CD	7208.51.91.10 7208.51.91.91 7208.51.91.92 7208.51.91.93 7208.51.91.94 7208.51.91.95 7208.51.99.10 7208.51.99.91 7208.51.99.92 7208.51.99.93 7208.51.99.94 7208.51.99.95 7208.52.90.10 7208.52.90.91 7208.52.90.92 7208.52.90.93 7208.52.90.94 7208.52.90.95	2003.06.13	74.6 74.6 53.2	74.6 74.6 52.6	100.00 100.00 100.00	2004.01.09
138	Wood venetian blinds and slats	A	CN MX	FI/CD* FI/CD* * FN/CN regarding blinds	4421.90.30.00 4421.90.40.40 4421.90.90.50 4421.90.90.99	2003.11.21	120.0 120.0	28.0 28.0	100.00 76.00	2004.06.18
139	Stainless steel wire	A A C A A A	CH IN IN KR TW US	FI/CD T/C FI/CD FI/CD T/C FI/CD	7223.00.11.00 7223.00.19.00 7223.00.20.00	2003.11.21	108.0 – 0.2 108.0 108.0 100.0	181.0 – 0.2 181.0 – 165.0	100.00 – 100.00 100.00 – 99.50	2004.07.30
140	Certain steel fuel tanks	A	CN TW	FN/CN	8708.99.93.90	2003.12.19	39.4 83.4	96.1 100.0		2004.08.31

	Goods	A/C	Country	Disposition	Tariff Classification	Initiation date	Preliminary margin	Final margin	Quantity dumped (%)	Date of Tribunal finding
141	Frozen self-rising pizza	A	US	FN/CN	1901.20.13.20 1901.20.15.20	2004.01.02	39.4	28.7	97.3	2004.08.18
142	Outdoor barbecues	A&C	CN	T/C	7321.11.90.30	2004.04.13	34.6			
143	Carbon steel and stainless steel fasteners	A	CN	FI/CD*	7318.11.00.00	2004.04.28	52	71.95	98.23	2005.01.07
		C	CN	FI/CD*	7318.12.00.00					
		C	CN	T/C**(Trib)	7318.14.00.00					
		A	TW	FI/CD*	7318.15.90.00		64	68.94	97.58	
		A	TW	FI/CD**	7318.16.00.00		64	68.94	97.58	
		C	TW	T/C						
				* regarding carbon steel screws ** regarding stainless steel screws						
144	Laminate flooring	A	AT	T/C	4411.19.90.90	2004.10.04	4.7			2005.06.16
		A	BE	T/C			6.6			
		A&C	CN	FI/CD			26.6/2.01	7.8/3.0		
		A	DE	T/C			2.2			
		A	FR	FI/CD			7.5	7.0		
		A	LU	T/C			–			
		A	PL	T/C			4.0			
145	Grain corn	A&C	US	FN/CN	1005.90.00.11 1005.90.00.12 1005.90.00.13 1005.90.00.14 1005.90.00.19 1005.90.00.99 1104.23.00.00	2005.09.16	Dumping 24.4% (or US$ 0.58/ bushel) + Subsidy amount of US$ 0.71/ bushel	Dumping 26% (or US$ 0.60/ bushel) + Subsidy amount of US$ 0.45/ bushel	Dumping 99% Subsidizing 100%	2006.04.18
146	Cross-linked polyethylene tubing	A	US	I/E						

Code	Explanation
A	Dumping investigation, anti-dumping duty
C	Subsidy investigation, countervailing duty
I/E	Investigation underway
T/C	Investigation terminated prior to final determination phase
U/E	Undertaking accepted, investigation suspended
UT/FE	Undertaking accepted, later terminated and investigation resumed
UX/EX	Undertaking accepted, now expired
FN/CN	Finding by Canadian International Trade Tribunal (CITT): no injury
FI/CD	Finding by CITT: injury; duties apply
FR/CA	Finding by CITT: injury; now rescinded
Country	See list of country codes on the next page
%	Margins of dumping are expressed as a percentage of normal value

Country codes

AR	Argentina	GB	United Kingdom	PH	Philippines
AT	Austria	GR	Greece	PL	Poland
AU	Australia	HK	Hong Kong (China)	PT	Portugal
BE	Belgium	HU	Hungary	PR	Puerto Rico
BG	Bulgaria	IN	India	RO	Romania
BR	Brazil	ID	Indonesia	RU	Russian Federation
CH	Switzerland	IE	Ireland	SA	Saudi Arabia
CL	Chile	IT	Italy	SE	Sweden
CN	China	JP	Japan	SI	Slovenia
CS	Serbia and Montenegro	KR	Republic of Korea	SK	Slovakia
CU	Cuba	LT	Lithuania	SG	Singapore
CY	Cyprus	LU	Luxembourg	TR	Turkey
CZ	Czech Republic	LV	Latvia	TH	Thailand
DE	Germany	MC	Macao (China)	TW	Taiwan Province (China)
DK	Denmark	MD	Moldova, Republic of	UA	Ukraine
EC	European Communities (AT BE DE DK ES FI FR GB GR IE IT LU NL PT SE)	MK	Macedonia, The former Yugoslav Rep. of	US	United States
		MT	Malta	VE	Venezuela
EE	Estonia	MX	Mexico	VN	Viet Nam
ES	Spain	MY	Malaysia	YU	Yugoslavia (This code is now obsolete. Refer to CS)
EU	European Union (AT BE CY CZ DE DK EE ES FI FR HU GB GR IE IT LU LV LT MT NL PL PT SE SI SK)	NL	Netherlands		
		NO	Norway	ZA	South Africa
FI	Finland	NZ	New Zealand		
FR	France				

APPENDIX II

Abbreviated example of dumping/subsidizing initiation: certain copper pipe fittings

Ottawa, 8 June 2006

Statement of reasons[1]

Decision. The President of the Canada Border Services Agency initiated an investigation on 8 June 2006, respecting the alleged injurious dumping of certain copper pipe fittings originating in or exported from the United States of America, the Republic of Korea and China, and the alleged injurious subsidization of certain copper pipe fittings originating in or exported from China.

Summary. On 25 April 2006, the Canada Border Services Agency (CBSA) received a complaint from Cello Products Inc. (Cello) of Cambridge, Ontario, concerning the alleged injurious dumping and subsidizing. CBSA notified the Governments of the United States, the Republic of Korea, and China that a properly documented complaint concerning the subject goods had been received. The complainant provides evidence that the subject goods have been dumped and that copper pipe fittings from China have been subsidized. Further, the evidence discloses a reasonable indication that the dumping and subsidizing have caused injury and are threatening to cause injury to the Canadian industry producing these goods. CBSA will extend developing country status to China for purposes of the subsidy portion of this investigation. Therefore, China is eligible for the higher insignificance (amount of subsidy) and negligibility (volume of subsidized goods) thresholds for the termination of a subsidy investigation involving a developing country.

Interested parties

The complainant, Cello, is the major Canadian producer of certain copper pipe fittings. CBSA has identified 43 potential exporters of the subject goods from customs import documentation and 77 potential importers of the subject goods.

For the purpose of this investigation, the subject goods are defined as:

> Solder joint pressure pipe fittings and solder joint drainage, waste and vent pipe fittings, made of cast copper alloy, wrought copper alloy or wrought copper, for use in heating, plumbing, air conditioning and refrigeration applications, originating in or exported from the United States of America, the Republic of Korea and China. The subject goods are properly classified in chapter 74 of the Customs Tariff.

---

1   The following is a summary of this statement of reasons. The authors have edited significant detailed information in the cause of brevity. For the complete statement of reasons in this case please contact:

Canada Border Services Agency
Anti-Dumping and Countervailing Directorate
SIMA Registry and Disclosure Unit
100 Metcalfe Street, 11th Floor
Ottawa, Ontario K1A 0L8
Canada

Like goods	Like goods, in relation to any other goods, are goods that are identical in all respects or, in the absence of identical goods, are goods of which the uses and other characteristics closely resemble those of the other goods. Copper pipe fittings compete directly with and have the same end uses as the subject goods imported from the named countries. The goods produced in Canada and the subject goods are completely substitutable. Therefore, CBSA has concluded that copper pipe fittings produced by the Canadian industry constitute like goods to the subject goods and that the subject goods comprise a single class of goods.
The Canadian market	Cello provided confidential data on sales of like goods from 2002 to 2005 and for the periods July to December 2004 and 2005. As Cello and Bow are the only manufacturers in Canada it is not possible to provide the companies' Canadian sales in this public document without divulging confidential information. CBSA's analysis of import data appears to support the complainant's claims that imports of subject goods from the Republic of Korea and China have been increasing and are substantial in nature. CBSA's analysis of import data for the United States shows a marginal decline from 2002 through 2005, but also discloses an increase between the first quarters of 2005 and 2006. The anti-dumping investigation will allow CBSA to refine its estimate of import data with respect to all three of the named countries.
Evidence of dumping – normal valves	The complainant alleges that certain copper pipe fittings from the named countries have been injuriously dumped into Canada. The complainant was unable to obtain information on domestic selling prices of the subject goods in the United States, the Republic of Korea or China. However, Cello indicated that in the United States market it routinely competes with the named exporters, and that it considers its own selling prices in the United States to be a reasonable indication of the selling prices of the named United States exporters in their domestic market. Given Cello's knowledge of the copper pipe fitting market and presence in the United States market, CBSA considers Cello's selling prices as an acceptable estimate for establishing normal values in the United States. With respect to the Republic of Korea, Cello estimated normal values for 10 benchmark products based on its costs of production at the end of its 2005 fiscal year (31 March 2005). CBSA considers it reasonable to use the complainant's estimate of cost of production. For China, Cello estimated normal values for 15 benchmark products as of 31 March 2005. CBSA considers it reasonable for the complainant to use its own cost of production with a downward adjustment to reflect lower wage rates in China. However, CBSA concluded that as GSA expenses would also be lower in China than in Canada, it would be more appropriate to estimate such expenses based on the 2004 financial results for the Korean manufacturer. On the basis that Cello's usage of a 5% profit was similar to the amount used to estimate normal values for the Republic of Korea, CBSA accepted Cello's estimate of 5% for purposes of estimating normal values for China.
Export prices	Cello used its own selling prices to a Canadian customer to estimate the export prices of subject goods from the named exporters in the United States. In its own determination of export price, CBSA analysed actual import data from customs documentation in 2005 and estimated the export price as the value on the invoice, less freight costs (based on the complainant's estimates of freight costs). For Korean and Chinese products, CBSA also analysed actual import data from customs documentation in 2005. CBSA was able to identify benchmark products and accordingly it estimated export prices for these products.
Margin of dumping	CBSA's estimated margins of dumping for the United States for the 14 benchmark products ranged from 2.3% to 196%, expressed as a percentage of export price. The overall weighted average margin of dumping of 20.2% is held

to be CBSA's estimated margin of dumping. The CBSA estimated margins of dumping for eight of the nine benchmark products from the Republic of Korea as one of the benchmark products had not been dumped. CBSA's estimated margins of dumping for the eight benchmark products ranged from 1.3% to 187.3%, expressed as a percentage of export price. The overall weighted average margin of dumping found for the eight benchmark fittings, 96.1%, is held to be CBSA's estimated margin of dumping. CBSA's estimated margins of dumping for the five Chinese benchmark products ranged from 20.5% to 109.4%, expressed as a percentage of export price. The overall weighted average margin of dumping found for the five benchmark cast fittings, 48.3%, is held to be CBSA's estimated margin of dumping.

The information available indicates that the volume of dumped goods from the United States and from the Republic of Korea and China would not be considered negligible and that the margin of dumping would not be regarded as insignificant.

Evidence of subsidizing

The complainant alleges that the subject goods from China are being subsidized. The alleged subsidies include:

❑ Special economic zone (SEZ) incentives.

❑ Grants provided for export performance and employing common workers.

❑ Preferential loans.

❑ Loan guarantees by the Government of China.

❑ Income tax credits, refunds and exemptions:

– Reduced corporate tax rate for export-oriented enterprises;

– Exemption or reduction of corporate income tax during designated start-up period;

– Income tax refund of amounts further invested in SEZs;

– Exemption/reduction in local income tax for SEZ enterprises.

❑ Relief from duties and taxes on materials and machinery.

❑ Reductions in land use fees.

❑ Purchase of goods from State-owned enterprises.

❑ Zhejiang Province – Strategic Plan for Local Copper Processing Industry. In addition, CBSA has also identified grants.

Based on the data available to CBSA with respect to these programmes, it was considered reasonable to conclude that the named subsidy programmes are available to exporters of copper pipe fittings in China. In examining these programmes, CBSA will request information from the various levels of the Government of China and from exporters and manufacturers of the subject goods to determine whether these programmes confer countervailable benefits on the subject goods.

Estimated amount of subsidies

In the absence of available information, the complainant has not been able to determine the value of the alleged subsidies on a per-unit basis, although these programmes are believed to significantly lower the cost of production and the selling prices of the subject goods exported to Canada. CBSA has estimated the amount of subsidies provided to copper pipe fitting manufacturers in China as follows: 'The overall weighted average margin of dumping and amount of export-contingent subsidy is estimated to be equal to 48.3%, when expressed as a percentage of export price. An additional amount for domestic subsidies is estimated to be equal to 17.4%, expressed as a percentage of export price. CBSA estimates that 100% of the subject goods have been dumped and/or have benefited from export-contingent subsidies, and that 100% of the subject goods have benefited from domestic subsidies. CBSA is, therefore, satisfied that the estimated amount of subsidy and volume of subsidized goods are well above the thresholds outlined above'.

Evidence of injury

The complainant alleges that the subject goods have been or are being dumped and subsidized, and that such dumping and subsidizing has caused injury or is threatening to cause injury to the production of copper pipe fittings in Canada. Based on its analysis of the data, CBSA considers the estimated margins of dumping and estimated amounts of subsidy to have had a significant injurious impact on Canadian producers of copper pipe fittings. Following an examination of all the relevant factors including exchange rates, raw material pricing and substitutability of non-subject goods, CBSA has not identified any significant non-dumping/subsidizing factors that have had a materially negative impact on the Canadian industry.

Conclusion

CBSA is satisfied that the complainant has sufficiently demonstrated that the injury it has suffered is due to the dumping and subsidizing of subject goods imported into Canada. CBSA considers reasonable the complainant's position that if the dumping and subsidizing of certain copper pipe fittings from the United States, the Republic of Korea and China is not rectified, Canadian producers will continue to suffer from price erosion and price suppression, lost sales, declining market share, reduced profits and profit margins, and reduced employment. Finally, CBSA is satisfied that the information provided in the complaint has established a reasonable indication that the dumping and subsidizing is also threatening to cause injury. Consequently, a dumping investigation and subsidy investigation were initiated on 8 June 2006 in respect of this matter.

Scope of the investigation

CBSA will conduct an investigation to determine whether the subject goods have been dumped and subsidized. All parties have been clearly advised of CBSA's information requirements and the time frames for providing their responses. On 5 June 2006, consultations were conducted between Canadian government officials and representatives of China, in accordance with article 13.1 of the WTO Subsidies Agreement.

Future action

The Tribunal will conduct a preliminary inquiry to determine whether the evidence discloses a reasonable indication that the dumping and subsidizing of the goods has caused or is threatening to cause injury to the Canadian industry. The Tribunal must make its decision within 60 days after the date of the initiation of the investigation, by 8 August 2006. If the Tribunal concludes that the evidence does not disclose a reasonable indication of injury to the Canadian industry, the investigation will be terminated. If the Tribunal finds that the evidence discloses a reasonable indication of injury to the Canadian industry and the ongoing CBSA investigation reveals that the goods have been dumped and/or subsidized, CBSA will make a preliminary determination of dumping and/or subsidizing within 90 days after the date of the investigation initiation, by 6 September 2006. Where circumstances warrant, this period may be extended to 135 days from the date of the initiation of the investigation.

Undertakings

After a preliminary determination, an exporter may submit a written undertaking to revise its selling prices to Canada so that the margin of dumping or the injury caused by the dumping is eliminated. Similarly, foreign governments may submit written undertakings to eliminate the subsidy on the goods exported or to eliminate the injurious effect of the subsidy, by limiting the amount of the subsidy or the quantity of goods exported to Canada. Alternatively, exporters with the written consent of their government may undertake to revise their selling prices, so that the amount of the subsidy or the injurious effect of the subsidy is eliminated. If an undertaking were to be accepted, the investigation and the collection of provisional duties would be suspended.

APPENDIX III

Abbreviated example of dumping or countervailing final determination: laminate flooring

Ottawa, 17 May 2005

Statement of reasons[1]

Concerning the making of a final determination with respect to the dumping of

Certain laminate flooring originating in or exported from China and France

and the making of a final determination with respect to the subsidizing of

Certain laminate flooring originating in or exported from China

and the termination of the investigation with respect to the dumping of

Certain laminate flooring originating in or exported from Austria, Belgium, Germany and Poland

Decision

On 17 May 2005, the President of CBSA made a final determination of dumping respecting laminate flooring in thickness ranging from 5.5 mm to 13 mm (other than laminate hardwood flooring where the hardwood component exceeds 2 mm in thickness) originating in or exported from the China and France, and made a final determination of subsidizing of such product originating in or exported from China. On the same date, pursuant to paragraph 41(1)(b) of SIMA, the President terminated the dumping investigation of such product originating in or exported from Austria, Belgium, Germany and Poland.

Summary of events. On 4 October 2004, the President of CBSA initiated a dumping investigation with respect to certain laminate flooring from Austria, Belgium, China, France, Germany, Luxembourg and Poland, initiated a subsidy investigation pursuant to subsection 31(1) of SIMA, with respect to these products from China; and did not initiate a dumping investigation with respect to these products from Spain as the likely volume of dumped goods from Spain was considered negligible.

On 3 December 2004, the Tribunal made a preliminary determination that the evidence disclosed a reasonable indication that the dumping and subsidizing of the subject goods had caused injury to the Canadian industry.

---

1   The following is a summary of this statement of reasons. The authors have edited significant detailed information in the cause of brevity. For the complete statement of reasons in this case please contact:

Canada Border Services Agency
Anti-Dumping and Countervailing Directorate
SIMA Registry and Disclosure Unit
100 Metcalfe Street, 11th Floor
Ottawa, Ontario K1A 0L8
Canada

On 17 December 2004, the President made the decision to extend the 90-day period for making a preliminary decision in the investigation to 135 days, because of the complexity and novelty of the issues presented and the number of persons involved in the investigation.

On 16 February 2005, the President made a preliminary determination of dumping respecting certain laminate flooring originating in or exported from Austria, Belgium, China, France, Germany and Poland, and a preliminary determination of subsidizing of such product originating in or exported from China. The President also terminated the dumping investigation of such product originating in or exported from Luxembourg as the volume of dumped imports from that country was considered negligible.

Interested parties

The complainant, Uniboard Surfaces Inc. (Uniboard), is the only known Canadian manufacturer of laminate flooring. CBSA had identified 91 known or possible exporters of the subject goods and 133 potential importers of the subject goods.

Given the unusually large number of exporters, CBSA calculated margins of dumping in relation to the largest percentage of goods that could reasonably be investigated. Ten exporters from the named countries accounted for over 70% of the value of all laminate flooring imports into Canada in this period. These exporters also accounted for over 60% of the total exports of subject goods from their own individual country. CBSA used the above criteria and sent a dumping Request for Information (RFI) at the initiation of the investigation to those 10 exporters (mandatory respondents).

All other exporters of subject goods were advised that they could ask for an RFI from CBSA and participate in the dumping investigation. However, these other exporters were also advised that due to the number of mandatory respondents and the time constraints, CBSA could not guarantee that a voluntary response to the dumping RFI would be taken into consideration for the investigation. During the investigation, CBSA received six voluntary dumping responses from exporters located in China and one located in the United States. All voluntary responses were reviewed for purposes of the final determination.

Product definition

For the purpose of this phase of the investigation, the subject goods were defined as:

> Laminate flooring in thickness ranging from 5.5 mm to 13 mm (other than laminate hardwood flooring where the hardwood component exceeds 2 mm in thickness) originating in or exported from Austria, Belgium, China, France, Germany and Poland.

Dumping investigation

Normal values are generally based on the domestic selling prices of the goods in the country of export, or on the total cost of the goods (cost of production, administrative, selling and all other costs) plus an amount for profit.

The export price of goods shipped to Canada is generally the lesser of the exporter's selling price or the importer's purchase price, pursuant to section 24 of SIMA.

With respect to each of those exporters whose company-specific information was verified and used for the final determination, margins of dumping were determined by subtracting the total export price from the total normal value of all of the goods shipped to Canada during the POI, including any individual sales that were made at undumped prices.

In determining the margin of dumping at the exporter level, CBSA had recently discontinued the practice of determining a margin of dumping in respect of models or types of product under investigation and the setting of any negative margins of dumping found in respect of a model or type equal to zero (commonly referred to as 'zeroing').

Table 1 – Summary of the results of the dumping investigation

Country	Weighted average
Margin of dumping*	
Austria	0.1% (insignificant)
Belgium	1.0% (insignificant)
China	7.8%
France	7.0%
Germany	1.1% (insignificant)
Poland	0.0% (insignificant)

In making a final determination of dumping in relation to goods imported from a country in the investigation, the President must be satisfied that the subject goods have been dumped and that the margin of dumping is not insignificant. Table 1 indicates that the margin of dumping was not insignificant for China and France. However, there was no dumping of subject goods imported from Poland and the margins of dumping from Austria, Belgium and Germany were insignificant. As a consequence, the investigation against Austria, Belgium, Germany and Poland was terminated.

Representations and other issues regarding dumping

Following the preliminary determination of dumping, CBSA received various written representations from counsel representing exporters and/or manufacturers involved in this investigation.

Denial of an effective right to participate in the investigation. CBSA received written representations from the complainant's counsel alleging that he was denied an effective right to participate in the investigation. It was argued that information was not disclosed in a timely manner and that certain information such as verification reports and internal working papers were not disclosed when they should have been.

As stated in a letter to the complainant's counsel dated 15 April 2005, CBSA acknowledged that there had been some instances where there was a delay in placing information on the exhibit listing but that as a rule, CBSA had provided all counsel with all of the information on a timely basis. With regard to verification reports and internal working papers, CBSA has no plans to disclose this material at this time.

CBSA policy on section 20. Counsel for the complainant provided representations that the CBSA policy on section 20, issued in June 2004, was 'wrong in law and in policy and ought to be reversed.'

CBSA did not find any information during its verification visits of the two largest Chinese exporters nor was any additional information provided to CBSA that would suggest that the Government of China was substantially determining domestic prices of laminate flooring.

CBSA's policy on 'zeroing'. In the SOR issued at the preliminary determination, CBSA invited interested parties to comment on the CBSA policy of zeroing. Counsel for the complainant provided several arguments and stated that the 'decision to abandon the practice of ignoring undumped product is illegal and ought to be reversed'.

CBSA believes its revised practice is consistent with SIMA and with Canada's obligations as a member of WTO.

Testing of transfer prices:. CBSA received written representations from the complainant's counsel concerning transfer prices by producers within vertically integrated corporate groups.

During their on-site verification, CBSA officers ensured that the transfer prices between related parties covered the total cost of the product being transferred, in accordance with SIMA.

Subsidy investigation

Based on the information obtained from the parties and the results of the verification of this information during the investigation, CBSA has determined that the following actionable subsidies exist in China and were used by the Chinese exporters of subject goods during the POI:

Preferential income tax programmes:

❑ Productive foreign invested enterprises (FIEs) scheduled to operate for a period not less than 10 years;

❑ FIEs in industries and sectors where foreign investment is encouraged by the State;

❑ Re-investment of profits by foreign investor;

❑ Enterprises located in special economic zones (SEZs) – excluding the Pudong area of Shanghai;

❑ FIEs located in coastal economic open zones or in the old urban districts of cities where the SEZs or the economic and technology development zones (ETDZs) are located or in any other regions defined by the State council;

❑ Enterprises located in the special economic zone of the Pudong area of Shanghai;

❑ Enterprises located in the western region and other specified locations;

❑ Enterprises operating in the forestry industry.

Relief from duties and taxes on materials and equipment:

❑ Refund of value added tax (VAT) for production of goods using fuel wood and other low-valued wood;

❑ Exemption on tariffs and VAT on imported equipment.

Grants:

❑ Loan interest assistance grant provided to enterprises with loans relating to investments in fast-growth-high-yield plantations;

❑ Grants from development zone management committees under the authority of town governments;

❑ Grants provided to companies newly established in the Pudong new area of Shanghai.

As a result of the investigation, the following programmes identified at preliminary determination have been determined not to have been used by Chinese exporters of subject goods during the POI:

❏ Advanced technology FIEs scheduled to operate for a period not less than 10 years;

❏ FIEs generating income from transferring technologies;

❏ FIEs exporting greater than 70% of production;

❏ Low interest loans to wood processing projects;

❏ Extended loan payback periods which include non-interest bearing grace periods on investments in fast-growth-high-yield plantations.

Table 2 – Summary of the results of the subsidy investigation

Country	Volume of importations (in m²)	Subsidized goods as a percentage of total subject goods imported	Amount of subsidy as a percentage of export price
China	4,736,364	99.8%	3.0%

Representations and other issues regarding subsidy

China's fixed exchange rate. CBSA received representations from the counsel for Uniboard stating that China's maintenance of an artificial exchange rate with the United States dollar is a de facto export subsidy and CBSA should have included this fixed exchange rate programme in its subsidy investigation.

As no new information was provided to CBSA regarding this issue since it was addressed at initiation, CBSA maintains that it is not convinced that the value of the conversion service as provided by the Government of China, or by bodies entrusted to it, would include the underlying value of the currencies being traded. In other words, it is not the rate of exchange *per se* that would be considered as conferring a benefit but, rather, the price charged by the Government in providing the actual currency conversion service.

In addition, no further information was provided by the complainant demonstrating how the granting of the subsidy is contingent, in whole or in part, on export performance in order to support its argument that China's fixed rate exchange system constitutes a de facto export subsidy within the meaning of article 3 of the SCM Agreement.

Subsidy investigation should not be restricted to practices identified by complainant. Counsel for Uniboard also stated that CBSA should not 'restrict its investigation of China's subsidy practices specifically identified by the complainant'. In particular, counsel requested that CBSA review China's banking system.

In conducting its subsidy investigation CBSA did not limit itself to the programmes identified by the complainant. In Part E of its RFI, CBSA asked for information on 'Any other programme not previously addressed' (item F). Any programme identified by the respondents was investigated to determine if it was an actionable subsidy.

Preferential income tax policies provided to foreign invested enterprises. CBSA also received representations from counsel on behalf of exporters and the GPRC arguing that preferential income tax policies provided to FIEs are not specific as FIEs do not constitute a 'particular enterprise' for SIMA purposes.

After considering the arguments above and other similar arguments made by counsel regarding the definition and interpretation of enterprise for SIMA purposes and its relation to FIEs and income tax, CBSA maintained that preferential income tax policies provided to FIEs were specific and constituted an actionable subsidy.

Subsidies based on geographic areas. Another representation received by CBSA from counsel on behalf of exporters argued that SIMA did not contain any provisions that addressed subsidies based on geographic area.

According to subsection 2(7.2) of SIMA, a subsidy is specific where it is limited, in law, to a particular enterprise within the jurisdiction of the authority granting the subsidy. When CBSA considers specificity in relation to subsidies provided to particular geographic or regional locations, it is determined based on the relationship between the enterprises and the granting authority that has jurisdiction over those enterprises. If the granting authority provides the subsidy to all of the enterprises under its jurisdiction, than the subsidy would be considered to be non-specific. However, if the granting authority does not make the subsidy available to all enterprises under its jurisdiction, than the subsidy is considered to be specific as it is limited to a particular enterprise.

Exemption of VAT for wood processing enterprises on purchase of fuel wood. Counsel for the Government of China also raised an issue regarding the specificity of the programme concerning the exemption from VAT for foreign and domestic wood processing enterprises on purchases of fuel wood and other low-value wood used in the production of other goods.

CBSA was of the opinion that this programme was indeed a specific subsidy, in that it was found to be limited, in law, to a particular enterprise. CBSA considered this programme to be limited, in this case, to a group of enterprises that produce 'comprehensively used products' using fuel wood and other low-value wood and sell these 'comprehensively used products' in the domestic market.

CBSA took note of the fact that this preferential VAT policy for enterprises using low-value wood was identified by the Government of China as being a specific subsidy in the subsidy notification that was made for purposes of China's accession to WTO.

Decision

The President was satisfied that certain laminate flooring originating in or exported from China and France had been dumped and that the margins of dumping were not insignificant. Consequently, on 17 May 2005, the President made a final determination of dumping pursuant to paragraph 41(1)(a) of SIMA.

The President was satisfied that certain laminate flooring originating in or exported from China had been subsidized and that the amounts of subsidy were not insignificant. As a result, on 17 May 2005, the President also made a final determination of subsidizing pursuant to paragraph 41(1)(a) of SIMA.

The President was satisfied that certain laminate flooring originating in or exported from Austria, Belgium, Germany and Poland had not been dumped or that the dumping of the subject goods was insignificant. As a result, on 17 May 2005, the President caused this portion of the investigation to be terminated pursuant to paragraph 41(1)(b) of SIMA.

Future action

The provisional period begins on 16 February 2005, and is to end on the date the Tribunal issues its finding. The Tribunal is expected to issue its decision by 16 June 2005. Subject goods imported from China and France during the provisional period will continue to be assessed provisional duty as determined at the time of the preliminary determination of dumping.

As of 17 May 2005, provisional duties will no longer be collected on imports of subject goods originating in or exported from Austria, Belgium, Germany and Poland. The provisional amount of dumping duty that has been collected on goods from these four countries will be returned to the importers in accordance with subsection 8(2) of SIMA.

The Tribunal's inquiry concerning the question of injury to the domestic industry is continuing with respect to China and France. The Tribunal is to issue its decision by 16 June 2005.

If the Tribunal finds that the dumped and/or subsidized goods have not caused injury and do not threaten to cause injury, all proceedings relating to this investigation will be terminated. In this situation, all provisional duty paid or security posted by importers will be returned.

If the Tribunal finds that the dumped and/or subsidized goods have caused injury, the anti-dumping and/or countervailing duty payable on subject goods released from customs during the provisional period will be finalized, pursuant to section 55 of SIMA. Imports released from customs after the date of the Tribunal's finding will be subject to anti-dumping duty equal to the margin of dumping and/or countervailing duty equal to the amount of subsidy. In that event, the importer in Canada shall pay all such duty.

Specific normal values and amounts of subsidy for the subject goods have been provided to the cooperating exporters. Should the Tribunal make an injury finding, these normal values and amounts of subsidy will come into effect the day after the date of the injury finding. Exporters who were not provided with specific normal values will have normal values established by advancing the export price by 9.7% for subject goods originating in or exported from China and 7.0% for subject goods originating in or exported from France. These amounts are based on the overall weighted average margins of dumping determined for mandatory respondents in each of those countries during this investigation.

For exporters that did not respond to the CBSA's subsidy RFI, a countervailing duty amount of 3.54 Chinese Renminbi per square metre will be payable on imports of subject goods originating in China.

Retroactive duty on massive importations   Under certain circumstances, anti-dumping and countervailing duties can be imposed retroactively on subject goods imported into Canada. When the Tribunal conducts its inquiry on material injury to the Canadian industry, it may consider if dumped and/or subsidized goods that were imported close to or after the initiation of the investigation constitute massive importations over a relatively short period of time and have caused injury to the Canadian industry. Should the Tribunal issue a finding that there were recent massive importations of dumped and/or subsidized goods that caused injury, imports of subject goods from China and France released by CBSA in the 90 days proceeding the day of the preliminary determination could be subject to anti-dumping and/or countervailing duty.

APPENDIX IV

Abbreviated example of dumping undertaking: Bingo paper

Ottawa, 27 September 2000

Statement of reasons

Concerning acceptance of an undertaking and suspension of the dumping investigation, pursuant to subsection 49(1) and section 50 of the Special Import Measures Act, with respect to bingo paper, in finished or unfinished form, originating in or exported from the United States of America and produced by or on behalf of Arrow International Inc., its affiliates, successors and assigns.

Decision. The Commissioner, Customs and Revenue has today accepted an undertaking and suspended the investigation respecting the alleged injurious dumping into Canada of bingo paper, in finished or unfinished form, originating in or exported from the United States of America and produced by or on behalf of Arrow International, Inc., its affiliates, successors and assigns.

Summary. On 20 March 2000, a dumping investigation was initiated respecting the alleged injurious dumping into Canada of bingo paper. The investigation was initiated in response to a complaint filed by Bingo Press & Specialty Limited, St Catharines, Ontario. On 15 June 2000, the Commissioner of Customs and Revenue (the President) extended the time period for completing the preliminary investigation to 135 days. Following a preliminary investigation, the Commissioner made a preliminary determination of dumping on 5 July 2000.

On this date, the Commissioner has accepted an undertaking from the exporter Arrow International, Inc., and has suspended the investigation. The undertaking accepted by the Commissioner covers all of the dumped goods and will eliminate the dumping of the subject goods into Canada.

Product definition

For the purpose of this investigation, the subject goods are defined as:

> 'Bingo paper, in finished or unfinished form, originating in or exported from the United States of America and produced by or on behalf of Arrow International, Inc., its affiliates, successors and assigns.'

Canadian industry

The Canadian bingo paper industry comprises companies that produce finished bingo paper from newsprint and companies that produce finished bingo paper from unfinished flat stock. Bingo Press is the predominant Canadian manufacturer of both finished bingo paper and unfinished flat stock produced for subsequent finishing.

Flat stock produced by Bingo Press is further processed into finished bingo paper by Bingo Press, Bingo Vézina, Montréal, Quebec, and British Confectionery Co. Ltd, Mount Pearl, Newfoundland. On 30 March 2000, BK Entertainment, the parent company of Bingo Press, announced the acquisition of Bingo Vézina.

Finished bingo paper is produced from flat stock by Servi-Jeux, Enr., Montréal North, Quebec, and by Arrow Canada, Calgary. Both companies use flat stock produced in the United States of America by Arrow and imported by Arrow Canada. Arrow Canada has also announced plans to begin producing flat stock as well as finished bingo paper in Brampton, Ontario, in autumn 2000.

Canadian market

During the previous decade the bingo industry had been in a growth stage. Bingo paper manufacturers across North America experienced significant increases in sales volumes as printing technology improved over the years. However, the bingo paper industry has now reached a plateau in North America and is operating in a mature market.

Since bingo paper is perceived as a commodity product, price is the major determining factor for switching from one supplier to another. In many cases, purchasers of bingo paper will switch suppliers on the basis of a difference of mere cents in price per 1,000 bingo faces. This is of particular significance in Ontario and Quebec, where commercial bingo halls are in operation and there is a greater incentive to lower operating costs. Ontario, with 38% of Canada's population, has a market for bingo paper which is considerably larger than in the other provinces.

The investigation. The investigation covered all subject goods shipped to Canada by Arrow from 1 March 1999 to 29 February 2000. Responses to the's requests for information were received from Arrow and Arrow Canada, and were verified at the premises of these companies.

Results of the investigation

Normal value. Where Arrow had profitable sales of like goods to more than one domestic customer, normal values were estimated based on the weighted average selling price of the like goods sold to customers in the United States of America.

Where Arrow's domestic sales were not profitable or where sales of like goods were to only one customer, normal values were estimated based on the production cost of the goods, plus amounts for administrative, selling and all other costs and an amount for profit.

Export price. The goods were generally sold to Arrow Canada on a delivered basis. Since Arrow Canada is a related company, the CCRA tested the reliability of the export prices. Export prices were estimated on the basis of the importer's resale prices in Canada, less all costs, charges and expenses incurred by the exporter in preparing, shipping and exporting the goods, all general, selling and administrative costs incurred by the importer and an amount for profit. Where export prices were estimated, an additional amount was deducted to account for the cost of processing in Canada. With respect to a limited number of resales in Canada, a further deduction was made to reflect the value of bingo equipment included in the selling price of the bingo paper.

Margins of dumping. All bingo paper exported by Arrow to Canada during the period of investigation was reviewed. Of these goods, 92% were found to be dumped. The estimated margins of dumping ranged from 0.1 to 98.9%, expressed as a percentage of normal value. The weighted average margin of dumping is 43.5%, expressed as a percentage of normal value.

Undertaking discussions. After the preliminary determination of the margin of dumping was made, Arrow's counsel indicated that it was interested in pursuing the possibility of concluding these proceedings by way of undertaking.

The CCRA received an undertaking offer from Arrow on 30 August 2000. The terms of the undertaking will ensure the elimination of the margin of dumping of the subject goods. Since Arrow Canada is affiliated with Arrow, the terms of the undertaking will also ensure that Arrow Canada's resale pricing in Canada will be at a level which will avoid any secondary dumping.

Decision. Based on the information obtained during the investigation, the CCRA is satisfied that the undertaking will account for all or substantially all of the dumped goods and will eliminate the dumping. Accordingly, the President has accepted the undertaking and has suspended further action in the investigation.

The CCRA will monitor imports into Canada of the subject goods to verify that such sales are made in accordance with the terms of the undertaking.

Contacts in the Canada Border Services Agency and the Canadian International Trade Tribunal

CANADA BORDER SERVICES AGENCY

Anti-Dumping and Countervailing Directorate

100 Metcalfe Street

Ottawa, Ontario, Canada K1A 0L8

Tel: +1-613 9547269

               +1-613 954 7390 (industrial products)

               +1-613 954 7390 (consumer products)

               +1-613 954 7349 (operational policy)

Fax: +1-613 9579723

Internet: www.cbsa-asfc.gc.ca/

CANADIAN INTERNATIONAL TRADE TRIBUNAL

Standard Life Centre

15th Floor, 333 Laurier Avenue West

Ottawa, Ontario, Canada K1A 0G7

Internet: www.citt.gc.ca

Secretary of the Tribunal:

    Tel: +1-613 990 2452

    Fax: +1-613 990 2439

    Email: secretary@citt-tcce.gc.ca

General inquiries:

    Tel: +1-613 990 2452

    Fax: +1-613 990 2439

Sample abbreviated exporter request for information

Information requested under the **Special Import Measures Act**
concerning Canada's dumping investigation

Instructions

Purpose of the RFI

RELEVANT PERIODS

The Canada Border Services Agency (CBSA) requires sales and costing information on all subject goods imported into Canada during the period of investigation (POI). CBSA requires sales and costing information for all identical or similar goods sold in the country of export during the profitability analysis period (PAP).

1.   This RFI specifies the information and documents required from your firm for the purpose of this investigation. CBSA will use the information to determine whether or not goods shipped to Canada by your company during the period of investigation (POI) were dumped. Accordingly, the RFI is intended to elicit the information required for purposes of determining normal values and export prices of subject goods in accordance with the provisions of the Special Import Measures Act (SIMA). If you decide not to provide the information or submit an incomplete response, duties may be based on the highest estimated margin of dumping found during the investigation.

2.   In order to determine the export prices and, where necessary, to construct a cost based normal value for the exported goods, CBSA requires detailed sales and costing information concerning the subject goods imported into Canada during the POI. In order to determine the normal values of the goods, CBSA requires detailed sales and costing information concerning your sales of like goods made in your domestic market during the profitability analysis period (PAP).

Confidential and non-confidential information

3.   SIMA provides for the disclosure of non-confidential information and, under certain circumstances, confidential information.

Disclosure of confidential information

SIMA states that information designated as confidential shall not be disclosed by any public servant to any business competitor or rival of any person to whose business or affairs the information relates. However, SIMA requires the President of CBSA to disclose confidential information submitted by a party to independent counsel for other parties in that proceeding or a subsequent related proceeding.

The President shall, on written request, disclose confidential information to counsel for any party to a proceeding, subject to any conditions that the President considers reasonably necessary to ensure that the information will not be disclosed to any person by counsel in any manner that is calculated or likely to make it available to any party or business competitor. As well, there is a limitation on such disclosure when the President is satisfied that the disclosure might result in material harm to the business or affairs of the person who designated the information as confidential.

Independent counsel will have to provide a Disclosure Undertaking when requesting the disclosure of confidential information. By signing a disclosure undertaking, counsel agrees:

❑ To use the information exclusively for duties performed in respect of the subject proceeding;

❑ Not to divulge the information except to personnel of the Anti-Dumping and Countervailing Directorate;

❑ To protect the information in a specified manner;

❑ Not to reproduce the information unless prior approval is provided by the President;

❑ To destroy the information on completion of the proceeding, and notify CBSA of the destruction of the information; and

❑ To report any violations or suspected violations of a Disclosure Undertaking to the President.

Under SIMA, 'counsel' includes any person, other than a director, servant or employee of the party, who acts in the proceedings on behalf of the party and is not limited to legal counsel. A party to a proceeding conducted by the President under SIMA is a person who is directly interested in a proceeding and who actively participates in the proceeding.

Certain information and documents provided to CBSA during the proceedings may be provided to the Canadian International Trade Tribunal, any Court in Canada or a bi-national or WTO Panel to permit them to fulfil their responsibilities under Canadian law, NAFTA Panel Rules or the applicable WTO Agreements. Such information submitted to these bodies is then subject to the rules of procedure of the particular body in respect to the treatment of confidential information.

Confidential and non-confidential submissions

4.   Your complete response to the RFI (the original) along with all of the attachments and supporting documents will constitute your confidential submission. This submission must be clearly marked 'CONFIDENTIAL' on the cover and on each page of the submission and all attachments.

If your company submits confidential information to CBSA, and the requirement for non-confidential submissions are not fulfilled, your information *cannot* be taken into account in these proceedings and the information *cannot* be used in reaching a decision pursuant to the Special Import Measures Act.

The Act requires that confidential information submitted to CBSA be accompanied by a non-confidential edited (public) version of the information.

The disclosure provisions of the Act stipulate that any non-confidential information submitted by your company shall be provided to interested parties upon request.

Non-confidential edited version or non-confidential summary

5.   Your non-confidential submission must include both of the following:

(i)   A statement which identifies the information that you want to remain confidential together with an explanation which explains why the information is considered confidential; and

(ii)   A non-confidential edited version or non-confidential summary of the information designated as confidential in sufficient detail to convey a reasonable understanding of the substance of the information.

Statement which identifies confidential information and accompanying explanation

6.   Where confidential information has been removed from your non-confidential submission, you must provide a **statement** which identifies the information you want to remain confidential together with an **explanation** which explains why the information is considered confidential.

A **comprehensive** statement(s) and accompanying explanation(s) may be provided for each part of the RFI. However, in any case where information designated as confidential is not obviously so by its very nature, CBSA requires a detailed reason for the designation in that instance.

Non-confidential edited version

7.   Generally, a non-confidential edited version contains the same amount of text or information as the confidential response with specific confidential details or data removed. As previously stated, it must be in sufficient detail to provide a reasonable understanding of the confidential information removed.

As an example, the confidential response to a question may state: 'The selling price of model ABC to our Canadian distributor during the POI was US\$ 25.99 per unit'. The non-confidential edited version of this response may be: 'The selling price of model ABC to our Canadian distributor during the POI was US\$ ____'. In this case, the text indicates the nature of the information that has been deleted.

Non-confidential summary

8.   **As an alternative** to providing a non-confidential edited version of the confidential information, **you may submit a non-confidential summary**. A non-confidential summary consists of a detailed description which describes the nature of the confidential information removed.

Using the above example, a non-confidential summary might be as follows:

'Appendix 1 is a listing of exports to Canada during the POI. It contains 20 pages and lists the following column data by transaction line: importer name; shipment date; invoice number; invoice date; quantities; gross invoice value; and net selling price. A one-page sample of this listing is attached'.

One-page sample of export sales listing

1	2	3	4	5	6	7
IMPTR	DATSHIP	INVNUM	INVDATE	QUANTITY	EXTSP	NETSP
	96/11/05	14064555	96/11/05			
	97/02/14	14179020	97/02/14			
	97/02/14	14179020	97/02/14			
	97/02/14	14179020	97/02/14			

As an example, a non-confidential summary of commercial documentation (i.e. commercial invoice, PO, sales confirmation, payment remittance etc.) would normally *be accompanied by at least one sample of the complete commercial documentation for one transaction (i.e. with the confidential data removed)*.

Please also ensure that the non-confidential summary contains a listing of all the attachments, exhibits and appendices described in a non-confidential manner.

Where a non-confidential edited version or a non-confidential summary cannot be provided

9.   There may be circumstances where, due to the nature of the information, you conclude that a non-confidential edited version or non-confidential summary of confidential information cannot be provided. In these circumstances, you must provide a written statement that a non-confidential edited version or summary cannot be provided together with an explanation of why it cannot be provided.

Similarly, there may be circumstances where, due to the nature of the information, you conclude that a non-confidential edited version or non-confidential summary would disclose facts that you wish to keep confidential. Again, in these circumstances, you must provide a written statement that a non-confidential edited version or non-confidential summary would disclose such facts together with an explanation which justifies the making of any such statement.

Non-confidential designation

10.   The non-confidential copy of your submission should be clearly marked 'NON-CONFIDENTIAL' on the cover and on each page.

If you decide that your entire submission is non-confidential, each page of your original response should be clearly marked 'NON-CONFIDENTIAL' and must be accompanied, in your covering letter, by a statement to the effect that you do not wish to designate any information in your submission as confidential. Information which is not designated as either confidential or non-confidential will be treated by CBSA as being non-confidential.

Due date for response

11.   Your response must be received by CBSA no later than the due date shown on the covering page of this RFI. If your company does not fully respond

to this RFI, duties assessed on subject goods exported by your firm may be based on the highest estimated margin of dumping found during the investigation as explained in item 1 above.

Required format of information submitted

12.   Replies to questions should be as specific as possible and clearly reflect the existing situation. It is essential to submit a complete and detailed response to each question. Where a question does not apply to your company, an appropriate explanation must be given as to why it does not apply. Note that 'Not Applicable' or an answer which only refers to an exhibit or an attachment does not constitute an appropriate response.

13.   When responding, the relevant question should be copied from the RFI and then followed by the full response to the question. Your submission should be in typewritten format and should:

❑ Be single-sided only and should not be stapled or bound (pages should be held together by clips or elastics);

❑ Be numbered consecutively from start to finish, including appendices and attachments;

❑ Use the YY/MM/DD format for all dates, e.g. 12 May 1998 would be expressed as 98/05/12;

❑ Quote all monetary information, such as costs, charges, prices, etc., in the currency in which they occur with the relevant currency clearly identified.

14.   Your response to this questionnaire must be in either English or French. Any source material that you provide with your response must be in the original language in which the transaction occurred and must be accompanied by a translation in either English or French.

Required format for submission of data on computerized media

15.   Please submit 2 (two) copies of the submission (including related databases) on separate diskettes. All diskettes must be checked for computer viruses before being forwarded to CBSA.

Your narrative responses to all of the questions in Parts A to D of the RFI should be provided on Word version 6.0 using 3.5" high density (1.44 MB) IBM-PC compatible diskettes. In addition, all data files used to produce responses to specific questions contained in Parts B to E should be provided on Excel version 5.0 spreadsheets using 3.5" high density (1.44 MB) IBM-PC compatible diskettes. A complete description of the contents of each diskette including the name of each file must be provided.

Information submitted in this manner is in addition to the information provided in a printed format and does not replace the requirements for the submission in printed format. Files can be submitted in a compressed format providing that a PKZip Version 2.04g or WinZip version 6.0 compatible system is used. DOS based or home designed backup systems will not be accepted.

Verification meetings

16.   A complete response, including all of the documentation requested, must be submitted to CBSA before a verification meeting will be considered.

17.   It is common practice for CBSA officers to visit exporters and the manufacturer(s) of the subject goods in order to verify the information

submitted. You will be contacted in advance of such a meeting to make arrangements as to the time and place of the verification meeting. Officers may wish to visit any location which has relevant data, such as your head office or sales office, mill locations, warehouses and any other location considered necessary by CBSA.

18.   If the verification meeting is delayed or cancelled due to the unavailability of company officials to meet with officers of CBSA, duty assessed on subject goods exported by your firm may be based on the best information available as explained in item 1.

19.   The purpose of the verification meeting is to verify information already provided to CBSA in your submission prior to the meeting. It is not intended to be a second opportunity for your firm to provide new or additional information. Accordingly, the original response should be complete and accurate.

20.   During any verification meeting with CBSA, each company official who prepared any part of the response and who has knowledge of the source documentation and the information contained therein must be available to meet with officers of CBSA and to provide additional clarification and explanation, as required.

21.   To satisfy itself as to the integrity, completeness and accuracy of the information supplied, CBSA may examine sales, costing and other information in respect of other goods not specifically included in the product definition for this investigation. For example, CBSA may require information on a product not covered by this investigation in order to validate costing allocations which were made in respect of the goods being reviewed.

22.   During the verification meeting, your office should be in a position to promptly retrieve requested documents and to provide photocopies of such documents when requested by the officers. During the meeting, your company will also be required to provide a non-confidential version of each document requested by officers of CBSA. Officers will require two copies of each document (plus one copy of the non-confidential version) requested during the verification meeting.

23.   Although the information requested largely relates to the time periods specified in the RFI, it should be noted that CBSA is not limited to the examination of information within these time frames. Information may be requested for periods outside the POI or the profitability analysis period in order that CBSA may satisfy itself as to the accuracy of the data presented for the periods of time which have been specified in the RFI. For example, current pension costs may include a portion of pension costs incurred in several previous accounting periods, but permitted to be matched against future revenues because of legislation or accounting standards. In such circumstances, CBSA will request information to support the current pension charges outside of both the POI and the profitability analysis period.

Source documents

24.   Source documents should be kept easily accessible at your business location for possible review during the verification meeting.

Failure to cooperate

25.   Failure to submit all required information and documentation, including non-confidential versions, or failure to permit verification of any information, may result in the assessment of duties on subject goods exported by your firm

equal to the highest estimated margin of dumping determined during the investigation. Such a decision will be less favourable to your firm than if full and verified information is made available.

Summary of the request for information

26.   There are eight parts to this RFI. Following is a brief explanation of parts A–F:

PART A
Requests basic information concerning your company, its products, its associates, and its domestic and export markets.

PART B
Requests information concerning your shipments of the subject goods to Canada during the POI that is indicated on the covering page of this RFI.

PART C
Requests information concerning domestic sales of like goods during the profitability analysis period.

PART D
Requests financial data with respect to your company as well as costing data in respect of both the goods shipped to Canada and the like goods sold in your domestic market.

PART E
Provides instructions to determine which domestic market sales meet the profitability requirements of the Act. This exercise is referred to as a profitability analysis.

PART F
A glossary which provides definitions and useful information concerning words, terms and phrases used in this RFI.

Requirements of respondent

27.   Your firm should fit into one of the following three categories. As a general guideline, the exporter for SIMA purposes is the person or firm who is a principal in the transaction, located in the country of export at the point of direct shipment to Canada, who gave up responsibility for the goods by knowingly placing them in the hands of a carrier, courier, forwarding company, their own truck or other conveyance, etc., for delivery to Canada.

It should also be understood that in cases where a vendor acts as an intermediary between the manufacturer and the Canadian importer, it is quite possible that the manufacturer will be held to be the exporter for SIMA purposes.

CATEGORY 1: An exporter of the subject goods to Canada who is also the manufacturer of the goods.

● A respondent in this category should respond to all parts of the RFI.

CATEGORY 2: An exporter or vendor of the subject goods to Canada who is not the manufacturer of the goods (i.e. distributor, trading company, etc.).

● A respondent in this category must respond to all parts of the RFI. You may conclude that certain questions do not apply to your company. You must nevertheless respond to each such question by explaining clearly why it does not apply. Trading companies and distributors responsible for export sales only should pay particular attention to the request in question D10 for information relating to the purchase price paid to the supplier of the exported goods and to other details requested concerning the acquisition cost of the goods.

At the same time, you must IMMEDIATELY forward a copy of this RFI to each of the manufacturers concerned and inform an officer identified on the covering page of this RFI of the name, address, telephone and fax number of the contact person of each manufacturer.

You should make every effort to ensure that the manufacturer(s) provide(s) the required information directly to CBSA by the due date indicated on the covering page.

Where the manufacturer (i.e. your supplier) fails to provide the required information, your submission will not be considered incomplete provided that you have submitted all of the requested information which is within your own ability to provide. CBSA will use other information in place of the information not provided by the manufacturer/producer. This **may** result in a decision less favourable to your company than if full information had been provided by the producer of the goods. (Category 3 provides instructions on the response requirements for a manufacturer that is not the exporter.)

If your company is a distributor (i.e. an exporter but not a manufacturer) the term 'factory' or 'production facilities' may be read as 'distributor' and the term 'produce' may be read as 'sell' throughout this document.

CATEGORY 3: A manufacturer of the subject goods that were subsequently exported to Canada by another party (i.e. distributor, trading company, etc.).

- A respondent in this category must respond to Parts A, D and H of the RFI. If the party responsible for exporting the goods to Canada does not, at the same time, also sell like goods in your domestic market (i.e. sales of the like goods in the domestic market are negotiated and completed by the manufacturer), then the manufacturer must also respond to both Parts C and E of the RFI.

Results of investigation and disclosure meetings

28.   The results of the investigation, including an explanation of the methodologies for determining the normal values, export prices and margins of dumping, if any, for goods shipped by your company to importers in Canada during the POI, will be provided to your company upon completion of each phase of the investigation. Should you wish to discuss the results and the decisions taken, officers will be available to meet with you or your representatives in Ottawa, Canada.

Establishing contact with CBSA

29.   You are requested to contact an officer indicated on the covering page of this RFI within a week following the receipt of this request, by telephone or by fax, to indicate whether your company will be responding to the RFI and if so, your firm's contact person. If applicable, indicate the name and telephone number of the counsel that will be representing your firm during this investigation.

Counsel

30.   If your company has retained counsel to represent you in this matter before CBSA, a letter of authorization must be provided. When such letter of authorization is provided, CBSA will, upon request, undertake to provide copies of all outgoing correspondence with your firm to designated counsel. Furthermore, if it is your wish that confidential materials relating to your company be released to or discussed with your counsel, the letter should specifically authorize CBSA to do so.

PART A

General information

The information requested in this part will provide CBSA with an overview of your corporate organization, the goods produced, and your domestic and export markets. It will also facilitate planning, scheduling and conducting the verification meeting at your company.

A1. Provide your company's complete mailing address, telephone and fax numbers, and email address. In addition, identify the name and position of the officer in your company responsible for your response to the RFI.

A2. Describe the nature of your company's business. Explain whether you are a manufacturer, a trading/sales organization, a distributor, etc., and provide a brief history of your company.

A3. Indicate whether you are replying to the RFI as a Category 1, 2 or 3 respondent (refer to item 28 in the Instructions). Explain why you have classified yourself in the category selected.

A4. Indicate whether your company is a sole proprietorship, a partnership, a limited liability company, or another type of corporate organization and provide information on whether it is privately held, a public corporation, a government agency, etc.

A5. Provide a chart showing all associated companies in order to provide an understanding of your company's place in the larger corporate structure.

A6. Provide a list of all associated companies with addresses, telephone numbers, fax numbers and contact names. Clearly indicate the relationship between your company and each of its associates, and the percentage of ownership held by your company and/or its associates. For each company, explain the nature of the business performed and the responsibilities or functions carried out by each associated company in respect of the goods shipped to Canada.

A7. Describe your company's internal organization and provide a complete internal organization chart. For each functional, divisional or other grouping depending on your particular circumstances, provide a description of the grouping and the activities performed within the grouping.

A8. Provide a list, including the names and addresses of your company's 15 largest shareholders and the percentage of shares that each of them holds. If not already covered, identify the names and addresses of any shareholder who owns more than 5% of the shares of your company.

A9. If your company is a subsidiary of another company, list the 15 largest shareholders of your parent company, including their names and addresses. If not already covered, identify the name and address of any shareholder who owns more than 5% of the shares of your parent company.

A10. If your parent company is a subsidiary of another company, list the 15 largest shareholders of that company, including their names and addresses. If not already covered, identify the name and address of each shareholder who owns more than 5% of the shares of your parent's parent company.

A11. Provide the details of any changes in the majority ownership structure of your company during the last fiscal year and during this fiscal year-to-date. Include details of any ownership change which has affected your costing, selling or pricing practices, and distribution practices within the last two years.

A12. For the last two years, indicate whether your company has been in receivership, has operated under any bankruptcy proceedings, has received protection from creditors, or in any other manner has been involved with bankruptcy proceedings as provided for in your domestic legislation. Provide full details of any such occurrences, including any proceedings which might currently be underway.

A13. For the last two years, indicate whether your company has been involved in any significant legal proceedings. Provide full details of any such occurrences, including any proceedings which are expected or are currently underway.

A14. Provide the address of each of your production facilities or factories that are capable of producing the subject goods. Identify each of your production facilities or factories where the subject goods shipped to Canada during the POI were produced. Indicate the location where the relevant sales data and costing data are kept in respect of your domestic sales and your shipments to Canada.

A15. Provide a list of all product lines produced by your company (i.e. both subject goods and non-subject goods).

A16. With respect to subject goods sold to Canada and like goods sold in your domestic market, provide details of the terms of sale that apply and explain fully how each term is defined by your company:

(a) Delivery (e.g. FOB, ex-factory, CIF, delivered, etc.);

(b) Payment (e.g. 2% 10, net 30 days; 180 days after bill of lading, etc.); and

(b) Method of payment (e.g. cash or money order, letter of credit, bank transfer, etc.).

A17. With respect to subject goods sold to Canada and like goods sold in your domestic market, is it your corporate practice to *discount your accounts receivable*? If it is, identify the methods of discounting employed, the cost to your company, and the timing associated with the discounting of the payment instrument.

A18. Provide a copy of the latest brochures, corporate publications, or any other such general literature concerning your company, its associates and products sold or manufactured both in your domestic market and in export markets.

REMINDERS

1.   If your company is not the producer of the goods, it is your responsibility and in your own interest to ensure that the producer(s) provide(s) CBSA with the necessary information as outlined in item 28 of the Instructions.

2.   If you have designated any information confidential, a non-confidential version of that information must accompany your response to this RFI. See items 3–10 of the Instructions for further details in this regard.

PART B

Export information

This part requests information concerning your exports to Canada. This information is required to determine your export practices and the export price of those goods imported into Canada during the Period of Investigation. It is recognized that you may not be in a position to know exactly when the goods shipped were actually imported into Canada. You may wish to contact the importer directly to confirm import dates respecting your sales or provide export sales information for shipments made well in advance of possible importation.

Much of the information for this part is required in electronic format. Refer to item 16 in the Instructions section of this RFI for guidelines respecting the submission of information in electronic format.

B1.   For each importer in Canada to whom your company shipped the subject goods during the POI, provide the:

(a)   Name;

(b)   Customer code;

(c)   Address;

(d)   Telephone number;

(e)   Fax number;

(f)   Name of the contact person;

(g)   Trade level;

(h)   Total quantity of each model shipped to that importer;

(i)   Total transaction value of each model shipped to that importer; and

(j)   Full book price (base book price plus applicable extras) for each model shipped.

B2.   For each importer identified in response to question B1, indicate:

(a)   The activities which the importer undertakes in respect of the subject goods prior to and following importation;

(b)   The sales activities that your company or any associate performs on sales to the importer in Canada;

(c)   The sales activities that your company or any associate performs on behalf of the importer in Canada;

(d)   The relationship between your firm and your Canadian customer. If your firm is **related** to the importer, elaborate; and

(e)   The details of any arrangements, financial or otherwise, in existence between your company and the importer in Canada of the subject goods.

B3.   Provide a detailed explanation of your company's channels of distribution to importers in Canada. Include a flowchart explaining the movement of the goods from the manufacturing plant to the delivery of the goods to the importer in Canada. Explain in detail any agency or distributor agreements and provide copies of each. At each step of the process, describe the functions or activities performed by the respective parties.

B4. Indicate who owns the goods at each stage of their movement described in response to B3.

B5. Explain in detail the order process used by your company with respect to your exports to Canada from the point of receiving an order, through to delivery and payment for the goods. Identify and describe fully the documentation used in each step of the process. Indicate the terms and conditions of sale, including the payment and shipping terms.

B6. For each shipment during the POI, provide the amount of any commissions incurred in respect of the sale and/or exportation of the goods. Identify the party receiving the commission. Explain the relationship between your company and the party receiving the commission. Describe the activities for which the commission was paid, the nature of the commission, the basis for calculating it, the method of payment, currency of payment, timing of payment, and any other relevant details.

B7. CBSA considers the date of sale to be the date that the parties establish the material aspects of the sale. The date of the order confirmation is usually considered the date of sale although the date of sale could be the contract, purchase order or invoice date, or such other date which establishes the material terms of sale. If any of the terms of sale are subsequently revised, the date that the revision was made is usually considered the date of sale.

(a) For your export sales to Canada, at what stage in the process (e.g. contract date, purchase order date) are the material terms of the sale established? In other words, what do you consider is the date of sale? Explain.

(b) If different methods are used to identify the dates of sale for different transactions (e.g. spot sales and short term and long term contracts), explain what you consider to be the date of sale for each type of transaction and explain why different methods are used.

(c) For your export sales to Canada, under what circumstances are terms of sale changed?

B8. Provide a list of all shipments of subject goods that were imported into Canada during the period during the POI. For each shipment, provide a separate line on the spreadsheet for every individual product included in that shipment. Provide hard copies of the listing in addition to the required electronic format.

B9. For each type of 'Other discount' you offer, provide line-by-line, the amount of the discount granted on each model/shipment to Canada.

Describe each type of discount you offer, including the terminology associated with the discount and the terms and conditions that must be met by the importer in order to receive the discount.

B10. For each type of rebate and/or allowance you offer, provide line-by-line, the amount of the rebate granted on each model/shipment to Canada.

Describe each type of rebate or allowance you offer, including the terminology associated with the rebate or allowance and the terms and conditions that must be met by the importer to receive the rebate or allowance.

If your company has any agreements with the importer respecting the payment of rebates and/or allowances, provide a copy of each agreement. If rebates and/or allowances are owing but have not yet been paid on shipments to Canada, explain how you determined the amount of the rebate or allowance reported in your response to B8.

B11. Provide copies of any catalogues, brochures, price lists, discount schedules, etc., relative to your shipments to Canada. Explain any product codes or other codes used by your firm on any documents submitted so as to permit a full understanding by CBSA.

B12. If the goods listed in response to question B8 conform to any government, association, international or other standard or specification, provide copies of the relevant standards or specifications.

B13. For each line listed in response to question B8, if there are any costs, charges or expenses incurred in respect of the goods by or on behalf of your company which are not already identified, indicate the amount of the item for each model in the shipment. The column names should clearly identify the nature of the cost, charge or expense. These costs, charges or expenses should relate to:

(i) Preparing the goods for shipment that are additional to those costs, charges or expenses incurred on domestic sales of like goods in the country of export, including additional packing costs for export;

(ii) The payment or future payment by you (or on your behalf) of any Canadian regular or special duties and taxes; and

(iii) All other costs, charges and expenses resulting from the exportation of the goods, or arising from their shipment to Canada.

Provide a narrative description of the cost, charge or expense identified. This description must be sufficiently detailed to permit a proper understanding by CBSA.

B14. For each shipment listed in response to question B8, compile and submit a copy of the following set of documents:

(a) The importer's purchase order and your acknowledgement or acceptance of the order, or the contract of sale;

(b) Commercial invoice and credit/debit notes issued in respect of the sale;

(c) Canada Customs invoice (if applicable);

(d) Bill of lading;

(e) Freight invoices covering any expenses incurred by or on behalf of your company for the movement of the goods from the factory to the final destination in Canada;

(f) Letter of credit (if applicable);

(g) Proof of payment (bank advice statement); and

(h) Mill certificate.

B15. With respect to your export shipments to Canada listed in response to B8, provide details of any foreign currency buying and selling decisions (hedging) made by your company to minimize the effects of exchange rate movements on your Canadian sales revenue, such as forward contracts, futures contracts or options.

B16. With respect to your export shipments to Canada listed in response to B8, did your company adjust the selling price to Canada in order to account for currency fluctuations? Explain.

B17. Are there any goods, services, rebates, warranties or guarantees provided directly or indirectly to persons who purchase the goods from the importer or from any person on any subsequent resale? If so, provide details concerning the nature and value of such benefits.

B18. Provide a listing by importer for the POI indicating the average number of collection days for your accounts receivable.

B19. In the event that your firm is not the manufacturer of the subject goods, provide the name, address, telephone and fax numbers and contact person of the manufacturer and your supplier(s), if different from the manufacturer.

B20. Identify all source documents on which you relied in preparing your response to this part, and indicate the business location where the documents are maintained.

REMINDERS

1.　If your company is not the producer of the goods, it is your responsibility and in your own interest to ensure that the producer(s) provide(s) CBSA with the necessary information as outlined in item 28 of the Instructions.

2.　If you have designated any information confidential, a non-confidential version of that information must accompany your response to this RFI. See items 3–10 of the Instructions for further details in this regard.

PART C
Domestic sales information

The information requested in this part is required to determine the normal values of the subject goods. Generally, where there are a sufficient number of profitable domestic sales of like goods to more than one unrelated customer, normal values are based on your firm's domestic selling prices of the like goods. Some factors which may be taken into account and for which adjustments may be made include the trade level of the importer in Canada compared to the trade level of your domestic customers, the quantities of goods sold to importers in Canada compared with the quantities of like goods sold to your domestic customers, qualitative differences, taxation differences and other differences in terms and conditions of sale.

However, if there are insufficient or no domestic sales of like goods, if domestic sales of like goods are to only one customer or if domestic sales of like goods are non-profitable, normal values will be based on your firm's total cost of the goods plus an amount for profit. Questions on your costs are found in part D of this RFI.

Like goods are goods that are identical in all respects to the subject goods exported to Canada, or in their absence, are goods that closely resemble the goods exported to Canada (similar goods). Some of the following questions require the identification of sales of identical or similar goods. In addition, to be considered like goods, goods must have been produced at the same production facility/factory as the subject goods exported to Canada.

C1.   (a)   Provide a detailed explanation of your company's channels of distribution to your domestic customers. Include a flowchart depicting the movement of the goods. Explain in detail any agency or distributor agreements and provide copies of each. At each step of the process, describe the functions or activities performed.

    (b)   Do the selling prices of the like goods sold in your domestic market vary depending on the channel of distribution through which you sell? If yes, explain how and why the prices vary.

C2.   Explain in detail the steps in the ordertaking and filling process and the commercial documentation used by your company with respect to domestic sales from the point of receiving an order through to delivery and receipt of payment for the goods. Sample documentation (e.g. purchase order, commercial invoice, shipping manifest, credit/debit note) should be provided to illustrate the complete documentation process. If you sell by short-term or long-term contracts, include sample copies. Explain any terms on the documentation which are specific to the industry or are of a technical nature.

C3.   (a)   Provide catalogues and/or brochures relating to the like goods.

    (b)   Provide the current price lists and all price lists for the like goods in effect during the profitability analysis period. Include any discount or rebate schedules used with each price list. Also provide copies of any internal price guidelines used by your salesmen during the profitability analysis period.

    (c)   If your company does not use price lists, describe how prices are determined. If price lists are not used, provide a detailed schedule showing each price change for each product during the profitability analysis period, and the effective dates of the price changes.

C4. CBSA considers the date of sale to be the date that the parties establish the terms of sale. The date of the order confirmation is usually considered the date of sale although the date of sale could be the contract, purchase order or invoice date, whichever establishes the terms of sale. If any of the terms of sale are subsequently revised, the date that the revision was made is usually considered the date of sale.

(a) At what stage in the process (e.g. contract date, purchase order date) are the terms of sale established? In other words, what do you consider the date of sale? Explain.

(b) If different methods are used to identify the dates of sale for different transactions, such as spot sales and short-term and long-term contracts, explain what you consider to be the date of sale for each type of transaction and explain why different methods are used.

(c) Under what circumstances are terms of sale changed?

C5. (a) Have there been price changes in your domestic market since the POI? If so, provide the percentage change in price for each product line within the subject goods definition and indicate the reasons for the price changes.

(b) Are price increases or decreases scheduled for the coming months? If so, provide the scheduled percentage change in price for each product line within the subject goods definition and indicate the reasons for the scheduled price changes.

C6. For each subject product shipped to Canada during the Period of Investigation provide the detailed information as requested for those products sold in your domestic market during the profitability analysis period, which are considered to be 'like goods' to the models exported to Canada.

As previously noted, like goods are goods that are identical to the subject goods exported to Canada, or in their absence, are goods the uses and other characteristics of which closely resemble those of the model exported to Canada.

NOTE: In the absence of domestic sales of like goods for a particular model, you should immediately contact one of the officers of CBSA identified on the cover page of this RFI to receive instructions regarding the selection of domestic sales.

The responses to questions C7 and C8 below must also be provided in electronic format as explained in item 16 of the Instructions.

C7. **First listing of domestic sales of 'like goods'**

Provide a detailed listing of all domestic sales of the like goods identified in your response to question C6 during the profitability analysis period. The domestic sales contained in this listing should be for ultimate consumption in your domestic market. Please clearly label this listing as *'All sales of like goods as per question C7 of the RFI'*.

Sales in this database must be adjusted for any credit notes issued respecting these sales, i.e. selling prices are to be net of credits. All remaining credits are to be removed from the database.

This information should be provided for each production facility or factory where the subject goods exported to Canada were produced.

The listing should be sorted in the following order:

(i)   Production facility or factory at which the goods were produced;

(ii)   Model; and

iii)   Date of sale.

C8.   Second listing of domestic sales of 'like goods'

There are certain legislative requirements in SIMA which must be taken into account in selecting like sales for the determination of normal values. In accordance with these legislative requirements, you are requested in this question to provide a second listing of *selected* domestic sales of like goods. The domestic sales contained in this listing should be for ultimate consumption in your domestic market. This second listing should be clearly labelled as *'Sales of selected like goods as per question C8 of the RFI'*.

Specifically, beginning with the database of sales of like goods prepared in response to question C7, please identify and list those sales of like goods which are:

1.   Sold to more than one unrelated[1] domestic customer; and

2.   Which are sold to the same trade level[2] as the importer in Canada; and

3.   Which are sold in the same or substantially the same quantities[3] as the quantities sold to the importer in Canada.

If you have no sales of a like good which meet all three of the above conditions, then you should examine sales of the like good which were sold at the trade level nearest and subsequent[4] to the importer in Canada.

Sales of the like good at this subsequent trade level may be substituted in your sales listing *only* in the absence of sales which meet the three conditions listed above. However, in order to be given consideration, the sales of the like good at this subsequent trade level must also be made to more than one unrelated domestic customer and must be sold in the same or substantially the same quantities as the quantities purchased by the importer in Canada.

In preparing the above listing of domestic sales of like goods, please sort the sales in the following order:

(i)   Production facility or factory at which the goods were produced;

(ii)   Model; and

(iii)   Date of sale.

C9.   Describe each type of discount, rebate, or allowance offered on domestic sales of like goods, including the terminology used and the terms and conditions that must be met in order to receive each one. For each type of discount, rebate and allowance you offer, add a column, with an

---

1   Refer to the definition of 'associated persons' and 'related' listed in part F (Glossary). Note that where two or more purchasers are associated with each other, they are regarded as single purchaser.

2   Refer to the definition of 'trade level' listed in part F (Glossary).

3   When the domestic sales are not sold in the same or substantially the same quantities as the sale of the goods to the importer in Canada, you should use those sales which are closest in quantity to the quantity of goods sold to the importer in Canada.

4   Refer to the definition of 'subsequent trade level' listed in part F (Glossary).

appropriate column heading, to your responses to questions C7 and C8 and indicate the amount of the discount, rebate or allowance granted on each sale. In addition, provide details of the methodology you have used to allocate each discount, rebate or allowance to the like goods.

C10. Indicate on what percentage of domestic sales of like goods listed in response to questions C7 and C8 each type of discount, rebate or allowance was granted to domestic customers. The percentage must be calculated on a quantity basis, i.e. the quantity of like goods on which the discount was granted.

C11. With regard to the sales listed in response to C8, provide a complete documentation package for every twentieth sale listed, up to a maximum of 30 sales. The package should include sales contracts, purchase orders, bills of lading, commercial invoices, credit/debit notes and proofs of payment.

C12. Explain any product codes or other codes used by your firm to enable a correlation between price lists, invoices, brochures, etc. and the listings of domestic sales.

C13. Provide a list of codes and the corresponding names for domestic customers listed in response to question C7.

C14. For each customer identified in response to C7, provide a listing indicating the average number of collection days for your accounts receivable during the Profitability Analysis Period.

C15. For each level of trade identified in response to C7, provide the following information:

(a)   A detailed description of each direct sales activity you perform in selling to your domestic customers (for example, sales representatives, travel, entertainment, advertising);

(b)   For each activity described in (a) above, indicate the cost of carrying out such activity in respect of the like goods;

(c)   For each activity described in (a) above, indicate whether the same activity is performed at all by your firm in selling to importers in Canada; and

(d)   If any of the like goods identified in response to question C8 were sold to customers at the trade level nearest and subsequent to the trade level of the importer in Canada, a trade level adjustment may be allowed. If you think that you are entitled to a trade level adjustment, explain why (refer to the definitions of trade level and subsequent trade level in part F – Glossary).

C16. Indicate the amount of any royalties or patent fees paid or payable with respect to each like good listed in response to question C7. A breakdown of the amount of payment to each firm is required. If applicable, explain why any such fees are not payable, or not payable in the same amounts, on models exported to Canada.

C17. If any applicable domestic commodity tax or any other domestic tax is included in the domestic selling price, the amount of the tax should be indicated in column 39. Indicate the manner of payment and method of calculation of the tax.

C18. If exports to Canada are partially or fully exempt from the payment of internal taxes and duties that are levied on sales for home consumption, or on the materials and components physically incorporated into the goods, or such internal taxes and duties previously paid are remitted on export of the goods, provide:

(a) An explanation of the legislation covering such exemption or remission, as well as a copy of the relevant regulations, with translation into English or French if required;

(b) The amount of duties and taxes refunded on the exportation of the goods and an explanation of how such amounts were calculated or apportioned to the exported goods;

(c) A record of the payment of the internal taxes and duties that were paid on goods sold domestically or on the material and components physically incorporated into the goods sold domestically but which were not levied on goods exported to Canada or other countries; and

(d) The calculated amount of such taxes and duties on a per unit basis. The allocation to each unit must reflect the basis on which the taxes or duties are calculated.

C19. Are there any goods, services, rebates, warranties or guarantees provided directly or indirectly to persons who purchase the goods from your company or from any person on any subsequent resale? If so, provide details concerning the nature and value of such benefits. Include an explanation of the associated terminology, and any terms and conditions that must be met in order to receive the goods, services, rebates, warranties or guarantees.

C20. Provide an explanation of any sales listed in response to C7 that are not made under conditions where price was established by the forces of supply and demand. Describe any price and/or wage controls or restrictions imposed by government bodies which may limit the price you charge your domestic customers.

C21. If you are not the producer of the goods, did the supplier of the merchandise know or have reason to believe that the merchandise you were purchasing was ultimately destined for the Canadian market? Was there any understanding restricting, discouraging or prohibiting sales in the domestic market, the Canadian market or any other market? Does the supplier have the right to review your sales records? Does the supplier provide after-sales service in Canada, participate in Canadian sales calls or activities or provide sales incentives to your customers?

C22. Identify all source documents you have relied on in preparing your response to this part, and indicate the business location where the documents are maintained.

REMINDERS

1. If your company is not the producer of the goods, it is your responsibility and in your own interest to ensure that the producer(s) provide(s) CBSA with the necessary information as outlined in item 28 of the Instructions.

2. If you have designated any information confidential, a non-confidential version of that information must accompany your response to this RFI. See items 3–10 of the Instructions for further details in this regard.

PART D

Financial data and costing information

The information gathered in this section will be used to determine whether your domestic sales are profitable. For models where normal values cannot be determined on the basis of domestic selling prices, the information provided in this section also will enable the determination of normal values based on the cost of the goods.

For this part, appropriate footnotes should be provided to explain (1) accounting treatment of any item(s) that deviate from established practices and (2) all corporate allocations. The information provided should enable CBSA to follow the audit trail from the unit product cost to the corporate audited financial statements.

D1. Provide a list of your general ledger chart of accounts. If your chart of accounts is in a language other than English or French, provide the original language version and a translation into either English or French.

D2. (a) Indicate the date of your company's fiscal year-end, and for the two most recent fiscal years, provide copies of:

(i) Your corporate annual reports including your audited financial statements (unaudited statements will only be accepted where audited financial statements do not exist);

(ii) Divisional income statements and balance sheets for each division of the company;

(iii) Income statements and balance sheets for each of the company's production facilities; and

(iv) Product-specific income statements and balance sheets for the like goods sold to your domestic customers, or if such statements do not exist, statements relating to goods sold to your domestic customers for the narrowest range of products which includes the like goods. These statements should be provided for the facilities where the like goods are produced.

(b) With regard to the following documents, provide monthly statements for each of the months of the profitability analysis period:

(i) Unaudited company income statements;

(ii) Divisional and/or product income statements for each division of your company. If your company does not compile divisional financial statements, any reports generated by the division should be provided, such as management reports, performance reports, production cost statements, operating reports or interim reports that contain the information requested;

(iii) Income statements for each of the company's production facilities/factories; and

(iv) Product-specific income statements for the like goods sold to your domestic customers or if such statements do not exist, statements relating to goods sold to your domestic customers for the narrowest range of products which includes the like goods. These statements should be provided for the production facility/factory that produces the like goods.

(c) If your company's shares are publicly traded, the last annual report and all year-to-date (e.g. monthly, quarterly) reports filed with the relevant agency charged with the regulating and control of public companies in your country.

D3. Explain your financial accounting practices with regard to:

(a) Valuation methodologies for raw materials, work-in-process, and finished goods inventories;

(b) Fixed asset valuation, revaluation, depreciation methodology, and treatment of idled assets;

(c) Inventory write-off and write-down methods for raw materials and finished goods;

(d) Income and expense accounts requiring year-end accruals and adjustments;

(e) Treatment of exchange gains and losses resulting from foreign currency transactions and translation of year-end asset and liability balances;

(f) Capitalization of general and administrative expenses or interest expense as part of inventory or fixed asset valuation;

(g) Plant closure, shut-down or restructuring costs (indicate whether any of your production facilities were restructured, shut down or closed during the profitability analysis period, or whether you incurred any expenses during this period as a result of shutdowns, closures, or restructuring during previous periods);

(h) By-products and scrap material from the production process (including method of valuation and disposition); and

(i) The effects of inflation on financial statement information.

D4. For each of the last two fiscal years and the current fiscal year-to-date, for the product line which includes the subject goods, provide, on a production facility/factory basis:

(a) Quantity produced (units);

(b) Quantity purchased from other suppliers/producers (units);

(c) Quantity sold (units);

(d) Gross sales (value);

(e) Cost of goods sold (value);

(f) Quantity (units) of goods transferred internally to other operations/divisions within the company for use in downstream operations; and

(g) Quantity (units) of goods sold to associated parties.

D5. For each production facility/factory producing the like goods, provide the following for each stage of production:

(a) A flowchart of the production process;

(b) A description of the activities undertaken during each stage;

(c)   A description of the type of machinery used during that stage and its standard useful life;

(d)   A list of material inputs used at each stage;

(e)   The production time, expressed in the industry standard;

(f)   Yield rates;

(g)   A list of by-products;

(h)   Details of scrap material; and

(i)   An explanation of how overhead is allocated.

D6.   (a)   Provide a detailed explanation and example of the methodology employed in costing the goods. For example, if you use standard costs, provide a copy of a sample standard cost as it appears in your product costing system. Explain each component of the standard cost, identify any allocations and explain how they were calculated.

(b)   Do you calculate costs separately for each type of model? If so, describe how precisely the product costing system captures the production costs of the goods.

D7.   Costs are sometimes affected by start-up operations that limit the level of production associated with the initial phase of commercial production.

Start-up operations are considered to be the use of new production facilities or the production of a substantially new product requiring new or different technology or production equipment.

(a)   Indicate whether your firm underwent start-up operations with respect to the subject goods and the like goods. Describe the nature of any start-up operations and identify the beginning and the end of the start-up period.

(b)   If start-up operations have affected the costs of the goods, explain why and how the costs of the goods were affected.

(c)   In responding to questions D10 to D16, where any costs have been affected by start-up operations that limited the level of production owing to technical difficulties related to the use of new production facilities or the production of a new product, do not provide costs incurred during the start-up period. Instead, provide costs that existed at the end of the start-up period. If the start-up period extended beyond the POI, provide the costs in effect at the end of the POI.

D8.   Where there are differences in quality, structure, design or material between a model exported to Canada and the like good sold in your domestic market:

(a)   Describe such differences and the production process that caused the differences;

(b)   Compute the value of the qualitative differences on a per unit basis; and

(c)   Explain the method of computation.

D9.   (a)   Describe any differences in the type, nature and value of any warranty against defect or guarantee of performance between any of the models exported to Canada and the like goods sold in your domestic market.

(b)   Describe any differences in the time permitted from the order date to the date of shipment between any of the models exported to Canada and the like goods sold in your domestic market.

(c)   Describe any other differences in the conditions of sale between any of the models exported to Canada and the like goods sold in your domestic market.

(d)   For any differences described in (a) to (c) which have an impact on selling prices, compute the value of the difference on a per unit basis and explain the method of computation.

RESPONSES TO QUESTIONS D10 TO D16 MUST ALSO BE PROVIDED IN ELECTRONIC FORMAT AS EXPLAINED IN ITEM 16 OF THE INSTRUCTIONS. ALL AMOUNTS SHOULD BE EXPRESSED ON A PER UNIT BASIS.

D10.   Provide the costs of production for each of the subject goods shipped to Canada that were listed in response to question B8 and each like good sold to your domestic customers that was listed in response to question C7. These costs must be provided separately for each production facility/factory where these goods were produced. If the cost of production of the subject goods exported to Canada differs from the cost of production of the like goods, provide separate cost of production statements for like and subject goods.

The costs of production for the like goods sold domestically will form the basis for conducting the profitability analysis. The costs of production for the subject goods shipped to Canada will be used, if required, as the basis for determining a cost-based normal value.

Actual costs are preferred. These costs are generally calculated on a monthly basis. However, if standard or budgeted costs are used, identify the variances that are recorded in the cost accounting system. For example, if variances are recorded monthly, the appropriate monthly variances should be provided. Indicate the frequency with which the standard costs are revised and the date of the latest revision. Explain how favourable or unfavourable variances resulting from production are assigned to the subject goods during each accounting period.

Where expenses are allocated, explain how you allocated the expense to the subject goods, and provide the supporting worksheets in your response. If expenses are allocated to subject and non-subject goods, explain the method of allocation and explain why this method of allocation is appropriate for the expense in question. An allocation based on annual data is preferable to one that will be skewed in periods of high or low production.

If costs have changed over the period, provide the various sets of costs with applicable dates and an explanation of the changes.

The costs of the following items should be provided on a per unit basis and should identify and include factors for yield losses:

(i)   Direct materials

Identify each major component and provide the quantities utilized and the full cost of each raw material input on a per unit basis of production. Note that materials or components that are obtained from another division, production facility/factory, or associated company should be identified.

The value of these materials should be the actual costs to the division, production facility/factory or associated company which produced or acquired the materials plus an amount for any corporate allocations, overheads and financial charges. In addition, the cost of engineering or design work incurred by another division, production facility/factory or associated company that is attributable or in any manner related to the production of the materials or components should be identified and included in the cost thereof.

If your company is not the producer of the goods, provide the following:

(a) The acquisition cost of the goods purchased from your supplier;

(b) The freight cost between yourself and your supplier;

(c) Rebates between yourself and your supplier;

(d) The commission between yourself and your supplier; and

(e) Any other cost incurred in relation to the acquisition of the goods.

(ii) By-products

Identify each by-product that results from the production process of the goods. Provide the value of each by-product expressed on a per unit basis of finished steel product.

(iii) Direct labour

State the labour cost per unit of production. In computing labour cost include overtime pay, all fringe benefits and payments for social programmes.

If you are not the producer of the goods, but incur direct labour costs, describe the relevant activities and state such costs on a per unit basis.

(iv) Factory overhead

State the factory overhead expenses per unit of production. For example, the expenses incurred for shop supplies and tools, utilities, indirect labour, supervision, maintenance, rent, depreciation, etc. Identify the accounts included in this category.

(v) Other costs of production

Identify on a per unit basis any other costs applicable to the production of the goods but not otherwise reported in your responses to D10(i) to (iv) above (e.g. research and development).

(vi) Scrap recovery value

State the total scrap recovery value per unit.

In presenting your company's full cost of production, CBSA recognizes that individual companies may not account for their costs in a manner that allows for the presentation of costs for each of the above listed cost components. Provided the costs presented are complete and represent the full cost of production, you may present your costs in a manner consistent with your own cost accounting reporting practices.

D11. For the profitability analysis period, itemize all administrative and selling expenses (A&S), including corporate overhead costs, that are directly or indirectly attributable to the sale and production of the like goods sold domestically. Allocate expenses over the like goods and explain your method of allocation. An allocation based on annual data is preferable to one that will be skewed in periods of increased or decreased sales.

If there were no like goods sold domestically, list all administrative and selling expenses that are directly or indirectly attributable to the sale and production of the subject goods exported to Canada on a per unit basis.

D12. For the profitability analysis period:

(a)   List and describe each source and amount of interest income earned on short-term investments or operational bank accounts that are related to the production or sale of the like goods;

(b)   List the amount and nature of each interest expense incurred on all forms of liability and indicate which of these interest expenses are directly or indirectly related to the production and sale of the like goods; and

(c)   Calculate an amount for net interest expense per unit. This amount is calculated by deducting the amount of interest income listed in (a) from the interest expenses that are directly or indirectly related to the production and sale of the like goods listed in (b). However, interest income may not offset interest expense beyond a zero net balance. Explain your method of allocation to the like goods.

If there were no like goods sold domestically, respond to (a) to (c) for the subject goods exported to Canada.

D13. For the profitability analysis period, list all other costs, charges and expenses that are directly or indirectly attributable to the production and sale of the like goods, allocate on a per unit basis to the like goods and explain your method of allocation. These expenses may be reported on the company's income statement below the operational income line and may include such items as losses from foreign exchange transactions, gains from foreign exchange transactions, etc. Report each gain, income, loss and expense separately.

If there were no like goods sold domestically, list all other costs, charges and expenses that are directly or indirectly attributable to the production and sale of the subject goods exported to Canada and allocate on a per unit basis.

D14. For the profitability analysis period, list the amounts of any expenses, including expenses incurred at the corporate level that have not been allocated to the like goods or the subject goods. Explain the nature of these expenses and why the expenses have not been allocated to the goods.

D15. Provide full information on all expected year-end adjustments that will have a material impact on the operating results of your company. These adjustments may be attributable to legislation, other government actions, a change in accounting methods, standards or practices, or may arise from any contingency, expected liability or extraordinary or unusual item which will be recognized during the current accounting period.

Identify the amount of any expected year-end adjustments on a per unit basis, and explain your method of allocation to the like goods or the subject goods.

D16. Provide the total per unit cost, on a model basis, of each subject good shipped to Canada that was listed in response to question B8 and each like good sold to your domestic customers that was listed in response to C7. For each model, the total per unit cost will be the sum of all the unit costs listed in your response to questions D10, D11, D12(c), D13 and D15.

D17. List and describe any production costs incurred by your company which are valued differently for cost accounting purposes than for financial accounting purposes.

D18. Provide a copy of the cost sheets as they appear in your product costing system for products representing the 20 top-selling models listed in response to question C7. This must be accompanied by a full explanation of the cost sheet and its contents, including a legend for any codes used. This will facilitate verification of the data provided in response to D10.

D19. Identify all source documents you have relied on in preparing your response to this part, and indicate the business location where the documents are maintained.

> **REMINDER:** *If you have designated any information CONFIDENTIAL, a non-confidential version of that information must accompany your response to this RFI. See items 3–10 of the INSTRUCTIONS for further details in this regard.*

PART E

Profitability analysis

Generally, normal values are based on your firm's selling prices of like goods where there are a sufficient number of domestic sales to unrelated customers that allow a proper comparison with the sales of goods shipped to importers in Canada. CBSA does not take into account unprofitable sales where the loss occurred over an extended period of time, where the volume of sales at a loss was substantial, and where the sales at a loss were made at prices below the weighted average per unit cost for the period. Therefore, in order to determine whether certain unprofitable domestic sales should be eliminated, it is necessary for your company to prepare and submit the following profitability analysis.

E1. Perform a 'profitability analysis' on domestic sales of like goods listed in response to question C8. This will form the database to be used in the profitability analysis and will be based on domestic sales of like goods provided in response to question C8, as well as the total cost figures for each sale. Sales in this database must be adjusted for any credit notes issued respecting these sales, i.e. selling prices are to be net of credits. All remaining credits are to be removed from the database. The database should be sorted by: 1. production facility/factory; 2. model; and 3. date of sale.

The following three tests must be performed on the adjusted database:

Whether sales are at a loss:

Test A: determines whether the net selling price for each sale is above or below the actual total cost of the sale. Sales at a loss will be further analysed using tests B(i), B(ii) and C.

Whether the sales at a loss are substantial:

Test B(i): determines whether the sale at a loss is substantial based on the total quantity of a specific model sold at a loss being equal to or greater than 20% of the total quantity of that model sold.

Test B(ii): determines whether the sale at a loss is substantial based on whether the weighted average net selling price of a model is less than the weighted average unit cost for that model.

Whether the unit selling price at a loss is below the weighted average cost:

Test C: is conducted on all substantial sales at a loss and determines whether the net unit selling price of the sale is less than or equal to the weighted average unit cost of that model.

You will find attached at the end of this part a flowchart which illustrates these tests.

Normal values for exported models where all domestic sales of the like goods have been found to be unacceptable based on the profitability tests described above will be determined pursuant to subsection 19(b) of SIMA, i.e. based on the cost of production plus an amount for administrative, selling and all other expenses, plus an amount for profit.

To determine whether a sale is at a loss, perform the profitability analysis according to the following:

Test A: Is the individual sale at a loss?

For each sale of each model, subtract the total unit cost from the total net unit selling price to find out if the sale was made at a 'profit' or a 'loss'. If the total net selling price is greater than or equal to the total cost, this sale is considered profitable and may be used to determine normal values. No further tests need to be done *for this sale*. If the total net selling price is less than the total cost, the sale is at a loss and must be tested further to determine whether it can be considered for determination of normal values pursuant to section 15 of SIMA; move to test B(i).

Test B(i): Is the quantity of the model sold at a loss greater than or equal to 20% of the total quantity of that model sold?

For each model, calculate the total quantity sold at a loss. Compare this to the total quantity sold. If the quantity at a loss is less than 20% of the quantity sold (the answer for the test for this sale would be 'No'), each sale at a loss must be tested further; move to test B(ii). If the quantity at a loss for the model is greater than or equal to 20% of the quantity sold of that model, the volume of sales at a loss is considered substantial (the answer for the test for this sale would be 'Yes'); move to test C.

Test B(ii): Is the weighted average unit net selling price of the model less than the weighted average unit cost of the model?

For each model, calculate the weighted average unit net selling price and the weighted average unit cost. If the weighted average unit net selling price is greater than the weighted average unit cost (the answer for the test would be 'No'), the sales at a loss of the model are not considered substantial and may be used to determine normal values; do not perform test C. If the weighted average unit net selling price of each model is less than the weighted average unit cost, the sales at a loss are considered substantial (the answer for the test would be 'Yes'); move to test C.

Test C: Is the unit net selling price less than or equal to the weighted average unit cost?

For each sale, compare the unit net selling price to the weighted average unit cost. If the unit net selling price is greater than the weighted average unit cost (the answer for the test for this sale would be 'No'), the sale at a loss may be used to determine normal values. If the unit net selling price is less than or equal to weighted average unit cost (the answer for the test for this sale would be 'Yes'), the sale cannot be taken into account in the determination of normal values.

For each domestic sale of like goods, determine if the sale may be used in the determination of normal values under section 15 of the Act. The status of each sale depends on the results of tests A, B(i), B(ii) and C. If the answer to Test A was 'PROFIT', then enter 'INCLUDE'. If the answer to Test A was 'LOSS', then determine the status of the sale (i.e. whether to 'INCLUDE' or 'EXCLUDE' the sale in the determination of normal values), according to the following table:

	Scenario 1	Scenario 2	Scenario 3	Scenario 4	Scenario 5
Test A	LOSS	LOSS	LOSS	LOSS	LOSS
Test B(i)	No	No	No	Yes	Yes
Test B(ii)	No	Yes	Yes	Do not perform	Do not perform
Test C	Do not perform	No	Yes	No	Yes
Status	**INCLUDE**	**INCLUDE**	**EXCLUDE**	**INCLUDE**	**EXCLUDE**

E2.   Provide a list of each model for which all domestic sales have been excluded from consideration in the determination of normal value as a result of the application of the above tests.

E3.   Provide a separate list (spreadsheet) containing all sales in your response to question E1 which had the test result, 'INCLUDE'. This list should contain the same columns as your response to question E1. This database must be sorted using a primary sort on production facility/factory, a secondary sort on model and a tertiary sort on date of sale.

Provide a list of each model where the sales which had the test result 'INCLUDE' were made to only one customer during the profitability analysis period.

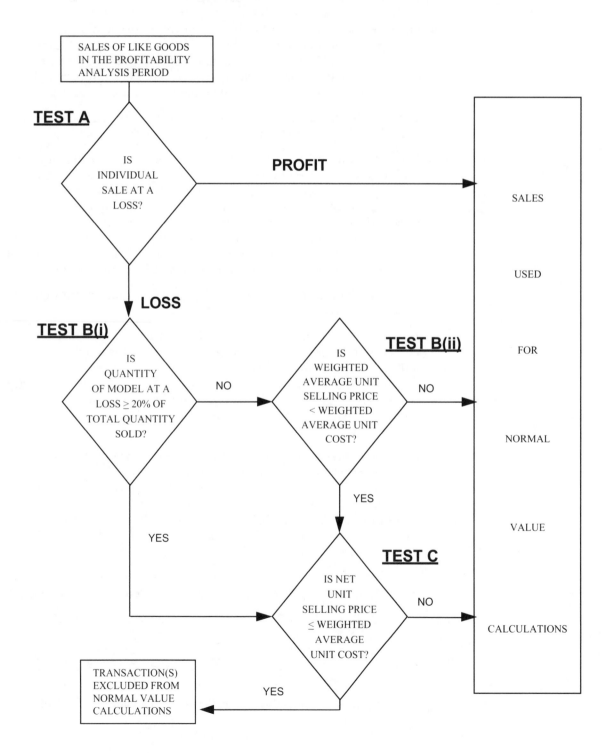

PART F

Glossary

Administrative and selling expenses	While the following list is not exhaustive, administrative and selling expenses include: directors' fees, management salaries and benefits, office salaries and benefits, office supplies, insurance, promotion, entertainment and depreciation expenses. Administrative and selling expenses also include corporate overhead.
Allocation	Allocation of expenses such as overhead, administrative, selling and all other costs; for example as a percentage of sales, percentage of direct costs, or a constant amount per unit.
Associated persons and/or companies	Persons or companies that are related to each other or do not deal with each other at arm's length. For example, individuals related by blood, marriage or adoption or companies that are directly or indirectly controlled by the same person or by the same company. See 'related'.
Associated purchasers	Where two or more purchasers are associated persons and/or companies, they will be regarded as a single purchaser.
Average number of collection days/ageing of accounts receivable	The average number of days between the invoice date and the date of receipt of payment for goods sold. Ageing reports provide details regarding the amounts due and those past due based on various predetermined time frames.
Bank charges	Any charge incurred as a result of services rendered by a bank or other financial institution in respect of the sale, shipment, financing, payment, etc. of the goods sold.
Brokerage fees	The amount paid to a customs broker for import/export services rendered.
By-product	A marketable product of lesser importance produced as an incident to the production of a major product.
Cash discount	This is a discount to the selling price of the goods which may be granted to customers by the vendor for the early payment of invoices. Sometimes called a prompt payment discount. *Example:* 2% 10, net 30 days.
Container freight charges	The charges normally associated with leasing or renting of a container and may include charges for packing or unpacking.
Cost of goods sold	Cost of goods sold is generally calculated by totalling the opening inventory and production costs and deducting there from the amount of closing inventory.

Date of sale	The date of sale is generally considered to be the date that the parties establish the terms of sale. The date of the order confirmation is usually considered as the date of sale, although the date of sale could be the contract, purchase order or invoice date. If any of the terms of sale are subsequently revised, the date that the revision was made is usually considered to be the date of sale.
Date of shipment	The date of shipment is the date the goods began their continuous journey to the customer. The selection of which shipments to include in response to question B8 is determined by the date of shipment to Canada.
Discounting or factoring of accounts receivable	Discounting of accounts receivable is the sale, usually at a discount, of a company's accounts receivable.
Dock charges	Any levy paid as a result of using dock or port facilities for movement of goods.
Dumped	Dumped, in relation to any goods, means that the normal value of the goods exceeds the export price.
Export price	Export price is usually the lesser of the exporter's adjusted selling price for the goods or the importer's adjusted purchase price. Where there is no exporter's sale price or no price at which the importer in Canada has purchased or agreed to purchase the goods, or where the price is considered to be unreliable because the sale is between associated persons or there exists a compensatory arrangement, the export price is based on the price at which the goods are sold by the importer in Canada to unrelated purchasers in Canada, less related expenses and an amount for profit.
Factory overhead	All production costs other than direct material and direct labour costs. Factory overhead includes all costs necessary to the operation and maintenance of the production facility/factory and is frequently divided into two categories namely, variable and fixed. Factory overhead does not include administrative and selling expenses but includes depreciation expense.
Forward sale/contract	A forward sale is a contract that commits the user to buying or selling an asset, such as a treasury bill or dollars, at a specific price on a specific date in the future.
Futures contract	A forward contract that is traded on an exchange.
Goods in question	May be either subject goods (goods sold to Canada which fit the product definition) or like goods (goods sold domestically that are identical or similar to the subject goods).

Harbour taxes	Taxes, duties or any other similar levy paid to a governmental body as a result of using a harbour or port for movement of goods.
Hedging/covering	Hedging is the purchase and holding of foreign currency for a length of time. Its purpose is to eliminate risks involved in dealing with foreign currencies. Also called covering and swap deposits.
Identical goods	Identical goods are goods that are identical in all respects to the subject goods exported to Canada.
Inland freight	All costs, charges and expenses associated with shipping goods via land but may sometimes include the charges and expenses associated with inland waterways.
Like goods	Like goods are goods that are identical in all respects to the subject goods exported to Canada, or in the absence of identical goods, goods the uses and other characteristics of which closely resemble those of the exported goods (similar goods).
Ministerial specification	A Ministerial specification is used to determine the normal values, export prices or the amounts of subsidy when the regular methods for making the calculations cannot be applied. It may also be used to cover new products or new exporters not covered by previous rulings.
Model	Model is the generic term used throughout this RFI to denote individual products.
Normal value	Normal value is usually based on the price at which an exporter sells like goods for domestic consumption in the ordinary course of trade to unrelated purchasers.
	Where normal values cannot be determined based on domestic selling prices, normal values will be determined based on the aggregate of the cost of production, an amount for administrative, selling and all other costs and an amount for profit. In the absence of the required information, the normal value is based on a Ministerial specification.
Ocean/overland/ port charges	All costs, charges and expenses associated with shipping goods via water.
Period of investigation (POI)	The POI represents the time frame selected at the time of initiation to delineate the *importations* into Canada for which information is required and that will be investigated.
Person	Includes a partnership, corporation or an association.
Profitability analysis period (PAP)	The profitability analysis period is the length of time during which the profitability of domestic market sales is tested.

Related	For the purposes of defining 'associated persons', persons are considered to be related if:
	– They are connected by blood relationship;
	– One is an officer or director of the other;
	– Each such person is an officer or director of the same two corporations, associations, partnerships or other organizations;
	– They are partners;
	– One is the employer of the other;
	– They directly or indirectly control or are controlled by the same person;
	– One directly or indirectly controls or is controlled by the other;
	– Any other person directly or indirectly owns, holds or controls 5% or more of the outstanding voting stock or shares of each such person; or
	– One directly or indirectly owns, holds or controls 5% or more of the outstanding voting stock or shares of the other.
Sale	Includes leasing and renting, an agreement to sell, lease or rent and an irrevocable tender.
Scrap material	Scrap material is material left over from certain production processes. Scrap typically has some measurable but relatively minor recovery value.
Similar goods	Similar goods are goods that are not identical in all respects but are similar in use and in characteristics to subject goods exported to Canada.
Standard cost	Standard costs are predetermined or budgeted (estimated) costs per unit of a product or process, comprising labour, materials and overhead. Standard costs are typically based on historical data and are the base against which actual costs are compared and variances measured and analysed.
Subject goods	The definition of subject goods is contained on the cover page of this RFI.
Subsequent trade level	Refers to the next lowest trade level, subsequent to the trade level of the importer in Canada, to which you sell in your domestic market. In this context, the producer is considered to be at the highest trade level and the end-user at the lowest trade level. In determining the normal value of the goods, adjustments may be made to your domestic selling price to account for differences in trade level between the importer in Canada and your domestic customers. See 'trade level'.

Subsidy	A financial contribution by a government of a country that confers a benefit to persons engaged in the production, manufacture, growth, processing, purchase, distribution, transportation, sale, export or import of goods. A subsidy does not include the amount of any duty or internal tax imposed on goods by the government of the country of origin or country of export from which the goods, because of their exportation from the country of export or country of origin, are exempted or are relieved by means of refund or drawback. A subsidy also includes any form of income or price support that confers a benefit.
Total cost	Total cost is the cost of producing the good plus administrative, selling and all other costs.
Trade level	The level which a company occupies in the distribution chain for a product. The predominant determining factor in establishing the trade level of an entity is the trade level to which that entity in turn sells the goods. The activities that the entity carries out may also help in distinguishing the trade level.
	Examples of typical trade levels are, in descending order: producer, national distributor, regional distributor, wholesaler and retailer. See 'subsequent trade level'.
Transfer price	The price charged by one division or section to another division or section of the same corporation, or the price charged between two associated companies, for products or services supplied.
Variance	A variance is the difference between actual cost and standard cost of a cost element, e.g. material price variance, material usage variance or labour rate variance.
Warehousing	All costs, charges and expenses associated with storing goods while on route to Canada, such as bonded warehouse fees.
Waste material	Waste material is material that either is lost, evaporates or shrinks during certain production processes and typically has no measurable recovery value but does have added cost.

Canada's anti-dumping and countervailing law is contained in the Special Import Measures Act (SIMA).

CBSA / CITT	The Canada Border Services Agency (CBSA) and the Canadian International Trade Tribunal (CITT) are jointly responsible for administering SIMA.
Anti-dumping duty	The amount of dumping on imported goods may be offset by the application of 'anti-dumping' duty.

Margin of dumping	Difference between the export price from the normal value.
Countervailing duty	The amount of subsidy on imported goods may be offset by the application of 'countervailing' duty.
Injury	Injury to Canadian industry caused by the dumping or subsidizing of imported goods.
Complainant	A Canadian producer of identical or similar goods to the competing imports can file a written complaint if it suspects that the imported goods are being dumped or subsidized and causing injury to Canadian industry. An association or producers may also file a complaint on behalf of its members.
Undertaking	Involves a commitment by exporters or foreign governments to change their pricing or subsidizing practices on goods sold to importers in Canada.
Safeguard inquiry	CITT determines whether or not a product is being imported into Canada in such increased quantities and under such conditions as to cause or threaten to cause serious injury to domestic producers of like or directly competitive goods.
Global safeguard inquiry	Considers the effects of imports from all sources on domestic producers.
Bilateral safeguard inquiry	Considers the effects of goods imported from a country with which Canada has a bilateral free trade agreement.
Material injury	CITT conducts inquiries into whether dumped or subsidized imports have caused, or are threatening to cause, material injury to a domestic industry.

References

The Economy in Brief, The Department of Finance, Ottawa, Canada, June 2006.

Opening Doors to the World, Canada's International Market Access Priorities, 2006, Foreign Affairs and International Trade, Ottawa, Canada.

Seventh Annual Report on Canada's State of Trade, Trade Update, 2006, Foreign Affairs and International Trade, Ottawa, Canada.

Grey, Rodney de C. The development of the Canadian anti-dumping system. The Private Planning Association of Canada, 1973.

Hart, Michael. What's next – Canada, the global economy and the new trade policy. Centre for Trade Policy and Law, Carleton University, Ottawa, Canada, 1994.

Hines, W. Roy. Uruguay Round Trade Agreements and the Winnipeg Principles on Trade and Sustainable Development. Ottawa, Canada. 1995.

Multilateral Trade Negotiations. The Final Act Embodying the Results of the Uruguay Round of Multilateral Trade Negotiations. Marrakech, 15 April 1994.

Ostry, Sylvia. Technological change and international economic institutions. April 1995.

Stone, W. Frank. Canada, the GATT and the international trade system. The Institute for Public Policy, Ottawa, Canada, 1984.

Various news releases issued by the Department of Foreign Affairs and International Trade, the Canadian International Trade Tribunal and Canada Border Services Agency (formerly Revenue Canada), Government of Canada.

Government of Canada, Canada Border Services Agency, Special Import Measures Act, regulations, operational handbook and anti-dumping and countervailing decisions. Ottawa, Canada. Numerous publications are available on the Act, administrative procedures, information requirements, decisions etc. from the Anti-Dumping and Countervailing Directorate on the intranet at *www.cbsa-asfc.gc.ca/*.

Government of Canada, Canadian International Trade Tribunal Act, regulations and rules and Guidelines, Ottawa, Canada. Publications dealing with this subject matter may be found on the Tribunal's web site at *www.citt-tcce.gc.ca*.